A WORLD ELSEWHERE

A World Elsewhere is Steven Berkoff's bold attempt to describe his multifarious theatrical works.

Berkoff outlines the methods that he uses, first of all as an actor, secondly as a playwright and thirdly as theatre director, as well as those subtle connections in between, when one discipline melds effortlessly into another. He examines the early impulses that generated his works and what drove him to give them form, as well as the challenges he faced when adapting the work of other authors. Berkoff discusses some of his most difficult, successful and unique creations, journeying through his long and varied career to examine how they were shaped by him, and how he was shaped by them. The sheer scale of this book offers a rare experience of an accomplished artist, combined with the honesty and insight of an autobiography, making this text a singular tool for teaching, inspiration and personal exploration.

Suitable for anyone with an interest in Steven Berkoff and his illustrious career, *A World Elsewhere* is the part analysis and part confession of an artist whose work has been performed all over the world.

Steven Berkoff is a renowned playwright, director, actor, photographer and author.

A WORLD ELSEWHERE

Steven Berkoff

 Routledge
Taylor & Francis Group

LONDON AND NEW YORK

First published 2020
by Routledge
2 Park Square, Milton Park, Abingdon, Oxon OX14 4RN

and by Routledge
52 Vanderbilt Avenue, New York, NY 10017

Routledge is an imprint of the Taylor & Francis Group, an informa business

British Library Cataloguing-in-Publication Data
A catalogue record for this book is available from the British Library

Library of Congress Cataloging-in-Publication Data
Names: Berkoff, Steven, author.
Title: A world elsewhere / Steven Berkoff.
Description: Abingdon, Oxon ; New York, NY : Routledge, 2019. |
Includes bibliographical references and index.
Identifiers: LCCN 2019029789 (print) | LCCN 2019029790 (ebook) |
ISBN 9780367356866 (hardback) | ISBN 9780367356873 (paperback) |
ISBN 9780429341144 (ebook) Subjects: LCSH: Berkoff, Steven. |
Dramatists, English–Biography. | Theatrical producers and
directors–Great Britain–Biography. | Actors–Great Britain–Biography. |
English drama–History and criticism. |
Theater–Production and direction–Great Britain.
Classification: LCC PR6052.E588 Z46 2019 (print) |
LCC PR6052.E588 (ebook) | DDC 822/.914 [B]–dc23
LC record available at https://lccn.loc.gov/2019029789
LC ebook record available at https://lccn.loc.gov/2019029790

Every effort has been made to contact copyright-holders. Please advise the publisher
of any errors or omissions, and these will be corrected in subsequent editions.

ISBN: 9780367356866 (hbk)
ISBN: 9780367356873 (pbk)
ISBN: 9780429341144 (ebk)

Typeset in Bembo
by Newgen Publishing UK

Dedicated to every actor
who has appeared in these plays, the talented
photographers who immortalised their images
for all time and all those gifted musicians
who gave the productions such an aura.
And also to the late Joe Papp, who left such
an extraordinary legacy and made space
for me in his legendary Public Theater in New York.

For Clara

CONTENTS

BIOGRAPHY

Steven Berkoff was born in Stepney, London. After studying drama and mime in London and Paris, he entered a series of repertory companies and in 1968 formed the London Theatre Group. Their first professional production was *In the Penal Colony*, adapted from Kafka's story. *East*, Steven's first original stage play, was presented at the Edinburgh Festival in 1975. Other original plays include *Messiah: Scenes from a Crucifixion*, *The Secret Love Life of Ophelia*, *West*, *Decadence*, *Greek*, *Harry's Christmas*, *Lunch*, *Acapulco*, *Sink the Belgrano!*, *Massage*, *Sturm und Drang*, *Brighton Beach Scumbags*, *6 Actors in Search of a Director*, *Actor's Lament* and a series of plays performed under the umbrella title *Anarchy and Religion – How to Train an Anti-Semite*, *Guilt*, *Roast*, *Gas* and *Line-up*.

Among the many adaptations Berkoff has created for the stage, directed and toured are *The Trial* and *Metamorphosis* (Kafka), *Agamemnon* (after Aeschylus), and *The Fall of the House of Usher* (Poe). He has also directed and toured productions of Shakespeare's *Coriolanus* (playing the title role), *Richard II* (for the New York Shakespeare Festival), *Hamlet* and *Macbeth* (where he also played the title roles), as well as Oscar Wilde's *Salome*. He directed and performed in *Massage* in Edinburgh and Los Angeles, and has performed *One Man* and *Shakespeare's Villains* at venues all over the world. His production of *On the Waterfront* had a critically acclaimed run in the West End. His plays and adaptations have been performed in many languages and many countries including Japan, Germany, Greece, Israel, Australia and America. His adaptation of *Oedipus* was recently performed at the Spoleto Festival in South Carolina following a run at the Edinburgh Festival. In 2015 Steven Berkoff played Saddam Hussein in Anthony Horowitz's *Dinner with Saddam* at London's Menier Chocolate Factory. He has most recently performed his own play *HARVEY*, which is now available on DVD.

Films Steven has appeared in include *A Clockwork Orange*, *Barry Lyndon*, *The Passenger*, *McVicar*, *Outlands*, *Octopussy*, *Beverly Hills Cop*, *Rambo*, *Revolution*, *Under the*

Cherry Moon, Absolute Beginners, The Krays, Fair Game, Another 9 ½ Weeks, Legionnaire, Forest of the Gods, The Flying Scotsman, Pu-239 and *44 Inch Chest*. He directed and co-starred with Joan Collins in the film version of *Decadence*. In 2010 he appeared in *The Tourist* with Johnny Depp and Angelina Jolie; and in 2011 in David Fincher's *Girl with the Dragon Tattoo*. Another 2011 credit is the independent film *Moving Target*. In 2016 he completed a film version of Edgar Allen Poe's 'The Tell-Tale Heart'.

Television productions include *West* (Limehouse/Channel 4), *Metamorphosis* (BBC), *Harry's Christmas* (Limehouse), *Silent Night* (Initial/Channel 4) and Edgar Allan Poe's *The Tell-Tale Heart* (Hawkshead/Channel 4). Television credits include *War and Remembrance, Michelangelo – A Season of Giants, Sins, Attila, In the Beginning, Hotel Babylon, The Borgias* and *Vikings*.

He has published a variety of books, such as the short story collections *Graft: Tales of an Actor* (Oberon Books) and *Gross Intrusion* (Quartet Books); the production journals *I am Hamlet, Meditations on Metamorphosis* (Faber and Faber), *Coriolanus in Deutschland* (Amber Lane Press) and *A Prisoner in Rio* (Hutchinson); his autobiography *Free Association* (Faber); a photographic history, *The Theatre of Steven Berkoff* (Methuen); and travel writing, essay and poetry collections *Shopping in the Santa Monica Mall* (Robson Books), *America* (Hutchinson) and *Overview* (Faber). Faber has published Berkoff's collected plays in three volumes, as well as *The Secret Love Life of Ophelia. Requiem for Ground Zero* (Amber Lane Press), Steven's tribute to September 11th in verse, coincided with a run at the Edinburgh Festival, followed by a one-year anniversary performance in London. His most recent books include *My Life in Food (ACDC)* a collection of paeans to food and comfort; *You Remind Me of Marilyn Monroe* charting personal thoughts pains and passions in verse; his memoir *Diary of a Juvenile Delinquent*; and in 2011 *Tales from an Actor's Life*, semi-fictional stories detailing the nuances of this profession. His collection of *One Act Plays* was published by Methuen in 2013. His novel *Sod the Bitches!* was published by Urbane in 2015.

Steven Berkoff has completed a variety of voiceover work and books on tape, including Kafka's *Metamorphosis* and *The Trial* for Penguin Audiobooks and Henry Miller's *Nexus* for Prelude Audio Books. Radio productions include the title role in *Macbeth* (Radio 4; available through Penguin Audiobooks) and his live music debut as the MC in *Cabaret* (Radio 2). He has also recorded *An Actor's Tale*, a selection of his short stories, for Radio 4.

Steven has exhibited his photographs of London's old East End at several galleries in London; his Glasgow 'Gorbals 1966' exhibition at Street Level Photoworks ran until 16 September 2018. Many of his books and DVDs can be found at www. stevenberkoff.com.

PREFACE

As I slowly crawl into the 'sere' of years, as Macbeth might say, I am forced to reflect on what has been my first occupation over the last six decades! My first occupation was that of an actor, but an actor must be malleable enough to embrace the limitless possibilities on offer in the theatrical canon.

Once can never tire of them. However, no matter what lurid, exciting or mysterious dramas exist, one's opportunities to play them are sadly rare. You are, after all, merely a hired hand. I was looking elsewhere, and I stepped away from the usual and well-worn path and devoted myself to reading works of drama and literature that made profound impressions on me (that went beyond those early 'earthy' dramas of domestic and social frustration). I was searching for something that reached into the deepest parts of my being, that amazed and even horrified me.

Having read Franz Kafka at an early age and found his work utterly inspiring, I was equally frustrated that little modern drama had the same hold on me. We need to wade into strange waters. In the following pages I have attempted to describe the path I took. How it was necessary to train myself to become both Director and Playwright in order to fulfil my own visions and to see and describe what Coriolanus refers to when he says 'There is a world elsewhere.'

1

IN THE PENAL COLONY

The Arts Lab, Drury Lane 1967

My very first production – when I read this frightening and brilliantly written tale I was sure that this would be my choice as the place whence to launch my directing and writing career. Most of the story is written in dialogue and so not too difficult to turn into a play. My eventual ambition was to stage Kafka's masterpiece, the novella *Metamorphosis*, and this was to be a curtain raiser. Today that would be felt to be quite unnecessary, but, in those far-off times, anything less than two hours was deemed to be short-changing the audience.

Customers expected it. They wanted drama that would engage them in the first act, keep them guessing in the second and satisfy them in the third with a *coup de théâtre*! The time of a dynamic play in one or two acts, lasting, much like a film, just under ninety minutes, was yet to come.

I had the very strong ambition to stage something that was utterly different from the kitchen sink dross that was Britain's current obsession.

I had next to no interest in the simple and somewhat dreary howls and moans of the class war.

I felt that too much theatre was becoming a mouthpiece for agitated playwrights to air their problems either with themselves or with society. I felt it was becoming a little tedious.

Kafka belonged to the world of imagination. I loved this strange and bizarre story and felt that there would be nothing on earth like it. This was my goal and I set to work.

Now, there are overwhelming and some daunting elements in the story. The central feature of the piece, if not the central character, is a machine. An extraordinary, barbaric machine designed to execute anyone working on the military base, where the play is set, for any offence deemed to lower the standards of military discipline. Its function is as bizarre and convoluted as the imaginative mind of Kafka himself. The machine punishes the 'sentenced' offender by the most extraordinary method that has ever been devised. The prisoner is strapped into the machine. The lid is closed and he waits. Very slowly and gradually needles puncture the man's flesh, water jets clear the blood and debris away leaving the back clear. Clear as a sheet of parchment, for this is exactly the function of the demonic contraption. Whilst the poor prisoner suffers the pain of the stabbing needle after some time, he begins to realise that there seems to be some form of logic to the incessant piercing of his flesh by the needles.

The needles are actually writing out the crime for which he has been punished! They are in fact writing out his 'sentence', the sentence in this case being all too literal. Now the prisoner, not yet being dead, even though on the brink and even in the dire situation he is in, struggles to interpret what these repetitive movements of the needles mean. A crowd of spectators have been invited to witness this gruesome execution, the highlight of which, unbeknown to the victim at this stage, is the moment of realisation. This is what everybody keenly awaits, when the prisoner gradually reads his sentence in the painful tattoos raining down upon his back. For the audience it is a most exciting moment and even perceived by many of them as a spiritual one. According to the officer who is relating the story, the tortured victim suddenly 'sees' the writing on his back. His expression is one of a terrible understanding as he then expires. This, for the protagonist of the story, is an almost holy event.

There are just four people in the cast. The protagonist is a fanatical officer, perhaps past his prime, who believes in the 'old way'. The machine has fallen out of favour in recent years and is now regarded as a rather outdated anachronism. It is no longer serviced or even repaired and is being allowed to gradually fade out of existence. However, the old-school officer is desperate to retain it for the values and tradition that it represents. He is trying very hard to persuade the 'explorer' who just happens to be on a scientific visit to the island to attend a real execution. The explorer is reluctant to recommend its continued use to the commandant even after much persuasion. The officer was hoping that the beauty and elegance of the execution might persuade him to put in a good word to the powers that be. He might even put the prisoner in the machine for one final magnificent demonstration.

The machine, having not been serviced for some time, lets the commandant down and the demo is flawed and comes to a stop. The officer is distressed that his carefully planned exhibition has not only failed miserably but has also humiliated him beyond redress. In bitter frustration he retunes the machine as best he can, then rips his uniform off and climbs into the monstrous contraption. He instructs his brutish assistant to fasten all the clamps and turn on the switch. This time the machine miraculously springs into action. It impresses for a moment or two but soon enough it shudders and breaks down. The officer, though, is thoroughly dead. The explorer completes his notes. The play ends.

Not only is this a most bizarre play, it is also very skilfully written and engages the audience from the beginning to the final shocking and climatic end. All sorts of interpretations are possible; although it was written well over a decade before Hitler's ascent to power in 1933, one can certainly sniff out the fumes of the oncoming order. The witches stew is bubbling in the pot and Kafka is naturally swift to detect it.

I badly wanted to do this play. The role of the derelict officer craving the good old days was a gift for an actor. It is passionate, nostalgic, lyrical, absurd and insane. But the real star of the play must be the infernal machine. It seemed like an impossible task to find someone to make such a complex piece, unless you had a budget for a film. However, as luck would have it, I had the great fortune to be courting a young lady named Alison Minto, whose rare intelligence and culture naturally attracted some very smart dudes around her. One of whom was a young fledgling architect called Alistair Merry. Alistair, just down from Oxford, was not only an architect but also a very talented carpenter and designer. He agreed to make it for me and he did, and what he built was quite incredible.

Kafka describes his horrific 'torture machine' almost lovingly, as the protagonist proudly guides his visitor into its unpalatable functions. 'Both "The Bed" and "The Designer" have an electric battery each – As soon as the man is strapped down, The Bed is set in motion – It quivers in minute, very rapid vibrations from side to side and up and down – The needles barely touch the skin, but once the contact is made, the steel ribbon stiffens into a rigid band – Then, the long needle does the writing and the short needle sprays a jet of water to wash away the blood … etc.'

Alistair Merry constructed a formidable interpretation of this machine. To my mind, it was a masterpiece, and as a skilled carpenter he constructed the machine in two main parts. The basic coffin-shaped Bed was beautifully made out of planed wood with slats for the 'prisoner' to lie on. That hinged to the top half, which had, embedded in its underside, row upon row of sharp, fine nails. Also, from this ran a series of vein-like wires down into The Bed, from which emerged transparent tubes to drain the blood. Holding the whole contraption in place were four large, steel poles, which helped to keep it stable while it vibrated. The stage management would do the rest, adding flashing light effects to complete the macabre illusion of the torture machine. It was most effective – a kind of Heath Robinson fantasy.

Now in Drury Lane, just off Covent Garden, was the aptly named The Arts Laboratory run by American maverick Jim Haynes. One day I happened to stroll in to this strange large studio and spoke to Mr Haynes. I left a script. He asked me when I would like to see it being performed. I hadn't a clue. But just to seem vaguely confident in my plans I suggested three months hence. He agreed to that even before reading the script and said he would get back to me.

Jim Haynes was an original on many different fronts and, having established the first fringe theatre in Edinburgh, called The Traverse, thought he'd do the same in London. The idea of Kafka, and his tale of torture and horror, was obviously 'catnip' to his alert entrepreneurial sense. A month later I looked in to get the feel of the place and there Jim was sitting at the same front desk where he had been a month earlier. He greeted me by drawing my attention to the wall on the left as you walked in. On the wall was a poster for *In the Penal Colony* announcing gloriously the premiere of the Kafka/Berkoff piece. It looked hand-done. Now, since somebody had gone to so much trouble to put this poster together I could no longer prevaricate. I had to do it.

Since this was my very first production and meant eventually to be a curtain raiser, the style was brutally simple. There were four in the cast, myself as the Officer, an Explorer, the Prisoner chained, sitting quietly and resigned and my thuggish Attendant.

My Attendant, it was felt, should welcome the audience as they come in with a blow torch in one hand that he had been using for a few minor repairs. The lighting was low and the Officer just waited casually leaning against the wall waiting for the spectators for the execution. The Explorer dressed in tropical fatigues is sitting in a chair making notes. When the Officer decides to make himself an example to prove the value of his wondrous machine, he strips down to his underwear. The climax at the end when the Machine finally shudders and dies should be suitably horrifying. Blood is seeping out of the machine as the Officer breathes his last. The machine has clumsily performed its last execution.

I had a first rate and loyal cast. Dino Shafeek was the condemned man. I had first met him at the YMCA when I would play handball most days. Asher Tsarfati, an Israeli actor whom I taught at drama school and who became a close friend, played the Attendant. Although he had no lines, he was very expressive and a character to whom the Officer could address much of his dialogue, especially when the Officer becomes intensely lachrymose and makes his final and desperate plea to the audience for understanding and respecting the 'ancient' traditions. And Christopher Hayden, a young actor whom I had auditioned, played the Explorer.

Dino Shafeek, a Bangladeshi actor, was well-built and possessed a strong muscular body, and there was a gentleness about him. He was struggling to find acting work and was generally cast as a low-grade native or servant when 'foreign or oriental types' were required. He was happy to do a play on stage, even though he did not utter a word, but sat there calmly awaiting his execution like a benign Indian deity.

Asher Tsarfati, a very powerfully built young man, said he relished my classes, since the school at that time was doing the kind of 'drinks table' plays that could hardly connect with his robust spirit. Although he had nothing to say in the piece, he was a very powerful presence. I addressed most of my passionate confessions to him as my ally. He stayed with me for the whole period, including the time when I mounted *Metamorphosis*. When he returned to Israel he swiftly rose in the ranks to become one of Israel's greatest actors.

Christopher Hayden as the explorer was a perfect foil to the arrogant, self-righteous officer. His elegant, even refined, looks were so apt for his role as my interrogator. I enjoyed working with him and we all sank into our roles.

So, two months later we opened my very first professional production in London. Nobody could have been more proud and the play, although only forty minutes long, was a resounding success. Eventually it was joined in a double bill by the wonderful dance and mime artist Tutte Lemkow, who had been performing his brilliant interpretation of Kafka's even more bizarre tale 'A Report to an Academy'.

FIGURE 1.1 *In the Penal Colony.* L–R: George Little, Steven Berkoff.

It concerned an ape giving his lectures on how he gradually became human. So now it was a perfect Kafka double-bill.

It was a most exciting beginning and I have never forgotten it. Sadly The Arts Laboratory is no longer there.

My two supporting actors I culled from the teaming mass of London's unemployed thespians. Dino, playing the hapless native about to be executed, I had become friends with in London's YMCA, a much-favoured gathering place for actors where we would play competitive games of handball or squash, or work out with weights. There is, or grows, a wonderful camaraderie between men in a gym. We sweated together, played together, laughed together and became gym friends … rarely meeting outside or even curious about each other's past or background. We were just men in the YMCA. Dino Shafeek as 'The Prisoner' was about to be executed, but, in the story's bizarre plot, that fact is not revealed to the condemned man. He learns it as the harrow in which he is placed face down slowly pierces his body. Dino's soft, dark, Indian face so perfectly captured the queries racing through his mind. Christopher, called 'The Explorer' in the story, perfectly exemplified the cool, reticent and guarded observer. Both were excellent in their respective roles.

2

METAMORPHOSIS

The Roundhouse, Chalk Farm 1969

This intriguing and horrid tale has fascinated me for many years. This had to be theatre and was to be my second production.

It had to be theatre because to my mind it demanded every ounce of imagination to bring it to life. The horrific tale of a human being trapped inside the body of an insect is a tale one would think impossible to stage. This of course means I would have to be far more creative to suggest the creature. Theatre allows you to do this – a simple gesture as the insect, its rhythm, its stillness, its sudden activity, demands that the audience uses its imagination. Thus they become participants in the ritual. This can only be achieved live on stage.

It's almost an involuntary act from the audience, the brain wishes to make sense and complete the story. Give the smallest gesture and the brain of the audience is compelled to fill in the rest.

Still naive in the methods of staging theatre, I had adapted it without the necessity of seeing the protagonist, the Beetle/Gregor. I just hadn't imagined how one could possibly put the insect on stage. However, one day I noticed that another company was actually showing their production of *Metamorphosis* in Oxford. I believe it was a young student group. Frankly I was astounded by what I saw! They had boldly and inventively put the Beetle centre stage. They had used the simple device of a box behind which crouched the actor, his arms crossed over each other resting on the box's surface somehow serving as an image or template for the insect. Brilliant, simple and so effective. I went home deciding to put my Beetle centre stage, but I would not use the box effect. I would use the whole body. John Abulafia was the creator by whom I was inspired. The end result bore little resemblance to his own inspired production. My creature moved, climbed the walls and actually hung from the ceiling. But the germ of it was his.

I had prevaricated for years, but now I was determined to do it. I had found a 'key'. As usual, indecision and fear fought each other for ascendency. Could I do it, direct it and play Gregor Samsa? I was determined. I had to make a decision and of course it was always down to me. The few theatres I had written to were too rearguard and conventional to even consider it. I did manage to raise a small amount of cash from a London film producer, John Heyman, famous for many of the better film efforts of the British screen. I was introduced to him by Wolf Mankowitz, playwright and screenwriter, chiefly celebrated for his West End musical 'Oliver'. I was very grateful for the £250 that got us all started, and so my first try-out was at the beautiful LAMDA Studio in Kensington designed by Sean Kenny, the brilliant stage designer.

During my weeks of indecision, when the contract to rent the LAMDA Studio had to be signed, I had a revelation. I was in the YMCA on Tottenham Court Road, which I frequented almost daily. They had a very primitive way of storing your old gym kit. They put it in a metal basket which was then shelved, stinking and moulding, until your next visit. On one occasion, as I drew out my basket, I saw a large black beetle sheltering amidst the odour. This was a most powerful sign to me and I knew then that I could not ignore the sign and I had to do it!

But before all this happened I had to find a cast. I seemed to remember having met Jeanie James socially and, having discussed this project with her, she decided she would like to play The Mother. She had a typically Eastern European face and was a first-class actress. She then introduced me to Petra Markham, who would be, and proved to be, perfect for Gregor Samsa's beloved sister Greta. By chance we found an excellent older actor to play Mr Samsa called George Little. He had a great deal of experience, a strong authoritative voice and moved well. For The Lodger and as Assistant Director I would use a very talented young American actor called Christopher Muncke. He had shown great promise at the Webber Douglas School where I had been teaching and also became a valuable assistant.

The actors all came round to my basement flat in Islington and sat around and read the script as it existed then. The fortunate element in the script was that all of the family roles, except of course for The Lodger and Chief Clerk, were almost equal in size, even larger than that of the insect. This was the result of my first draft of the play when I had put many of Gregor's meandering thoughts about life in their sad, drab apartment and how they were slowly decaying into the mouths of the family. Much of the original novella was conveyed through Gregor's thoughts as he lay neglected and bitterly lonely in his room.

I did, however, invent a flashback when he was able to enter the room as a young enthusiastic brother to his beloved sister, who he was funding to send to the Music Academy. She was an aspiring violinist. Kafka's relationship with his sisters was very close – it seems natural that he would create a loving and devoted sister in the character of Greta.

The actors were indeed enthusiastic since this would be something that they had never done even remotely before. I then told them all that as soon as I had found a space to show it we would begin. Well I did. So I decided that it was imperative that I play the tortured young man, Gregor Samsa. I felt such an overwhelming kindred spirit with him. It struck me when I first read Kafka's terrifying story. His pain, his loneliness and his sense of isolation, I felt, were mine too. I had found the key, and it was quite obvious. Since it was so obvious, why hadn't I thought of this before – I who was such a passionate advocate of the miracles that could be achieved with the human body? The simple reason was that it did not occur to me. How could we show the audience a creature like some gigantic repulsive bug. But my trip to Oxford to see the student production was the starting point. I was astounded at its raw simplicity. A simple box behind which crouched the actor with only his arms and head revealed.

I did not choose to do this, but it gave me the courage to take a bolder step and reveal the beetle. And so I set to work on myself as Gregor. Only in my case I would design a scaffolding set that would allow the 'bug' to climb the walls and even the ceiling. I had been teaching movement and mime at the Webber Douglas School of Drama in South Kensington, now just a fading memory, but my experiments with the young students taught me as much as I hope it did them. I had been working with the metronome for part of my experimentation, to free us from the predictable and naturalistic theatre through our mime classes. I would put this to good use. I felt that Gregor Samsa was, to a certain extent, a pathetic victim of his daily deadening routine of a travelling salesman, scurrying around the city not unlike a scurrying black insect. His daily life was predictable. When the family awake, I would use the metronome to break their movement up as if they were clockwork dolls, mechanically repeating the same actions each and every day. This was far more interesting than watching a family just eating their breakfast and wondering why their son Gregor had not risen for his. The actors revealed themselves as it were in a series of swift images. At the same time the insect's movements are naturally mechanical. I incorporated the Gregor/ Insect awakening movement to match the family's.

That's how we staged the play. The insect was slowly revealed, on his back, his flailing limbs helplessly crossing and uncrossing before he begins to speak. It certainly holds the attention of the audience from the very beginning. I also had the family on three equidistant metal stools facing the front. We are able to see all three of them at all times. The rest of the production followed a very physical style throughout. Music was most important, although I did not use this at the very beginning, but only after the second revival. Music was an element I was slowly discovering as I became aware of its fantastic persuasive power. Not being a musician, I had tremendous respect for those who, while watching rehearsals, could instinctively draw from their instruments the perfect sound to heighten the mood or the action. While we rehearsed in a dusty old studio in Islington in my early days, I was tempted to pluck the strings in the back of an old upright piano. The sounds of a plucked piano are indeed eerie, and I did find that they heightened the scenes for which they were used. My present musician, Mark Glentworth, has been my steadfast composer for the last thirty years. I also used a gigantic cyclorama that, back-lit, would accentuate the limbs of the insect as it struggled desperately to turn onto its belly. It was also used to most dramatic effect when the actors were front-lit and their giant shadow or silhouette was cast on the back.

I rented LAMDA's beautiful arena stage when the students were down during a spring break. I told the actors that we had little money, but that we would share the box office. But since this would be a unique event in London, it would be to little avail unless the public knew about it, and I had the audacity to ask the actors whether they would like to contribute to a largish ad in The Guardian. To my utter amazement, they so believed in the project that they all chipped in willingly, and for that I am ever grateful to them.

We opened at LAMDA for our week's try out and spent the morning erecting the set and then focusing the lights. I have to say that it looked stunning. The family sat on the three metal stools, which were perfect for the movement, spinning around, leaning into each other as when the Chief Clerk came to enquire why Gregor hadn't turned up for work. In the dream world of Kafka, time is compressed and the Chief Clerk is already there within minutes. As he threateningly leans in on the family they reflect their own anxiety by shrinking away from him. The effect multiplies the terror and helplessness they feel in the face of cold-blooded authority.

When Gregor actually bravely decided to try and open the door, the actor mimes gripping the key in his jaws. The mimed door opens and the light signifies that the creature is now exposed. The secret of enacting a creature is to capture its rhythm and, even if you are able to produce just a tiniest gleam of it, the audience will fill in the rest, since the human imagination does this automatically. Also as a reflex action, the human imagination loves to play. So as the door 'opens' the family and Chief Clerk react by suddenly pulling away in horror. They freeze, eyes locked on the thing on the floor. Actually the floor is a ramp. This is to allow the audience to see past the family when they are seated on their stools. Gregor too is frozen, but only as a large black beetle would be before he decides to move. The actor now merely runs his fingers along the floor and then suddenly, in one move, lowers his body. His face is motionless. The effect was utterly terrifying. The audience actually seem to freeze. As the creature moves, the family group also move away from their stools to the cage, where they try to persuade Gregor in unison to 'Please open the door.' Begging, cajoling, then angry and then deeply worried. He now very slowly slides down the ramp. And abruptly stops. The family now scream and spin away from him, in short, percussive moves to reflect the movement of the creature. But they are unable and unwilling to let their eyes wander away from the monster before them. Gregor, not wishing to disturb or frighten them, tries with his insect-like shrunken chords to call out 'Mother' and very slowly moves towards her in small jerky moves. Nobody appears to be able to do anything. Mother, Mrs Samsa, faints. Mr Samsa now appears to come to life and grabs a huge bamboo pole, the kind you use to open high windows. He thrusts it under Gregor's belly and pushes him back into the room. Gregor is slightly wounded as the large cane impales his softer underbelly and is turned over and back into the room. The Chief Clerk screams and flees as fast as his legs can carry him. The family almost stumble back to their stools. Throughout the play the movement seemed to reflect Gregor's, even while it gradually became more humanised. So that was the end of the first scene. I knew that we had something special on our hands.

All during the lighting rehearsal that morning I heard the phone ringing non-stop and it frustrated me since the box office was unmanned! Our Guardian ad had worked, but I was mightily relieved when the staff eventually showed up. The first night of my first production came and it was as successful as it could be, and the whole cast and I felt that we had achieved something that was quite special.

So now we were ready to open at The Roundhouse, but this time I was going to include the curtain raiser *In the Penal Colony*. It was a very tough double bill made far worse on the Saturday matinee when I would be obliged to perform the double bill twice. In other words, four shows in a day!! However, such was my faith in what we had created at the try-out, that my set designer Martin Beaton and I went to a West End money lender to borrow the deposits for the theatre. Though the interest rate was colossal, we were convinced we would pay it back after one month.

The first night came and we were ready. The reviews were utterly faultless. I was triumphant. All the actors were flawless and I could not have been happier. Only when *The Times'* Harold Hobson's rave review came out were we absolutely sold out. Of course, word did get around and in the next few years I was asked to direct it all over the world. First in Australia, where again I was blessed with a brilliant cast, then in Israel, which followed on straight from Australia. Then my first production in Germany at the renowned Düsseldorfer Schauspielhaus. Later Los Angeles with the sadly departed actor Brad Davis, the brilliant star of *Midnight Express*. Then on to New York some years after with Mischa Baryshnikov, as a result of him having seen Roman Polanski, whom I directed in Paris.

I did revive it at The Mermaid Theatre in 1986 in London, with Tim Roth as the bug, which played for sixteen weeks. The last production and I believe probably one of the best was the Japanese-language production in Tokyo, where I was again blessed with an exceptional cast. The Japanese company enjoyed having to accept my choreography and took to it with great enthusiasm, marking the gestures very carefully and practising them endlessly, particularly the mother and daughter. I felt it was an opportunity for them to explore the endless potential of mime and movement. There was even a touch of Kabuki about their performance! And of course in Kabuki they only use men.

I even revived it there several years later with a young Japanese actor called Mirai Moriyama who was spellbinding. Strangely enough the play was received enthusiastically all over the world, except the good old USA.

In the arid wastelands of New York with just one or two theatre critics whose reviews just might sell seats, it is a game of Russian roulette. We were sadly cursed with a review from Frank Rich, whose dirty, wretched comments put a bullet in its heart and it slowly died even with the wonderful Mischa Baryshnikov at its helm. So sad, since I did believe that this was one of my very best revivals. All that work, the constant rehearsals and vocal training for Mischa, the four-week try-out at Duke University in North Carolina, and then to be shot down by one irresponsible critic is so disgraceful. Yet such is the unending enthusiasm for live theatre that producers will continually risk fortunes and the careers and livelihoods of writers and actors to be judged by one man in the *New York Times*.

FIGURE 2.1 *Metamorphosis* at The Mermaid Theatre, 1986. L–R: Linda Marlowe, Steven Berkoff, Tim Roth, Saskia Reeves.

If the *New York Times* had the slightest glimmer of the fragility of modern theatre, they might think it would nourish American theatre to at least reflect the diversity of the theatre-going public … What a splendid idea.

I am always happy to revive my productions and there is hardly a time when new ideas have not grown out of this. So that the production should be fresh, I used a different musician on each occasion. Likewise, I rarely toured the production, but cast afresh in every city it plays. I've been blessed with some remarkable actors and I am deeply grateful to all of them.

> Cast of Gregor Samsas
> London 1969 – Steven Berkoff
> Australia 1976 – Ralph Cotterill
> Israel 1978 – Asher Tsarfati
> Los Angeles 1982 – Brad Davis
> Düsseldorf 1983 – Bernd Jeschek
> London 1986 – Tim Roth
> Paris 1988 – Roman Polanski
> New York 1989 – Mikhail Baryshnikov
> Tokyo 1992 – Amon Miyamoto
> Tokyo 2010 – Mirai Moriyama

3

MACBETH

The Place Theatre 1970

I was really hungry to do a Shakespeare having just immersed myself in two of his plays when directing at Webber Douglas Drama School. However, I could never direct, if one could call it that, in that rather traditional old-fashioned way that I had seen in London theatre for too many years. The actors were usually good and making an effort, but the productions were so hide-bound, so stilted, so terribly uninventive. They had learned absolutely nothing about theatrical techniques of movement, grouping, ensemble, choral, mime etc. and relied on the same old worn-out routines and therefore I felt they were missing out a great deal. They were indeed a curse to the British theatre with just one or two exceptions. Chiefly, Peter Brook and John Dexter. Brook for his extraordinary and eclectic imagination. Dexter for his dynamic and disciplined staging, which I had the privilege of experiencing first hand. I had been cast in his production of Arnold Wesker's semi-autobiographical play *The Kitchen* at The Royal Court in 1963

Again it was my great fortune to have been teaching at the Webber Douglas School, which was a godsend for me to unravel the mysteries of movement with live young human bodies. It was possibly frustrating for some of them at the time, since, before the actors could start speaking lines, I had to make sure that we had the mysteries of the structure in tow. For many hours we struggled to find it. I was desperately looking for the 'key' that would unlock the production and one day I felt that I had found it, and if not completely, at least was on the road.

Now, it so happens that we were living and breathing the heady experimental atmosphere of the late sixties and, like some wondrous spore flying in on the wind of liberation, sexual and otherwise, the American groups were really showing us simple Brits how it is done. I had, as did many others, heard about the mind-boggling play and production of a work called *Futz*. A play of wondrous daring and boldness by American playwright Rochelle Owens. It was showing at the modest Mercury Theatre in Notting Hill. The audience were stunned, shocked, enlivened, and we watched them believing that we had seen the future of theatre. The director was Tom O'Horgan. Briefly, it was a hilly-billy story of a man who has fallen in love with his pig. He is just so devoted to it, that the red-necked locals are disgusted and they are determined to kill him. The play started with the actors entering the stage half crouched down, moving forwards in a very animalistic way. They were each carrying in one hand a large, empty wine jug, which they then proceeded to play rhythmically. The effect was stunning. We had never seen anything like this. O'Horgan had found the key to his production. As we drifted out, stunned by what we had seen, we just stared at each other as if bereft of words to describe it.

Naturally I stole the clever movement of the beginning of 'Futz' to use in *Macbeth*. This became the key to the play's primitive origins. I had the actors slowly enter, one leg striking out and then the other, almost like a witches' gathering, and it was quite compelling. After *Metamorphosis* I did feel that I was now daring enough to try anything and everything.

I had always felt very strongly that movement in a theatrical production intensified the story and enhanced the meaning. I was indebted to the lessons I had learned with the supreme maestro of movement Jacques Lecoq. The foremost lesson he had taught was to show us that the body had the possibility of a visual language and that an entire play can be staged using only the massive contribution of the actors' bodies. Not only will the movement of the actors tell the story with far more vividness than a director who relies on sets and props, it will clarify it. Having seen theatre in the Far East, especially in Bali, I could not for a second imagine these brilliant performers needing anything else but their bodies and voices. Sometimes a few select props might be used that were vital for the function of the play, possibly masks or iconic and dramatic costume. Of course, it is well known that Antonin Artaud, the visionary writer and director who witnessed it during the Paris Exposition in 1900, was so stunned by the Balinese monkey dance that he felt that all other French theatre was bourgeois and deadly. He wanted to bring some of that spirit to his own company, but died before he could achieve it. Besides, he lacked the physical training to accomplish it. However, Jean-Louis Barrault did train furiously as a mime, along with Étienne Decroux, working together for long hours and creating their own theatre techniques.

So I decided that Macbeth was to be my next production and I was to both play Macbeth and direct it. No easy task, but in many ways I had little choice. No one was asking me. So, still inspired by the production of *Futz*, I decided that our bodies would tell the whole story in tandem with the text. I auditioned for many weeks until I found a group of actors who would work for no wages until such a time when we had a production to mount in a theatre and would be paid. There was a church hall opposite my house in Devonia Road, Islington, and that was where we met every night at 5pm and worked until 10pm. I was very lucky to have found my cast gradually. First I recruited Pip Donaghy from Drama Centre. He was an extraordinarily gifted actor and mover, and then he brought in Glyn Grain, also from Drama Centre. I once again used Chris Muncke, whom I had trained at Webber Douglas, and slowly the cast came together. Lady Macbeth was a strong, attractive actress I had met at the Citizens Theatre in Glasgow called Eliza Ward. And most of all she was adaptable and responsive to ideas, which made it easy to work with her. I often wondered what happened to her. She was a very dynamic and rather sexy lady, which I felt suited the character of Lady Macbeth to the ground and would partly explain Macbeth's obsession to please her.

And so we began. It seemed to be the fashion in those days to do endless workshops to 'loosen' us up, so I did a mime class first and then we began the arduous task of blocking the play. I was still at the beginning of my directing career and the early stages were painful. I didn't let it just flow and if it didn't look 'wonderful' I would fret and keep at it until the cast were sick to death of it. My mistake was that I was too desperate to see thrilling effects and so didn't allow a sense of improvisation to take place – I was too impatient. I curtailed the actors' imaginations by imposing my own. When I reversed this, the results were staggering!

The early scenes talk about the battle, although you don't see it. I was determined that we should enact what normally is off stage. What is 'off stage' is usually related by an actor 'on stage' due to the difficulties of bringing a violent scene to life. But in this case showing it on stage was far more revealing and more creative for the actor.

After the actors did their animalistic crawl on stage, they slowly formed into a vertical line of bodies one behind each other, facing the audience to give a dynamic image of a fighting machine. This is always effective. To a drum beat they moved from left to right or up and down. This took a while to achieve but eventually, as the actors got used to it and put all their energy into it, it was an exciting beginning. The witches were also an unnoticed part of this line and as the battle slowly dissolved the witches rose as if born out of the battle.

The witches were a group of very sweet young ladies who weren't too witch-like, but I gave them a slow, percussive drum beat to move to and also had them behind each other like a six-limbed Indian goddess. The drum beat slowed and they moved to it from side to side. It was very simple but also very effective. A multiple image is always impressive and disturbing, in this case the women playing the witches echoed Shiva, the goddess of destruction. And so we worked on and on, week after week in this fashion, and gradually it was coming together, very gradually. When we came to a problem, since we were a democratic group, everybody was encouraged to come up with ideas. Sometimes too many! But Pip always had great ones, such as crouching and placing one's arms behind one's back like the wings of a giant bird and moving by bouncing from one leg to another. Painfully difficult at first, but when he did it, it was quite inspiring.

We enter the castle and slowly form a circle as if we are seated at a round table enjoying a ritualistic feast for our honoured guests, these being King Duncan and his entourage. We toasted each other, laughed while Lady Macbeth slowly circled us, pouring the drinks for our visitors. Slowly, very slowly, the guests succumb to sleep. As Macbeth readies himself for what is to come, he rises from the sleeping group. We are a perfect circle, our feet all facing inwards. But just when Banquo himself rises, catching me out so to speak, we exchange a few sentences and then slowly, very slowly, allow ourselves to lie down.

Now after a few moments a single arm raises itself from the group, clutching a dagger. Macbeth rises in horror. He very slowly circles the sleepers, beginning his famous speech 'Is this a dagger that I see before me?' We make real what is imagined. For now as Macbeth slowly follows the dagger it is passed from hand to hand and, just as he goes to seize it, the dagger is then passed again. It was such an effective piece of theatre and I have to admit we were all proud of this since it could only have come from physical theatre. Bodies are so flexible and can change on the instant. Eventually the dagger is 'floating' at the head of the table. Macbeth now seizes it and does the act.

The sleeping figures now writhe in their death throes, suggesting that the King and all his retinue, or even the kingdom itself, have been slain.

After Macbeth's next scene with his wife, the dawn is rising, the lark is singing and we hear the most lyrical words on the rising of the dawn from the King's agents who are coming to escort him. Now comes the infamous 'Porter' scene where he in his apparent 'drunken' haze admits all the demons of hell and those punished to damnation. He imagines himself to be the gate keeper of Hell as he hears a knocking at the gate.

Now our team of actors rising from their 'sleep' become the apparitions imagined by the porter. As he bellows out drunkenly 'knock knock knock' he opens the doors and introduces each of the unfortunate souls described so vividly by Shakespeare. Glyn Grain performed this so brilliantly that I have never forgotten it. This talented young actor came from Drama Centre, a radical, free-thinking drama school in North London, which seemed very much to focus on the actor's physical abilities. He worked the scene like a fairground barker, exhibiting his line-up of ghouls. As he introduced each one to us, they became the creatures he described.

This also shows Shakespeare as a master craftsman, since, having witnessed the ghastly killing of the King and his two poor drugged minders, plus the dripping bloody hands of the Macbeths, Shakespeare puts in a scene of comic abandon. Yet, with this still, a sly message about what we had just witnessed.

The Porter scene is one of those scenes which regrettably rarely works on stage since the actor is trying so desperately to be funny. Of course, the next scene is a real nail-biting one since the King's men are now requesting to see their Master and here Macbeth has to put on the show of his life! This is a tough one, but at least here he has the most magnificent language to hold on to.

Macbeth has no choice but to say 'I'll take you to him' ... Now here is where mime really comes into its own since the actors, previously the sinners in hell, now use a method called 'figuration mime'. It is a method whereby the human body, with a little skill and imagination, substitutes for a prop, chair, stairs or a wall. As the actors walk to the King's chamber they form a long wall. As Macbeth walks along the castle wall the last pair of actors, arms outstretched, suddenly become a double door opening. As the door 'opens' the third walker links up to continue the wall and so it continues until they reach the King's chamber. This not only worked superbly well, it also gave a sense of foreboding as they continued their journey. Macbeth now reverses the journey at speed and then begins his speech while the actors have dissolved back into the chorus. I will not bother to describe our production further, except to say that this is the method we used for the whole play and this made the production at least visually exciting.

I'll finish with just this – Banquo, sensing that Macbeth is losing his haggis, decided to bolt for it. Now Shakespeare, knowing that you can't put a dynamic horse race on any stage, substitutes the words of how Banquo usually takes such and such a route. But of course we young, inventive, passionate actors take this opportunity to put it on stage, since we knew how to convincingly mime horses and that is what we did. It was beyond thrilling to do.

Once the two murderers had mastered the galloping horses, they rode like the very furies pursuing Banquo. The drama of the scene was in observing the pursuers and pursued. They had not moved more than a foot or two and were racing on the spot. As they become closer, one of the assassins strikes Banquo, thus ending the scene.

The creation of a creature, animal or insect requires that you first find the rhythm of the animal you are hoping to portray. For a horse, it begins with the snap of his hooves, left foot, right foot, ball heel, ball heel. Making a rhythmic pattern, which incidentally can be sped up to a gallop or even slowed down to a trot.

Now, I do not mean to say that all other methods of playing Shakespeare are dull as piss-water. Though most are a little bland. I could not imagine that Olivier's was anything but magnificent. I was simply overjoyed that Jacques Lecoq had opened so many doors for me to help make drama a significantly visual experience as well as an exciting oral one.

We worked on Macbeth for about four months. Part of that time was consumed by healing an ankle that I had fractured in two places by practising full somersaults from a springboard and catching my toes into one of those straw-like gym mats. It was rather unfortunate; however, after a couple of days my group, headed of course by Pip Donaghy, insisted that I direct for a while from a wheel chair. I shall never forget my wonderful team hoisting me up the stairs from my basement flat and back again. What a team I had! Fortunately I had been able to find a splendid rehearsal space just opposite the church hall. A really first-class space with clean pine floorboards and so convenient. It became our rehearsal space for several years. Chris Muncke, who helped me put *Metamorphosis* together, was again helping me and, when I was in doubt, never failing to encourage me. I was lucky in my choice of cast and I will never forget them. They came nearly every night from 5pm until 9/10pm and they were paid not a penny.

I had now formed a relationship with Sussex University and their splendid arena stage designed by Sean Kenny. Alwyne Scrase Dickens was the administrator and so the Gardiner Centre became the first base of our operations. And at least the actors were now paid. After Brighton we booked the theatre at the London School of Contemporary Dance. We had booked a three-week run, which was quite ambitious for us, and we were most encouraged by the praise from the dancers. That was praise indeed, since they live and breathe movement.

We did have some critics in, and I confess I was disappointed with their lack of vision or comprehension, but they were mildly praising of the endeavour. On the first Saturday night, after the first week's run, I hastened after the show to Fleet Street to buy the Sundays, which I felt beyond any doubt would support what I was doing. The first paper I picked up was, as far as I can remember, *The Sunday Times*. The critic was J. L. Lambert and I read it aghast. The idiocy of the man was beyond belief. The snide comments, the sarcasm, all so absolutely unnecessary. But one sentence I still remember from the pathetic man – 'We must have a moratorium for those "groups" who always seem to get into circles.' We did form that particular shape, but just twice in two and a half hours! Once for the sleeping scene when the dagger was passed round and once for the banquet scene when I see the ghost. Still, Lambert has gone to his grave and let him rest in peace, if he can. I loved playing Macbeth. Eliza Ward was a splendid partner as Lady Macbeth. This was early days for us, and we made do with our 'wrinkled tights' but our spirit was anything but wrinkled. I would love to do it again. Maybe I will.

We now had an Arts Council grant. I had little knowledge of the procedure required for receiving this, but I admired those that did. I had to know what strings to pull or what methods to use. I felt, maybe unjustly, that other groups had been wheedling for cash their whole lives from Uni onwards – I had worked for my wages all my life but was not yet in the groove. But eventually I did apply, showing my determination in already having produced three shows without asking for a penny. I had to put in a detailed application itemising each and every cost. This would be set against the potential income including nationwide tours, etc. Also one must include potential losses and profits. Campaigning for Arts Council money really made you run the gamut and, if you could and did, it was worth it.

So I was thrilled when my application was accepted. This had to be used and it was the great motivator and I was proud as Punch to have received it and always grateful. So I decided to try and tour a slightly cut-down version of *Metamorphosis* with a new curtain raiser we called *Knock at the Manor Gate*, a collection of some of Kafka's most curious and imaginative stories. I didn't wish to play the 'Beetle' again, having suffered aching and bruising knees for months, so we auditioned some actors and came across a handsome red-haired actor called Terry McGinity.

We actually began workshops on the great Jacobean writer John Ford's masterpiece *'Tis Pity She's a Whore*. This I was inspired to do after reading Antonin Artaud's seminal book on theatre called *The Theatre and Its Double*. A breath-taking read from start to finish, and I shall be ever grateful to the actor Peter Brett who introduced me to it. Thank you, Peter. I fell in love with Artaud. He said everything that touched a nerve inside me.

To me, the book was a cry of the heart and it echoed everything I felt about 'theatre' and a lot more. But what really struck me was his passion, his audacity, his reverence for the body of the actor as a malleable and dynamic expression of the play. 'Actors' voices have shrivelled from merely being the mouthpieces of bourgeois inanity.' His ambition was to stage violently controversial works such as the aforementioned *'Tis Pity She's a Whore* or his adaptation of Edgar Allen Poe's

The Fall of the House of Usher, in which he saw himself as the insane and tortured Roderick Usher. In fact he even confessed there was no one else who could play it but him, but I believed I was number two! Very sad that Artaud eventually died insane.

Our workshops were very exciting but also quite demanding. Nevertheless, I was so impressed with Terry McGinity that I asked him to take over the role of Gregor Samsa in *Metamorphosis*.

This would be for our first tour as a company. Stephen Williams, also a Webber Douglas student, now took over the role of The Father. I was still missing The Mother when, walking down Camden Passage in Islington, I came across an actress I had worked with during a wretched time I had in Nottingham. Her name was Maggie Jordan. I hardly knew her there and in fact hardly knew anyone there except, by chance, the director John Neville's lovely wife, whom I met in the theatre coffee shop, where we had charming informal talks and I could pour out my heart to her. So I told Maggie Jordan that we were desperate to find a Mother for *Metamorphosis* and lo and behold she was free!

I now redirected *Metamorphosis* with a vengeance and was deeply impressed by Terry. His voice was like silk, almost unnatural, and so very persuasive. Maggie was a marvel and entered the spirit of the play. Her voice was classically brilliant like cut glass, with a light but musical Scottish accent. I had a perfect cast. I could not believe how lucky I was. I really did feel that Maggie could become a really great actress. She reminded me of the images I had seen of Sarah Bernhardt. She was made for fame at a very high level.

But to fulfil our mandate with the Arts Council we did need a new show as a curtain raiser and so we began acting out the short stories. They were quite surreal and we loved doing them. Maggie opted not to be in them, which was alright with me, she was doing enough as the Mother and great she was.

For the time being I stepped out and played the Chief Clerk and Lodger and was now producing sound effects on the back of the strings of a piano. We toured around the crustier theatres and towns in England before ending up at the Hampstead Theatre Club for a four-week season under the auspices of the manager David Aukin. I was now learning how to endure dreary tours and ghastly digs and that was a valuable learning curve.

4

MISS JULIE VERSUS EXPRESSIONISM

National tour and the ICA 1971

I just wanted to do some acting, since I had virtually stepped out of *Metamorphosis*, except for taking over the role of Mr Samsa for four weeks whilst Terry was stunning the audiences with his 'bug'; I needed, wanted, craved, was desperate to act again. I thought that playing Jean the manservant in Strindberg's savage drama of the sexes would be a good choice. But how? Obviously I could not do it as it is written. There had to be more than that. We had to take this drama to pieces, to tear it up, to express the torment inside the belly of the beast.

Miss Julie is a conventional play, though at its time it was considered quite revolutionary. The language is nothing less than magnificent, but I found the staging with tables, chairs and kitchen utensils a little cluttered and strongly needed to find its pure essence. There had to be a way to escape from its heavy naturalism, and so I did. But it would take time before I found the 'key', since there is always a key to a work that will release its inner life. I was completely unsure when I started, and hoped that with patience and playing with the materials something would come to life. Any fool can design a set and any fool director can obey the stage directions, and they can be well-acted, if not passionate, productions, I have no doubt. But for some reason I could never go down this deadly conventional path. Something in me forbade it.

To travel along a well-worn path will bring you little, except the familiar and aching boredom of convention. However, for some plays, such a conventional approach may be unavoidable. I can recall, in my 'rep' days, the director bringing into the first rehearsal a prettily crafted model of the 'set'. The actors all gathered dutifully around, gazing like shy brides at their 'new' home.

The director then happily pointed out 'This is your entrance, the stairs to the bedroom, the door to the kitchen, etc. etc.' I stared at the little pile of cardboard slats and the tiny figures he had placed on the set to give it the correct scale, and something in me said, or rather shrieked, 'If I ever direct, I will never, ever go down this path.' There is a world in our unconscious which will never be tapped in this way. That world has to be stressed out of us.

Usually, I love to start with space … Actors on an empty stage. Then the words, where we are and why. Then the music; I feel there should always be the sounds that encourage and underline the play. Then, in the absence of ephemeral garbage, an idea, a sensation will arise from your unconscious to the surface. And what surfaces will be so much more extraordinary, more relevant than a group of actors staring meekly at a set.

In contrast, putting actors in front of a theatre maquette means that any spontaneous eruption of creative instinct will be automatically vetoed by the structure in front of them.

So one day Maggie Jordan and I went to a rehearsal room above a pub in the Angel, Islington and began. We just spoke the lines, moved around the room, but try as we may it just wasn't happening. Something was wrong. I do believe that Maggie and I were too far apart. Maggie was a brilliant classical actress and wanted to be moved or choreographed. Wished to know where we were going. Wanted the play blocked so that she could release her performance. I was dreaming of other worlds, fantasy, electric visions. Danger.

One day she had had enough and walked out, and I could not blame her. She had tried. She was so brilliant in *Metamorphosis* because she was taking over a role in a production that was shaped to a gesture, since the role had been created by Jeanie James and we had worked it out together. I kept looking at the play and realised that something in it was trapped. I needed to take it apart and I felt so excited by this that I got up each night at midnight and worked in my kitchen. I knew that if it didn't work I could just go to sleep. Nothing lost. As I started I can still remember to this day that I trembled as I was writing it.

I didn't want actors to be offstage and when we spoke about Miss Julie she would be there almost as if she were listening to us. When I spoke about Miss Julie heading the dance with the Gamekeeper on midsummer night festivities we saw Miss Julie sweep across the room, take me (as the Gamekeeper) in her arms, dance me around the room and disappear while I continued telling the story.

One night while thinking about it I had an epiphany. I felt that the play was begging for music. My then friend Shelley Lee, a dancer with the contemporary dance company, introduced me to a cellist called Colin Wood. Such an elegant young man with his thick curly hair, aquiline nose and shyish disposition.

The first day of the rehearsal I told Colin that I didn't really know where I was going. He replied comfortingly that neither did he. I was so in awe of musicians with their years of training and skill compared with us lazy actors who seldom train their bodies or their voices with the same ruthless discipline as musicians. I was quite nervous, but as soon as he drew his bow across the strings my heart melted. It was so powerful. I thanked God for him.

I gave him few directions or notes, for I wanted the special gods of inspiration to just guide. As we moved across the stage Colin followed with inspiringly beautiful notes on his cello. Then my adaptation kicked in, what I had been staying up so many nights for. I felt I had to break the form up, leaping from scene to scene almost like a collage. My god, it seemed to really work. It felt right even if it wasn't the form Strindberg wrote it in, but it had our form, and scenes flew into each other followed by the fierce plangent sounds of the cello. After the initial shock of the play shattered from its usual slow beginning and deadly exposition it started to settle and we continued the play as per scripts. For the few props I needed I chose a giant pair of boots. A bell that is rung from time to time, which is the master bell compelling John to spring to attention and furiously clean his boots. Three white cubes for seats.

As I said, I always have a penchant to bring on stage that which is spoken about as happening off stage or in the distant past. It's Walpurgisnacht. Mid-summer night evening when all the demons and sprites are released. When Julie is tempted into a sexual alliance with Jean I felt I had to show it. I had Jean and Julie merely stand against a wall, in fact in two bright white lights shaped as door frames. Jean's domestic wife, who is also the servant, uses Jean and Julie as models. Smearing lipstick all over Jean's face and doing the same with Julie. She ruffles me up, pulls the shirt out of my trousers, undoes my zip, pulls Julie's blouse out of her skirt and makes her hair thoroughly dishevelled. Whilst this is going on I had projected large blow-ups of Victorian French erotica. Meanwhile Colin is playing the appropriate music. It was a striking and exciting effect. Jean and Julie never had to touch each other. The full stage lights come on and they both rush from the lit door-like spaces, hurried and adjusting their clothes, tucking in shirts and blouses. That's all we did and it told us everything. The pornographic photos I had converted into slides came from an old book of French pictures. Their starchy black-and-white images were quite wonderful.

When we first tried the production out in the Gardiner Centre at Sussex University I must admit that I sank down in my seat as the lighting man asked to see the erotic slides, so as to check that the light didn't fade them out. No they were perfect. The lighting man, bless him, took it all in his stride … 'Is that the lot?' … 'Yes, thanks' and we continued.

In this production I was so fortunate to have the amazing talents of dancer and singer Carol Cleveland as the servant girl Christine, as well as Eliza Ward, my Lady Macbeth. Both ladies were quite wonderful to work with and I counted myself lucky to have them.

Eliza Ward, whom I had met at the Glasgow Citizens Theatre, was a striking Miss Julie. She had within her a sense of freedom and desire to experiment. Carol Cleveland was perfect as Christine. She had been a dancer, and that skill opened up a whole tranche of possibilities as the maidservant. Many actresses wished to know the 'reason' for every move or suggestion and would be resistant until they were convinced of its worthiness. With Carol, she would just hurl herself into it until the reasons became apparent.

Now, there is a really passionate scene that follows, starting with the enthusiasm of Jean, fired up by his unexpected romance and his fantasies about starting a small hotel with Miss Julie after they leave. It's a really powerful scene full of hope and the tempting seeds of adventure. Perhaps in post-coital leavening down of his enthusiasm Jean backs down on doing anything too radical. But Julie insists. She has now been devalued and can no longer stay in the house for another moment. Jean reluctantly agrees and tells her to swiftly pack some things. But Julie cannot leave her precious pet bird behind and insists on taking it with them. Jean's fury at the pathetic, as he thinks, feminine sentiments, makes him rage and, in his frustration and brutishness, he says he'll kill the little bird. Such a very horrible decision. Now, I didn't want to fake the killing of the little bird, so I devised the following: Miss Julie will *enact* the bird.

Julie has wrapped a large feather boa around her neck and arms. As she pleads to save the bird, her arms flutter in protest. As she flutters the precious small feathers of the boa, she slowly but surely takes on the rhythm of a bird in panic, moving forwards and backwards as she cries out in alarm. Jean has now a large cut-throat razor in his hand. As she moves frantically in her 'bird' state he thrusts out with the weapon. Eventually he strikes her. Blackout. Jean in the blackout has donned a satanic Devil mask. Now Miss Julie makes her speech, which has to be one of the most powerful feminist speeches in all drama. The bird is dead. The stage is black. Only her powerful voice rings out in the darkness of the stage. Now the master has returned. Christine takes the bell and rings it furiously. Jean is paralysed by the sound, like a Pavlov dog, and furiously attacks the boots.

The second production of *Miss Julie* was one of the most satisfying and exciting plays I had ever done up to that point in time. The reviews were mixed, with some dismissing it as an indulgence and some saying it was one of the most exciting evenings that they had had in the theatre. We played it at the Institute of Contemporary Arts (ICA) in Pall Mall for several weeks and then took it on tour. Since the tour was some months hence we sadly had to change the actors, and I chose Teresa D'Abreu for Miss Julie. Teresa was a dynamic Julie. She was in fact not too dissimilar from her role. Well educated, well brought up, with an almost aristocratic voice and a sheer delight to work with.

She almost slid into her role as if she was to the manor born. And even had the slight gaucheness of a high-bred lady. Whereas Eliza was far earthier, yet both sides of their characters suited the role.

Christine, Jean's wife, was played by Judith Alderson, who was equally good. She was far wilder than Carol Cleveland, but lacked her beautiful elegance. However, like the other cast change, it worked just as well. Teresa worked with me as a rather young Clytemnestra in my first production of *Agamemnon*. She then went on to play Leni in my adaptation of Franz Kafka's *The Trial* at The Roundhouse, Chalk Farm.

Teresa died a few years ago at far too young an age to be taken from us, and so few members of the public would get to know her. This young, bright and vital woman.

We toured several towns in England with *Miss Julie*, but eventually it came to an end, as my early shows often did, without a good producer to encourage its longevity. I never did work with Maggie Jordan again, which was sad as she was a unique actress. Certainly one of the best.

5

AGAMEMNON

National tour and The Roundhouse, Chalk Farm 1973

Now, as it so happens on very rare occasions, I was offered a directing role from RADA of all places. The director of RADA, a most charming and cultivated man called Hugh Cruttwell, apparently saw one of my early productions and picked me as a movement person. We met and had a very pleasant chat and I was booked to direct the *Oresteia*. All three plays. This was a nightmare, since one play I can cope with, but the three of the trilogy was just a little too much. Well, the long and short of it was that I had to back out of the trio of plays. At the end of the day, a whole day spent reading the stuff tediously translated and boringly read, I went downstairs and almost tearfully told Mr Cruttwell that it was too much for me. 'Then why not just do the first part, part one, *Agamemnon*. Have a drink.' he said, and this most elegant and sensitive of men went to the drinks cabinet and poured me a whiskey and water. I felt better already and happily agreed to do the first part. Another director would direct the final two parts, *Orestes* and *The Furies*.

I was happy and went to work with a will. Now, I was always looking for the key, my own particular key to unlock the puzzle, and this was becoming difficult. We spent many days doing workshops and exercises as if I were testing the lock on a safe. One number will reveal all. Eventually I started blocking. It was slowly working, largely due to the exercises and physical improvisations with the actors. These improvisations not only tap our imagination and make us more inventive, but also bring the actors closer together. Sometimes the exercises appear to have nothing to do with the play, but in a curious way the impulses and themes of the play will reveal themselves

This time I did not always use live music, but added recorded music and some rock music. One piece in particular fascinated me, and it was by King Crimson, a group fronted by Robert Fripp. Notably, their weirdly wonderful *In the Wake of Poseidon*. We continued very slowly, but it was gradually coming together. I felt that the translation was stuffy and archaic, however, and to be quite frank the actors were struggling with it. But two still stand out. The chorus leader was Henry Goodman and Agamemnon was Jonathan Pryce. Jonathan was a very gentle soul and, since my style of working was so slow, I didn't get up to his entrance scene, at the end of the play when he returns to Argos, for some time. I always apologised to him, and his response was to say that I shouldn't worry and that he was fine waiting. Eventually I did come to the scene when he arrives at the head of a troop of cavalry, expertly mimed by our young actors. When he opened his mouth – 'First I hail Argos and her Gods …' – he suddenly let out a sound on 'Argos' that I had never heard before. It was stunning, like a great trumpet blast that could have felled the walls of Jericho. This young man was a star. Where did this young Welshman develop such a powerful instrument? Wherever it came from, it was part of his armoury. It was part of his Welsh village, part of his dad's mining history. For the production I was allowed to use as my assistant my young student from Webber Douglas, Christopher Muncke. I think we were both stunned by Jonathan's vocal chords.

The show was more successful than I could have imagined, and one day I decided to do a professional production, since I had invested so much in this Greek play. Also I would rewrite the whole thing. About one year later I began a few words of my version. By some happy chance I decided one summer to go to a Greek island called Skyros, an amazingly beautiful island, with my girlfriend at the time, a charming young woman called Anne Cheatle, Annie. The island of Skyros was and still is like a mini-paradise, and I started keeping a journal and, of course, being of a rather romantic nature, my writings reflected the environment. I loved writing about that mystical isle. I wanted to give heartfelt thanks to this wonderful accident of nature, an island heaved out of the sea millions of years ago. I wanted to embrace the waves, the surge, the colours, the sun, the heat and I started then to rewrite *Agamemnon*. When I returned to London I continued, and it just flowed out of me in a storm of language.

Then one day I was writing out the Herald's strident speech about the war and I couldn't stop, I felt it deep inside me as if I had been there. I wrote almost as fast as I could think, and when I finished the page the ends of my sentences made a perfect vertical line down the page as if it had been drawn using a ruler.

The time came to start working on it. I put an advert in *Time Out* for actors, and Teresa D'Abreu became my assistant and played Clytemnestra. Dozens of actors applied, and we found at least ten pretty efficient ones, several of whom were foreign. As chorus leader and Aegisthus we were blessed with the splendid German actor Wolf Kahler, who was once in Nancy Meckler's Freehold Theatre Group, Alfredo Michelson, an Argentinian actor who became a staunch ally, and then an actor called Barry Philips turned up who was quite remarkable. A young Londoner/cockney, though he spoke English immaculately and the text with tremendous verve and clarity. At the last minute an actor called Hilton McRae joined us, an attractive, slightly wired young man with a beautiful soprano voice.

We had a team and we started. This time, however, I would play Agamemnon.

The young Jonathan Pryce's performance was a distant memory, and I felt compelled to play Agamemnon as a dynamic warrior, expressing all the elements of

FIGURE 5.1 Hilton McRae in *Agamemnon* at Greenwich Theatre, 1976.

movement which I had learned in the mime school of Jacques Lecoq. I loved the character of Agamemnon, he was a bold and fearless warrior. A powerful, if confused soldier obliged to sacrifice his own daughter to free the winds for his sails. I feel the story carries an ironic undertone, that if you go to war for a worthless cause (the elopement of Paris and Helen), you are obliged to taste a bit of personal pain or don't join this wretched Armada! However, it certainly fits his karma, since his wife Clytemnestra will ensure his death on the very day he returns from the wars.

Eventually we found an astounding musician who was so inventive that I didn't have to give one note! His music just inspired us. His name was Paul Burwell. We began rehearsals over a pub in the Angel, Islington. It was a nerve-wracking, nail-biting time to begin with this largish group, but, having spent weeks doing workshops, they were swift in adapting to any situation. I felt so strongly that this had to be a visually exciting play and the challenge to their physical invention would be fairly demanding. But this was Greece. Everything is physical, lived through the body. Sea, ships, oars, battles, worn toothless villagers who were the chorus.

We began with the story of the curse, a longish speech detailing the macabre feast when one of the two brothers in conflict not only slays the children of his siblings but tricks his rival into eating them. It's a disgustingly vivid speech, but curiously it brought the best out of me. Terry McGinity did this opening prologue when we did it in Greenwich Theatre, and his reading of it was extraordinary. But for now I was just getting a first draft together, so to speak. And we jettisoned the long opening prologue.

We began as I did at RADA on the very first day with the chorus in a slow march on the spot, gently swaying from side to side.

> *Ten years since Agamemnon and Menelaus,*
> *Those twin bronze fists from the house of Atreus,*
> *Sent forth a thousand ships to the doom of Troy.*
> *Screaming like eagles/ maddened for the prey/ clawed hate/ wings beating, they*
> *swooped/ they ripped and tore/ the Gods above heard the furore/ their song of blood*
> *stung the air/ and so the House of Atreus swept on to crush the House of Priam.*

I matched their voices in rhythm to the movement and even composed a rhythmic beat to it, which gave the movement power. Behind this was a slow drum beat. It felt right. As the men gathered to prepare for battle the last thing in the world I wanted was any simulated punch-up on stage. I do believe audiences have had quite enough of poorly simulated battle scenes, when valuable days have been spent employing choreographers to put together a vague image of conflict. It wearies the poor actors, injures quite a few. However, to 'symbolise' it is far more effective and infinitely more exciting. I simply used the words of weaponry: 'Javelin! Arrow! Spear! Sword! Axe! Cut! Thrust! Tear! Bleed! Hack!'

Two groups of warriors faced each other, four to a side. One actor comes out and goes to the opposite side. He approaches a second actor who's standing perfectly still. He then sharply calls out 'Javelin!' The actor he approaches reacts as if he had just been mortally wounded. Then the same actor goes to one after another, calling out the names of the weapons as he approaches each man. A drum beat accompanies him at each strike. Just before he finishes the next actor is stating his ritualistic recitation. Then the third. A slight pause, then two actors working in unison beginning their action and so it continues. The slain ones are now recovered, to be able to increase the number on the battlefield. Now the drum is building up speed and the actors have formed into a vertical line. And as they now shout out the words, they move their bodies alternatively left or right or leaping up, but still in the same spot. It was most effective, so much so in fact that it thrilled me each time I saw it. The head of the line was Wolf Kahler, who let rip a scream which signified the end of the movement.

We had created an exciting battle simply using words and movement, sans swords, spears, blood and all the other rather simple props of the conventional theatre. I knew we were on our way and that it would just flow from then on. We had found the key!

The scene then returns to the village folk, waiting at home and whining for news of their battling heroes. So, immediately after the first sword battle, the cast swiftly took large staves as if they were spears and held them aloft. To a drum beat they swiftly clashed, retreated, then to the beat clashed again. As they did so, they became fatigued, worn out, ancient and the staves were then the old staves of the villagers, holding themselves up, bent over double as ancient crones; and then they began their speech.

> *Meanwhile we wait.*
> *For years we wait.*
> *For a sign …*
> *For a sign from Agamemnon.*

They continue as the old villagers to recount the story of how Helen was stolen or seduced by Paris. They reflect on their hopelessness until suddenly the Queen enters, which causes great excitement, jubilation and some cynicism until she says the remarkable words that she has news. 'News!?,' they cry. 'What news?' Now comes one of the most remarkable speeches in the whole of the *Oresteia*, which I of course adapted to make it not only more rhythmic but also more demotic, unlike the stilted translations that exist of Greek tragedy.

After a scene of mocking, clowning and disbelieving, after the fact that she is still a woman and liable to exaggeration and invention, she then shuts them up. It is an awesome speech, requiring the actress to be at her very best. They continue to taunt Queen Clytemnestra, until, when one of the crabby old men says 'News travels fast but not that fast, what travels so fast?,' she lets rip …

> *Fire travels/ Fire speaks/ The God of fire raced from peak to peak/ The God of fire leapt/ scorched crackles and shrieks/ I had a hundred watchmen trained for years on highest peaks/ from here to Troy/ to light their fires when they see the smoke begin to rise from Trojan streets/ their eyes they focused on infinity did not dare blink! They must not miss the faintest wisp that tells them something's burning/ something lives on fire/ the tunnel in the water of their eyes must pass the picture back to me/ from Ida/ Lemnos/ Athos/ Skyros/ across the Aegean Sea/ A whiplash of lightning like molten gold/ the sharks danced to see the beacons glow/ each sleepy watchman fired his sticks in turn/ so a current of flames streaked over Euripus/ hill to hill/ crackle scorch and burn/ it soared it swung it came/ like an avenging angel across a frozen forest of*

stars/ Aesopus/ it burned on to Kitheron/ burn/ the great marsh of Gorgopis/ burn burn burn/ raced on like fiery stallions to Aegyplantus Peak/ lightning strokes lit the skies/ jagged veins of flame/ dancing fireflies/ then shook its beard of shimmering red/ leapt headlong across the Saronic Gulf until at last/ on Arachnus burst into bloom/ then flew like a meteor/ on to the house of Atreus/ my fire runners ran/ relay to relay/ unbroken/ my marathon of flame/ that is my news/ what have you to say?

The chorus have suddenly become quiet, they are listening fascinated. Now, our method of working is not to let the queen begin and end her great monologue while actors stand idly by, giving the odd nod of acknowledgement. As they listen they are slowly caught up in her story. Slowly, very slowly, they join her, becoming and reflecting the extraordinary things she is saying. Their eyes face front as if they are totally spellbound by her, and when she talks about a 'whiplash of lightning' their bodies reflect hers. In this case they are not acting it out so much as reflecting, being her orchestra, her children and her servants. This of course has to be done very carefully so that a member of the chorus doesn't do something that does not support her. But curiously none of them ever did, they were so caught up in it. They are fascinated since she tells them how she placed watchmen on the peaks of every island from Troy to Argos. And as soon as Troy falls, a watchman in the city has been primed to light a beacon to telegraph the news. It is thrilling to hear it. And so each watchman lit his beacon in turn until a current of flame leapt from isle to isle.

Her own watchman in Argos on the roof of the palace has been patiently waiting for ten years, or thereabouts, for this moment and excitedly relates the news to Clytemnestra. She not only describes it with deep relish and emotion but acts as if she herself embodied the fire. Racing from isle to isle spitting out the expressive Greek sounds as the islands are named. What follows after the momentarily stunned villagers recover their senses is truly a Greek epic, as in the distance they can see the bare outline of a figure running. It is the Herald, of course. Now begins a second crescendo, or if you like scherzo, as rhythmically they all fasten their eyes on this small moving dot as it grows larger and larger.

I think I see a dot begin to grow into something moving/ slow/ now fast/ now faster still/ its shape suggests a man running/ telling us/ what?/ Chaos/ disaster/ more?/ A herald running from the shore.

Now follows their description as he comes closer and closer, spoken, shouted in the rhythm of his strong legs. Now here I felt something completely new and radical had to introduce his entrance. The speech of the Herald is for me one of the highlights of the play, since he not only relates the story, but encapsulates it. I did not want a Herald to merely rush on from the wings with a few mild simulated pants, I felt it necessary that we see him from the beginning of his journey, and this would be an epic moment, since he would be not only eagerly awaited by the sedentary townsfolk, but would also be corroborating the extraordinary revelations of Clytemnestra. There are certain moments in a Greek tragedy which are climaxes in the play, the entry of the Herald is one of them, when he is able to reveal the horrors he has just witnessed. Such moments must invite an intense and dramatic revelation. So we see the Herald as he is approaching the village, as he arrives and as he delivers his heart-rending account.

Many years ago, Peter Brook, the most celebrated director, organised a bus for forty or so spectators to go to a medium-sized church hall in London's East End to see a performance of Grotowski's Polish Laboratory Theatre group.

I was fortunate enough to get a ticket. We all patiently waited outside the door, building up a great sense of anticipation while the group finished off their warm-up. Mr Brook waited with us like a patient school master. Eventually we were let in. We all sat silently, expecting that we were to see the wonders of the theatre world. Of course, not knowing Polish, the language bits went right by us and so we concentrated on their physical style. To speak true, while they were very good, I was not over-impressed except for one moment. A man is running with urgency to reach his destination. He runs on the spot. He runs for a long time and I was most impressed by this. It showed the dedication of the actor and his physical prowess. This moment sowed a seed in my head that was to flower in the awesome and compelling run of the Herald.

As our group of villagers are facing ahead, watching and encouraging the Herald on in rhythm, slowly from the back appears the man playing the Herald. Here we use a simple film technique. The chorus face front and very slowly part, still chanting, when the Herald begins. He begins very slowly, starting with a mimed walk which breaks into a run. The chorus chant, the drum begins a different beat, the wind instruments of the musicians begin to make their weird eerie sound, he continues running. And now we hear only the runner. This was performed by Barry Philips. He gave life to it that was utterly enthralling. There was no other word for it. We hear his breath, and when I play the tape, since we always tried to at least make a sound tape of our productions, hearing it over forty years later it is hearing not only his pounding feet but this young man's breath that almost makes me weep.

The Herald eventually stops running, breathing heavily, and the chorus joyfully mock his beating heart, pounding their own chests in rhythm to it. Now begins the second most powerful speech in the play, as the Herald describes the fall of Troy. Barry's voice rings out powerfully and this is just after he had had to run continuously on stage for at least five minutes, on the spot, which is no easy thing. He relates the story of Agamemnon's mighty military success.

> *Oh, this good soil of Argos/ I never dared to dream that I would see my blessed earth again/ Great Agamemnon's coming back/ render him the welcome he deserves/ Troy has toppled down/ her shrines dissolved in dust/ her seed exterminated by chattering machines of death that spit from iron mouths/ by the hot breath of napalm/ scorching the sins that stank to heaven/ while howitzers screeched arias in the streets/ then ack-ack-ack-ack/ and Dum-Dum shells explode/ their scattering claws of steel/ explore men's veins and arteries/ and spread confusion in flying brains/ and guts that fell like hail and slimed the rooves/ a panoply of armour ripped the sky apart/ as Zeus*

unleashed missile after missile/ and anti-missile missile missile/ equal to the weight of ten thousand tonnes of hate/ ploughed the fields/ destroyed the crops/ forever/ lay waste even the waste/ bore holes the size of mountains/ while our brave boys/ burning under a monstrous sun/ and seizing what they had/ gleaming bazookas/ Patton tanks like Trojan horses made from heavy steel/ rasped deadly snorts into the walls/ which fell like flaking skin/ that's nuclear scorched/ and Zeus laughed and laughed and laughed and spat out deadly gasses from his guts/ and men collapse like flies/ heaved out their entire wet insides/ we sloshed around a slaughterhouse of guts/ then in we marched/ with masks of death/ protected 'gainst that burning breath around us/ grasping in fists our automatics proudly cocked/ small fat grenades packed in our crotch/ and ricocheted around the town our tuneful whistling bullets/ smooth bore/ cannon/ trench/ mortar/ shrapnel/ tommy gun/ and blowpipe/ RAT TAT TAT/ RAT TAT AT/ KA BOOM/ KA BLAST/ KA BLAM/ SPLAT! PHUTT! SMASH! PHAM!!! WOW!

Now he is asked by the astounded villagers what happened to Menelaus, 'the other half of Agamemnon'. Here the Herald agonisingly tells of the fateful consequence of their actions.

Not quite so fortunate, a storm did hit the fleet/ the first day out/ the last crap on the beach/ the sails repaired/ hoist up the rig/ release the hawsers/ a soft wind fills our sails/ like the giant cheeks of Cyclops' ass/ all's well/ the sea's as calm as thick as syrup/ the sky a halcyon sheet of baby blue … Then one black night/ we felt a team of elephants begin to move beneath our boughs/ that sudden lurch which brings our supper foully back into our mouths … And as the dawn arose we saw the Aegean thick with bloated Greeks/ like flowers scattered by the wind and lazy sharks unbelieving their good luck/ were having breakfast/ the fleet was smashed except for us/ we sailed through that infernal nightmare/ with not one timber sprung.

This is as remarkable as the first half of his speech. Of course I rewrote this from the translation that I had, since what on earth can replace the original Greek language? I tried to make it vivid, powerful and expressive in my own language. For some reason I was so caught up in the story that my 'version' just poured out of me and I wrote it in one session without stopping, as if the muse was sitting with me.

The text (after Aeschylus) brought something out of him which was almost elegiacal. It touched on that cell of mankind where the essence of our humanity lay. I do believe that it was certainly Barry Philips' finest hour. I am so glad I have a tape of those fantastic moments and so it will never die.

Now Clytemnestra chides the woolly, untrusting and pathetic townsfolk. I felt I had to have just as powerful and dramatic an entrance for Agamemnon and his troops as for the Herald, who of course had announced their imminent arrival just a few minutes earlier. As I have said, one of the virtues of studying the mechanics of the body is that you can translate a story via the use of that wonderful instrument most of us are blessed with. The human body.

We, the cast and I, would become the horse and riders proudly charging into Argos. Why not! Paul Burwell's brilliantly evocative music began. As if to signal the beginning, a strange piercing but low note was sounded, our feet made one strong pounding of the wooden stage with our heels and then slowly repeated it, gaining more and more pace. Then he played or shook some bells, which were the horse harness and buckles in the distance. And our feet started to pound until we established the rhythm of a trot. The drum now added its dramatic, fierce sound, slowly matching the rhythm of our feet. Now, and gradually, we added our voices, in rhythm … 'A-GA-MEM-NON … A-GA-MEM-NON.' This goes on for a few moments, but now from the trot we speed into a regular and ordered canter and following this into a gallop. The actors were able to accurately beat the rhythms of those separate speeds as it built up. Eventually it stops; the actors/horses paw the floor. Agamemnon slowly walks to the front of the group and makes his speech. I felt that this was a pivotal moment.

Eventually I finish the speech. My captive Cassandra, played immaculately by Australian Anna Nigh, makes the terrifying warning speech as I reluctantly tread the red carpet. My wife makes a speech preparing to slay me, which she does as I lie naked in a bath. Aegisthus, her lover, now reveals himself and makes his triumphant speech. Curtain.

Agamemnon struggled somewhat in England. However, it did make it to Israel, where it had been translated into Hebrew, which expressed so well the Greek spirit. The sounds in Hebrew were sharp and abrasive and onomatopoeic. There is something in the Hebrew language that is emphatic when it needs to be and dramatic when it reaches a high moment of passion. There was also the relief that someone else was producing, in this case the Haifa Theatre Company under theatre director Amnon Meskin. It was an exciting period of work, and I could put everything I had learned so far into this new production. For the costumes I was inspired by the built-up and padded bodies of American football players. Clytemnestra was played by the Israeli American actress Joanna Peled, a very strong, beautiful red-haired actress who had recently been working with La MaMa in New York. She brought that work ethic with her and she was quite wonderful. Agamemnon was played by an old friend of mine whom I had taught at the Webber Douglas School of Drama in London in 1968. Asher Tsarfati had now grown over the years since I worked with him in *In the Penal Colony* and was perfect for the role, powerful, strong-limbed with great vocal power. And the percussion was by Zohar Levy, whom I had used in *Metamorphosis*, also done in Hebrew, the year before.

I had a third outing of the play when I directed it in LA for Susan Lowenberg at the Olympic Arts Festival in 1984. The arts committee had requested plays with an Olympic theme, and of course what could have been better than a great Greek drama? Having staged it in Israel with Israeli Jews and Israeli Arabs, I felt that I needed a sense of community, a group with a feel of cohesiveness. I suggested we stage it with Afro-American actors. Even from the first days of the auditions I knew I had made the right decision. They were a dynamic group, and I was very proud of the production. There was such a feeling of camaraderie that I remained in touch with many of the actors for years after the event. Clytemnestra was played by Dianne Sommerfield, whose voice was electric and whose fluid movement was like that of a dancer. Curiously enough, after that magnificent performance she left Los Angeles and was never heard of again. A not uncommon occurrence in LA. Roger Smith played a brilliant Herald and went on to become a unique actor creating his own dynamic and controversial one-man shows. That was the last time it has been seen and that was 1984.

6

THE TRIAL, BY FRANZ KAFKA

The Roundhouse, Chalk Farm 1973

This book had been on my 'bucket' list for many years. It is an astonishing work of fiction which taps into all the thousand and one fears that flesh is heir to. It touches one so deeply by its utter simplicity and honesty. There are few of us who cannot relate to its story of guilt. The uniqueness of Kafka is that he begins his tales with a climax and then works through the repercussions.

> *Somebody must have been lying about Joseph K, for without having done anything wrong he was arrested one fine morning.*

Thus we the readers are hooked from the very beginning. This is a most strange and yet epic book, and I decided to adapt it. It felt absolutely right for my method of work.

An exercise that Jacques Lecoq gave us was the following. A group of actors are gathered on the stage. At a signal, one of the actors will be captured in a special situation which he or she will instigate. The actor may be sitting in a café ordering a meal. Within seconds, the entire group are in the same café, totally absorbed in the situation and creating a scene. A second actor now changes the environment, e.g. to the interior of a train. Again, within a few seconds or less, we are strap-hanging in the Underground. This exercise can go on indefinitely.

The Trial has a similar pattern as it moves through a myriad of scenes, almost like the fleeting images of a dream. We are able to change the scene even in a split second. Another of the most exciting techniques Jacques taught was 'mime-figuration', where the bodies of the actors become the environment and thus we have a 'metaphysical' theatre. This was very suited to Kafka's paranoid novel.

No one in Britain had adapted it before, and in France it was of course very tempting for the French maestro Jean-Louis Barrault, who adapted it with André Gide. Quite a pair. I thought their adaptation interesting but not detailed enough and so I would create a new one. The Jean-Louis Barrault adaptation was very inventive, but seemed to skate over many small but important scenes, which I thought were essential for the plot. I had always known Barrault to be a brilliantly inventive mime, making full use of the body in all of its miraculous parts. The ensemble are the backbone, heart and viscera of the play. Joseph K, meanwhile, is the brain, but of course they need to work together. *The Trial* is one of those works that stays with you all your life, so much so that it permeates your entire being. I even began to think like Joseph K, the unfortunate victim who never discovers for what reason he is 'guilty'. But what fascinated me above all was its mysterious European flavour. I began working on this magnificent novel during a period of time when I was teaching Drama at Webber Douglas Drama School. I had spent some months teaching mime and movement when the school governor, Raphael Jago, asked me whether I would like to do a production. No British drama inspired me too much in those ghastly days of kitchen sinks and ironing boards. I asked my students to buy themselves each a copy of *The Trial* and read the first page. I felt I had to try it out or at least explore it. My first fumblings were a little incoherent. But I stayed with it. I had no performance script and had worked nothing out. I merely opened the book and read the first page to them. I then asked our young group of actors to act out what we had just read. I saw in *The Trial* a perfect novel for Jacques Lecoq's methodology.

Not exclusively, but a perfect way to interpret this mysterious and labyrinthine work. The technique he taught us was mime figuration. It's a natural technique which demands that we use our imagination to create the environment. We used to practise this with the use of two or three bodies to convey any situation we wished. But it has to be conveyed figuratively. A body, if skilfully used, can be a staircase which the other actor climbs. When Joseph K is searched, his whole body becomes a set of drawers merely on curling his hands, keeping his arms by his side. The other actor seizes his partner's hands and pulls the drawers open, and then brusquely shuts them. In the book his room is searched. The room is the victim. The victim is being assaulted, hence he becomes the drawers and the violation is all the more potent. You are what you possess. The technique is of course far more complex than this, since one goes from image to image and you have to smartly and succinctly melt from one to another. It is a breathtaking concept. Sometimes we could use another form with a simple prop, like, for example, a rope which became very significant for us – a rope was thrown across stage and unwound from one actor to another. It is now taut. Joseph K walks along the rope accompanied by a simple drum beat. As soon as he reaches the end of the rope the actor holding one end swiftly takes a portion of the rope and turns at right angles. Joseph K follows the wall or rope downstage, but as he gets to the end he turns round and retraces his walk, though on the other side of the rope.

As he reaches the end Joseph K has to turn right and continue, meanwhile, before he reaches the end of the rope, the first actor now steps swiftly at right angles, thus shortening the rope even more. Joseph K simply and calmly continues his journey. As he gets to the end of this smaller section of the journey, the actor holding the rope merely lifts one side, which K will now use to mime climbing a staircase. The second actor waits whilst the first actor torments K, by now changing the direction of the stairs, first up and then down. Meanwhile the steps taken are speeding up, the drum beats swifter and with greater urgency. You could say the rope symbolises K's hopeless and repetitive journey. His rope shortens to its final length and the two actors very swiftly cross each other, and as they do they have K in a stranglehold. While it may not be quite so easy to describe, the effect, carried out by two swift-thinking and capable actors, is breathtaking.

K falls to his knees, the rope held on the two opposite sides. With his last breath he calls for help. It is heart-breaking. Finally the two guards do the final pull as K slowly intones … 'like a dog'.

The Trial has ruled my life, in the sense that I have done it a number of times and each time it never failed to enthral me. It meant something. It is a profound work. Günther Beelitz, the Intendant of the Düsseldorfer Schauspielhaus, asked me to do it there, and that was probably the most exciting version of the play I have done. It suited the actors, and of course it was in its original language. I was directing in one of the major theatres in Germany and the play was very well received.

Everything slipped into place. I lived in a tiny apartment and my landlady brought my breakfast each morning at 8am sharp, as did the landlady of Joseph K. That was my first experience of directing abroad and in another language, and I have never forgotten it.

I was always searching for ways to express the drama. Ways that would break down the conventional and simple methods of naturalism, which is the most often used method for those who either have few theatrical skills or even lack a desire to learn them. There is no need for huge cumbersome sets merely because the novel is set in houses, streets and offices. That is written. But the essence of the story is within the mind. At the time I had the great opportunity to see a dance company led by Alwin Nikolais, a remarkable choreographer who made great use of abstract structures and forms like stretch fabric wrapped around the dancers. In the show I saw at Sadler's Wells he used free-standing frames covered in fabric. When several were put together they made a wall. When one was shifted it revealed a scene going on behind it. These screens were moveable and flexible. I had found my set for *The Trial*. I was most excited by this 'discovery' since scenes could be revealed and just as easily wiped out as in a film. I shared my idea with my actors, all of whom were enthusiastic, and we set about buying the wood to make the frames. The frames were about two inches wide, an inch thick and about six foot six inches in height (all old measurements). Then I bought some metal brackets to stand them on so that they could be free-standing and would not wobble, and could easily be transported by the actors into any position we chose.

Then something most bizarre happened. We stood all the finished frames upright, about ten of them, just waiting to be covered in a thin cloth. As I stood staring proudly at the empty frames I found them so beautiful in their present 'unclothed' state. I could walk through them and when they were placed in a line that became a corridor. Placed side my side, north and south or horizontally, they became a busy office, each actor in their cubicle, or one standing alone became a painting for Titorelli, the court painter.

A chair behind a screen became the room for the tenement. The screen was then easily moved to the off-stage area, creating a neutral area for the 'chorus' or ensemble. For us it was a profound discovery since we did not now need the cloth to cover the screens, and we had such a very stimulating time working out all the possibilities of the manipulating screens. It was exciting, as well as highly symbolic. We were now all very aware that we had found something quite unique.

Also they were perfect for use with our mime figuration. When at the beginning of the play two guards appear, they merely step through the door in ultra-slow motion as if stepping through some eerie substance. Then they search K's room, a detail which I had added, since in the novel they just question him. However, since accused people are usually brusquely searched, we added that detail. Now the chorus are watching, sitting on chairs on either side of the stage. Here they can act as a chorus of voices, commenting on the action and being Joseph K's worrying thoughts. It worked well. It worked so well in fact that it seemed as if the door frames were a symbol for the play. Especially since, at the beginning, we intoned the speech usually said by the Priest at the end of the book: 'Before the door stands the doorkeeper. Before him stands a figure of a man waiting to gain admittance to the law …'

Nothing could have been more appropriate. We had found it. We were on our way. I had attained a capable team of actors who were working for nothing, and gave themselves to it. Especially Pip Donaghy, Paola Dionisotti and Bill Stewart as a magnificent Joseph K. He has left us as I write these words and I miss him terribly. These actors worked for nothing because they were highly imaginative actors, who saw this work as an opportunity to do something that few other theatres seemed to be doing. Our work was radical and inventive. Some would have sold their souls for such an opportunity, but eventually, once we became successful and started touring, they were all paid. We also had the talented actor from the RSC Barry Stanton. Barry Stanton was an ex-RSC stalwart. A large, powerful man, who was a force of nature on stage. I wanted such a gargantuan beast for the role of Huld, the useless, pompous lawyer, bloated with his own opinions, on whom K places all his hopes. Also, Barry was a comic genius. Others came and went and gave great contributions, like Stephen Williams, whom I taught at Webber Douglas. Actors will work for no pay if they feel that there is nowhere else on earth they will gain the benefits of a unique experiment. It is of course much easier to work for wages, even if your soul is being starved. We were young and idealistic, and everybody gave themselves to it wholeheartedly.

We worked at our studio church hall in Islington every day or every evening for at least six weeks. I played the court painter Titorelli, the role that Stephen Williams had played at Webber Douglas when he was a student. He was brilliant in a Marx Brothers' style. I shamelessly emulated him.

Titorelli's description of the various stages of guilt is amongst the most brilliant comic writing in the whole of Kafka. Kafka parodies the pettifogging complexities of the law in a brilliant satiric way. At times you could be reading pure Marx Brothers! There is such a clown-like temperament in Titorelli that I played him in a harlequin half mask. It suited the character enormously, and as soon as I put the mask on I felt totally at home within my character. The only trouble was that I sweated like a pig and in the end I had to abandon it. Like a lot of ideas that we had after an initial period, we found a lighter ballast. Finally I just painted on a Dalí moustache and played him as a kind of Dalíesque clone.

No theatre in London could have suited us more than The Roundhouse in Chalk Farm; a magnificent palace of a building that had once been used for turning railway engines. This time it was winter and the nights were long and suited to performing. There was never a night when we didn't get ovations. One matinee a very charming Viennese producer who was in charge of the Vienna Theatre Festival (Wiener Festwochen) came to see us. He came backstage to talk to me about performing at the Vienna Theatre Festival next June.

That was the first major festival we had been invited to, and I accepted gleefully. We all turned up at the Künstlerhaus, which gave our cast the opportunity to make no end of smirky comments, but we opened to highly enthusiastic reviews. One paper even wrote that it wished the Burgtheater – their own highly celebrated National Theatre – should try to emulate the dynamism and invention of our production! Vienna was indeed a ravishing time for all of us. On our one night off the producer took me to see an utterly astonishing production that was choreographed by Maurice Béjart. I believe it was *La traviata*. So our charming producer knew what he was doing. Alas he is no longer with is. His name was Ulrich Baumgartner. I so appreciated him coming to see us at The Roundhouse.

I was so in love with Vienna, and the fact that they paid our entire fee in cash so I was able to pay the actors off immediately, I decided to stay, just to explore the environment for a while longer. I took one of those small puffer trains that go up into the mountains and visited a glorious mountain village called Wank – and I'm not making it up! But after a couple of days I got a bit lonely and made my way home. I took the long route and boarded a ferry boat from the continent to England. I was so happy. We had achieved so very much and I was so proud that we achieved all this with a splendid cast who gave their all.

The Trial didn't seem to pick up much attention from Great Britain's critics, still much enamoured with the detritus of the kitchen, but we were continually receiving invites from Europe. One was a tour of Holland, which was a rather painful time since little was spent on announcing us. Sometimes there were more of us on stage than in the audience, but the fewer there were, the more we played our hearts out, as if to compensate.

In German it all melded together and was mightily popular. Now there was only I and my skilled translator and assistant Estella Schmidt. The cast were highly skilled German actors, especially the lead, a most charming and good-looking young man called Hans Christian Rudolph, who went on to run his own theatre in Hamburg. Alas, no longer with us but lodged deep within my memory. My wife Shelley Lee came to the first night and I could not have been more proud. Eventually

I directed it in Israel at The Habima Theatre, Tel Aviv. For the first time it was not very well received and the audience were wondering where the set was! Curiously I cannot remember a single rehearsal. It must have been awful. Nevertheless, when the Habima were invited to take a production to some international festival they chose to take my production of *The Trial.* I saw the reviews! The company and Israel were congratulated on creating such innovative theatre! I was not even invited to warm it up for the tour.

Many years later I did do it once more, this time at the National Theatre. I took on my usual part of Titorelli even though I was concerned that I was taking on too much and maybe another actor should do it. However, I was persuaded by Tony Sher, whom I had taught at Webber Douglas. He said it would be 'sexy' to have both of us on stage together and so I was persuaded, and I am so grateful to him at least for that. This was the best production of the play I had ever done. Matthew Scurfield now took on the part of Huld, the Lawyer, and also played the Chief Inspector. There were standing ovations each night but, as usual in our sceptred isle, the reviews were scandalous. Never mind, we were sold out nearly every night. So I conclude from this that it was indeed 'sexy'.

An attractive Canadian actress, Myriam Cyr, played Miss Bürstner beautifully, and the horrendous Miss Gruback, the landlady, was played by Imogen Claire, a wonderful actress who is also sadly no longer with us. While I was very proud to have a production at the National Theatre, one cannot help but notice and be affected by the deeply traditional way they have of doing things. As in most theatres, a great emphasis is placed on the 'sets'. Naturally all of this has to be decided before the play

FIGURE 6.1 *The Trial.* L–R: Steven Berkoff, Anthony Sher.

is even in rehearsal for the simple reason that it takes many weeks to build it. One does not have the luxury, which I of course take for granted, of experimenting with the company until the physical needs make themselves felt. The poor director has to take 'pot luck' and create the set before the play has come to fruition. When the set arrives, it may not quite fit the show it was designed for, thus many exhausting hours are spent cutting, reshaping, while the poor players pitifully sleep in their dressing rooms during these hellish overnight dress rehearsals! Not us. However, we were proud to be there and were well supported, and proceeded to a first-class dress rehearsal, whereas usually in traditional theatre it's a total mess, with great overlong and overnight lighting sessions. I was very grateful to Richard Eyre for this opportunity.

Michael Jenn was a splendid Block and Paul Bentall was a simply brilliant priest. I remember every rehearsal, especially the first one. Of course we were now at war with Iraq and fastened to our TVs each night. Now on the first rehearsal I was at pains to show Tony Sher how the play was shaped by movement. He threw himself into it and within minutes was pouring with sweat. I was aware of how in traditional theatres the director sits down with the cast and bores them to death for the first week and even more! But soon he really got into it and seemed to relish it. Our cast, most of whom I had worked with before, were well up to it. By the end he was a splendid Joseph K. Sadly he was struck down with appendicitis and Alan Perrin was obliged to take over as understudy. Perrin was perfect; a true Joseph K figure, and I thought he took over from Tony very well. At this time, Tony was a 'star player' on the British stage and was concerned with getting the text absolutely clear first. Perrin was more concerned to make the movement the key element, and the clarity of the text would follow and be more relevant. Both were brilliant in their own, very different, ways.

I had known Alan Perrin for some years, and saw in him a bold and inventive actor, totally on my wavelength. Sher, although I had a great rapport with him when I taught him at Webber Douglas two decades earlier, had become more beholden to the text, and continuously probed and questioned it.

This in itself was quite right and proper for an actor; however, I may have been impatient for him to embrace the style, which was for me as important as the text, since it was another language, albeit a visual one.

Eventually an invite came from Japan to take two productions, so we did. We took *Salome* and *The Trial.* But that's another story.

But at least we have a first-class video of both shows courtesy of NHK Japan.

7

THE FALL OF THE HOUSE OF USHER

Hampstead Theatre Club 1974

Having performed Poe's *The Tell-Tale Heart*, I felt that here was a remarkable author, whose work I should mine for more of his exquisite insights that so aptly illuminate the drama. *The Fall of the House of Usher* did appeal to me, as it had all the elements of gothic horror. It was bizarre, verging on the insane, and touched those parts of me that felt strange familiar echoes. It centres around the character of Roderick Usher.

Here was a man whose feelings lay just beneath a thin parchment-like skin and who seemed to register the slightest tremors, the faintest sounds and the lightest touches. The house referred to in the title, the House of Usher, is the family ancestral home that over the centuries is reaching its demise, as is its owner, the last surviving member of that dynasty. The house is crumbling, slowly decaying and soon to be swallowed up by the bleak and dark tarn over which it rests. Therefore the theme of the story seems to be that the house is a symbol of its master.

Decay and a slow death await both of them. In a way, Usher is a reflection of the house as it gradually warps and cracks, suffering from years of neglect and isolation. A perfect role for me, I felt, and was even further encouraged by reading that Antonin Artaud, the extraordinary French actor and theatrical theorist, declared that for him there was one role that only he could give life to, that only he was born to play, and that was Roderick Usher.

I needed no further encouragement, since my identification with Artaud at that time could not have been greater. Early in my career as a budding actor, I had been given his startling book *The Theatre and Its Double* and I was transfixed. Here was a blueprint for theatre that spoke loudly to me, and I now knew which way I was to attempt to go.

I would play Roderick Usher and of course I would also adapt and direct the play. In this I am grateful to Terry James, a writer who helped me with the initial script. At that time I was soon to be married to dancer Shelley Lee, an American lady who was studying in London at The London School of Contemporary Dance. It was there that she met a voice teacher called Vladimir Rozienko, who was experimenting with the dance company to see how dancers could also use vocal technique. He was at the same time working with a radical theatre group called The Roy Hart Theatre Company, who used only their voices to create utterly wild theatrical pieces. I was invited to see one of their works in rehearsal and frankly I was astonished. Shelley had arranged a meeting between Rozienko and myself.

One of the teacher's claims was that he could free the human voice to reach many octaves, which would not only liberate the performer, but enable them to expand the simple threshold of the naturalistic drama.

I took several classes with Rozienko, during which he tried to release my voice from the jail in which it had been suffocating over the last few decades. Slowly, with utter patience, he encouraged me to learn how to scream, something that women have the ability to do so much more easily than men. I believe that the female voice, when released, has an awesome potential to express a power unknown to men; perhaps women are emotionally freer biologically, while the male is by social necessity more guarded. We began gradually, with the smallest of sounds just to open the throat, and after each session it was as if I were walking on air. We worked together for many weeks and I wish it could have been months. Roy Hart perished in May 1975 in France in a fatal car crash and shortly afterwards I lost touch with Vladimir.

I wanted my voice to be able to act out the tremors of the house, the creaking, the crumbling, the slow torturous decay, as well as the hysteria of Usher himself. Usher is living in the house with his sister Madeleine, who is also showing many of the same symptoms of loneliness and decay as her brother. They decide to invite an old school friend to the house for some company. The friend becomes the narrator of the story.

Shelley became Madeleine and actor Alfredo Michelson the visiting friend. But how to start? I knew that *The House of Usher* would not only need live music, but would positively thrive on it. So Shelley, again using her contacts at the dance school, brought in harpist David Ellis, who would follow the movement, and the harp would be the perfect sound for Usher's frayed nervous system. I wrote the stage play quite simply and we began.

We worked very closely together, making suggestions and experimenting with the movement, and I was lucky in having Shelley as a partner with consummate gifts of movement and in Michelson a brilliant mime.

Beginning a production is always a challenge, and the four of us, now that we had the harpist, would experiment and decided that it would begin simply with Roderick Usher enacting the house itself. A bizarre idea, but it seemed to work. The narration became my words as I slowly came downstage and began speaking the opening lines with the added difference of my voice, which thanks to Rozienko had become a formidable instrument. A single spotlight lit me from above, and I began while David Ellis on the harp plucked the most sensuous and yet chilling notes.

The House of Usher,
My walls are bleak … Walls
Vacant eyes like windows
Set amidst a few rank sedges.
White trunks of decayed trees …
I have stood here for years,
My principal feature is excessive antiquity.
Minute strands of fungi overhang my whole exterior,
Hanging in a fine tangled webwork
From the eaves.
Only a barely perceptible fissure extends from my roof
Making its way down the wall
In a zig-zag direction
Until it became lost in the sullen
Waters of The Tarn.
I hear someone coming to me …
Strengthen yourself house.
Make yourself ready to receive him.

I attempted to use my voice every which way to express the soul of the house, which I was now enacting. Deep, sepulchral, rasping, high and light, deathly low, and for whatever reason it made a strange kind of sense.

Now Madeleine floats into view looking pallid and ghostly. She falls into my arms, which then becomes a very slow dance as she begs for news of the friend whom we have invited to stay with us for a few days. 'Is your friend coming today?,' she plaintively asks. I reply 'He said he would, today is the day he is expected.' We continue speaking to each other, overlapping our sentences since we are so bonded together, while I am reassuring her that once more we will have company and she concurring how wonderful that will be. I pull on the invisible bell rope to summon my servant Oswald to explore the grounds to see whether he is on his way.

The light upstage summons Oswald. He makes his way from the very bowels of the house, where he has his quarters. While Madeleine and I continue speaking, we can observe the servant slowly and with effort making his way to us. Now it is as if we could see right through the walls of the house as he walks along corridors, all mimed of course, turns and faces a closed door which he now opens, traverses further corridors, opens further doors. Now he climbs the stairs, spiral stairs of course, and on reaching the top opens yet more doors, closes them, carefully thus demonstrating the immensity of the house. All this takes at least five minutes. Eventually he comes to our room where we are speaking and opens the double doors with both hands and simply says … 'You rang?'

The audience appreciated our little stab of humour. I now ask him to see whether our friend is coming. He walks to front stage and opens the large windows.

FIGURE 7.1 Steven Berkoff in *The Fall of the House of Usher.*

As the windows are opened, a huge gust of wind blasts into the room, which causes Madeleine and I to be swept back as if reacting to the wind as it howls its way into the room. With effort Oswald closes the windows, but during the gust we still, albeit with some difficulty, enquire whether he can see any sign of our friend, to which he replies in the negative.

The servant is dismissed, while Madeleine and I continue our conversation, which centres around whether our 'friend' is lost. But we now see the friend upstage riding his horse as he comes closer and closer to his hosts. His mime is slow and expert as he rides and speaks.

> *During the whole of a dull dark*
> *and soundless day in the Autumn*
> *of the year, when the clouds hang*
> *oppressively low in the heavens,*
> *I had been passing alone on horseback*
> *Through singularly dreary tracks of country*
> *and at length, found myself in view*
> *of the melancholy House of Usher.*

Madeleine and I now create the doors he enters. We take two large poles, which we extend from our hands, which become the long corridors that the 'friend' traverses even as he describes his environment.

> *Conducted in silence through*
> *Dark and intricate passages.*
> *The carvings of the ceilings,*
> *The tapestries of the walls,*
> *The ebony blackness of the floor,*
> *The phantasmagoric armorial trophies*
> *Which rattle as I strode.*
> *Feeble gleams of light make their*
> *Way through the trellised panes*
> *I felt that I breathed an atmosphere of*
> *Sorrow, an air of stern, deep, irredeemable*
> *Gloom pervaded all.*

Now we have come to the end of our journey, and I collect the two sticks together and make the two arms of the banisters as we all climb them. My friend just in front and I behind holding the poles. Madeleine is just behind me as we make the upward movement of the climb. As I reach the 'top step', I merely open my arms and the staircase has miraculously become a double door through which our guest freely enters.

The production continued in this fashion, with each scene seeming to provide its own answer once we had discovered the 'key'. The 'key', of course, was the techniques Jacques Lecoq had evolved over decades, which simply amount to being able to think in another dimension. How freeing it is, how liberating, to be able to create solid matter out of the air. And not just to create the illusion of it but to become one with it. And not just to be one with it, as our bodies turn into the environment that we are using, but also to be its servant, so very carefully sculpting the forms we wished to use.

Australian artist Silvia Janson designed my costume, which was frail and diaphanous, suiting a being for whom the slightest touch is a minor invasion of his being. Her designs for Madeleine and the 'friend' were also perfect and in keeping with the theme of the work, but Roderick's was spectacular, light and frail and bound with a ruffle at the neck which seemed to frame my face.

We opened at the Edinburgh Festival in 1974 and received positive reviews. The theatre was a stalwart of The Fringe called The Traverse, which was then situated in The Grassmarket, an exotic square in Edinburgh. Naturally we were given a late slot since the festival was the best time for drawing audiences that were slim during the rest of the year. Consequently The Traverse picked all the best slots for themselves.

After Edinburgh, which I shall never forget since it was such a spectacular festival, we were invited to The Hampstead Theatre Club in Swiss Cottage. There we did a four-week season and earned a few more glowing reviews. Except for one idiot in the Sunday papers who didn't have a clue what was going on, but fondly compared Usher's voice of ageing decay to a 'squeaky lawnmower'.

We were then invited to tour Holland for a three-week run in twenty-two towns and cities, which was less pleasant since the story had become a text for studying English in Dutch schools. Still, we battled on through some appalling young audiences and were glad when it came to an end. While most of the audiences were respectful and even fascinated by our show, it was when we played in 'industrial' towns that we felt the full erosion of cultural life. In one town, the young audience were seated on 'flip-up' seats, which of course meant that every young arse signalled their total disinterest by rising abruptly, with the accompanying 'thwack'.

This increased during the performance, and every 'thwack' broke the intense concentration we had worked months to achieve.

We were then invited to perform at a fringe theatre in Munich, and so we all climbed into the lighting man's battered old German limo, much to the disgust of the German passers-by, who were alarmed to see their beautiful Mercedes being so appallingly abused by its savage English owners.

We were given a pleasant flat to share and opened to an enthusiastic audience. At the evening's end, the theatre owner would leave our 50% share of the box office on the desk in the lobby, which was just about enough to pay for the company's dinner in one of the large Viennese restaurants. Those nights were unforgettable as well, since we were famished by this time and really felt like strolling players.

Now, the sister of the man who ran the theatre was living in New York and worked in the diamond trade. When I visited New York a year later and met up with her, her boyfriend shocked me by handing me a cheque for $5,000 in appreciation of our efforts in Munich. He had seen the show and confessed that it had frightened him to death. Obviously he must have also witnessed how we were paid and wanted to help our company. I was never so moved in my life, and determined to prove myself a worthy recipient of his generous offer.

By now the show was gaining a reputation, and we were invited to tour Australia. It was to be a twelve-week tour, beginning in Melbourne, but this time I would be doing a curtain raiser, which was my other Poe work, *The Tell-Tale Heart*. This made for a rather exhausting but altogether exhilarating evening. The role of the friend had now been taken over by an old company stalwart, Terry McGinity. The role of Madeleine was taken over by the great Scots performer Annie Stainer, whose work I had held in awe on the few occasions I had seen her.

I had worked with Terry for many years, and we had a close symbiotic relationship. He had a remarkable voice. Annie Stainer was one of a rare breed of solo female performers. I first saw her work at the Edinburgh Festival and confess I had seen no one like her before. I knew I had to work with her, and of course one day I did.

We toured Australia successfully, performing in Perth for the whole three weeks of the Perth Festival, and it was now beginning to wear us all down, especially me with the job of doing two shows per night, although I have to confess I really enjoyed doing *The Tell-Tale Heart*.

I found I was becoming obsessed, not unlike the character I was playing. I was becoming Roderick Usher! Paula DeBurgh, my assistant and production manager, tried to help every which way she could, but I was so very glad when I finished the tour.

Finally, we played at the Cottesloe Theatre in London. Peter Hall had just opened the National Theatre and was burdened with having to fill three theatres at once. He sought radical theatre groups for the National's third space, so we were invited to show our work there and we did three productions, *East*, *Metamorphosis* and *The Fall of the House of Usher*. That was the last time we played it, but as writing about it has stirred up so many memories, I feel it's about time to revive this strongly exotic work.

8

RANDOM THOUGHT

The dressing room

There are two or three places where you pass the greater part of your life. One is the bed-room of your home, and, if you are an actor, another will be your dressing room in the theatre. There, you might spend the most intense hours waiting for the inevitable knock on the door. Inevitable, since the moment cannot be put off, or postponed, until you feel a little better, a little more confident … But no, there is no escaping from the knock … none.

The knock is inevitable, as is the warning voice accompanying it. The first raps on your dressing room are just a little warning that your time is slowly coming and the countdown has begun.

Some actors are obliged to share dressing rooms as they are junior members of the company, and will not have their own private dressing room until they have risen in the ranks. However, a crowded dressing room also can be comforting, allowing sharing of your concerns with your fellow actors, and thus the tension is shared. Much light gossip ensues, where merits or demerits of other actors are discussed and reputations shredded. There actors, though lacking space, still have their own special area where their reflection in the mirror is their main concern. Your reflection even becomes a comfort to you as you stare back at the person you have become.

But if you are alone in your room, you have freedom to indulge yourself, either to be silent, or to meditate in those last minutes before the fall of the guillotine. You might run through a few lines, which are a nightly ritual to reinforce those cells of memory, for no matter how well you know your part, it feels reassuring to run through the piece again and again. To make sure that the demon of forgetfulness just doesn't slip in. So you sit and wait, staring at the self in the mirror, or reading snippets of the 'best wishes' cards you have been sent for the first night. If you are in a number one dressing room, you might reflect on those who have been there before you, since their shades may still permeate the walls; they too have sat facing that same mirror, have gone through the same pre-show thoughts, some with terror, others with sublime confidence, but all knowing that the time will come. All putting their souls on that stage, all praying to whatever god they believe in that those precious words will come. Yes, of course they will.

Some nights you have booked a table for dinner after the show in some smart showbiz restaurant ... Sometimes I did this, but often I just couldn't since it would make the assumption that I will survive the night. I'll get through it. I will not be shot down in flames. How can I assume this? So, after the show, you might be walking home passing the bar next to the theatre and take a swift glance at the diners all enjoying themselves and happily discussing your show, whilst you traipse back to an empty home ...

But this night you have thrown caution to the wind and have a guest coming in. Coming to see you bare yourself on stage ... However, that knowledge may also fire your performance somewhat ... May give you life or purpose beyond a theatre full of strangers. I think again of all the great stars who have sat in this very room, preparing themselves for yet another night, not retiring at home and eagerly seeking what programme is on the TV that night ... No, that is for the aged or the meek, for the timid who feel that they just cannot bear to wake up in the morning knowing that they will have to go through it all again that evening. And again, and again ... No, you cannot be one of those, not really, since that is a form of death, in a way ... Your soul has been put in limbo, you are no longer being challenged, challenged so much that you might pray for the days to pass so you no longer have to bear this constant noose hanging over your head each night. But then, you would miss the after-effects when the curtain comes down and it is all over ... Have you ever experienced such bliss, such joy, such sweet relief? You have sacrificed yourself and have been granted life ...

The final knock on the door ... 'Beginners, Act One ...'

9

EAST

The Kings Head Theatre, Islington 1975, Regent Street Poly and the Cottesloe Theatre 1977

East was my first original play concocted out of my head with no reference to other influences either historic or adaptations from novels. I felt that my forte was adapting theatre works from strangely exotic literature. However, one day an actor with whom I had worked for many years and whose opinion I respected named John Joyce suggested that I write an original work. I brooded on this for a while, feeling I had really nothing to say. No great or profound thoughts filtered through my mind. But then one day it occurred to me that, on the contrary, each one of us is a professor of who we are and our experiences are an endless storehouse.

The point is not to be profound, but to be honest. And so I began. The theme of the play would be based on describing in detail the most intense experiences I had gone through in my life. Key moments in my growing years and the other characters' key and intense moments in their middle years. Therefore my own memorable events became the template for the characters I invented. However, the invention, while having its base in true events, can be enlarged and even exaggerated to make their points more salient. I called the play *East*, not just because it was set in the East End of London, but also because east was where the sun rises, east sides of cities are where the immigrants first land when escaping from their rotten hellholes in Russia and Romania. My own grandparents fled in the latter half of the nineteenth century. They first landed at the eastern ports of London, and where once they set foot on East London soil they stayed. Then grew the dynamic working-class societies in the slums and ghettoes of East London.

The desires of second-generation immigrants were simple, but no less passionate for that. Our wealth was minimal, and in consequence the things which brought us the most divine pleasures were uncomplicated. The young men simply revelled in each other's company, and petty differences were solved with violence of language if not of bodies. We were a post-war generation who felt that sex had only just been discovered, and our greatest joys were in the perpetual hunt for the ladies, whom we pursued with such passion lest it would suddenly become illegal. For our pastime nothing could be more enthralling than to master the mysteries of 'jive' … Which we pursued endlessly until we became the masters of that intricate art. But following on closely after that was the need to adorn ourselves in the height of fashion, and nothing was more thrilling than to save for at least a year to have the money to enter a tailor's shop and be measured for a suit. To stand there and be measured for the suit of your dreams and then return at least two or three times for fittings.

At that time I wore stiff collars which were detached from your shirt until we resembled little Lord Fauntleroys. Then on the weekends we strutted to our palace of delights, The Lyceum dance hall (since restored to its original use as a theatre) in The Strand. We were utterly different from those suburban yokels who also called themselves 'Teddy Boys' but whose style was anything but sharp, as we were. They looked like poor parodies in their huge shirt collars and 'Slim Jim' ties and thick crepe-soled shoes. Yes, we did dance the 'jive', but it was our own style which had the suave movements of an eighteenth-century minuet.

I of course had no money to even think about possessing a car, nor frankly the desire. My method of locomotion had to be a motorbike, although this fulfilment came many years later. I nevertheless included a motorbike scene in the play, and this actually became one of the production highlights although I had never ridden one before. I had to buy a motorbike manual to glean the relevant technical information.

Our parents in 'East' were simple to the extent of grossness and 'dad' was an out and out thug who revelled in the escapades of the Nazis.

Sylv, the young lady in the piece, for whom Mike yearned, was no less passionate and very much turned on by Mike, and her 'moment' was in fact her bilious stress in doing the worthless daily job just to earn some cash. Watching Mike battle on clearly turned her on and made her his devoted and adoring slave …!!

> *At it they went … It weren't half fun at first*
> *It weren't my fault those jesting, jousting lads should*
> *Want a tournament of hurt and crunch and blood and shriek*
> *All on my dress it went … That's Mickey's blood, I thought …*
> *It seemed to shoot out from something that cracked*
> *… I saw him mimicking an oilwell … Though he'd take off*
> *Many things for a laugh, this time I did not laugh*
> *So much … They fought for me, thy blood my royal*
> *Mike wast shed for me. And never shall the suds of Persil*
> *or of Daz remove that royal emblem from that skirt*
> *That may times you gently lifted in the Essoldo, Bethnal Green.*
> *I was that monument of flesh they wanton hand would smash and grab*
> *I only clocked the other geezer Mike and can't help if my*
> *Proud tits should draw their leery eyes to feast on them …*
> *… But now the bastard blameth me for all*

And seeks vile vengeance on my pretty head. Which if he does
Will surely grieve my brothers Burt and George who
Will not hesitate to finish off the bits that Les did leave
But all this chat of violence I hate
Is ultra horrible to me that thrives on love and tongue
Wrenched kisses in the back of the MG Sprites, with a
'Stop … I'm not like that! Oh just for now' which
Doth ensure a second date … So hold a morsel
Back girls … And he'll crave it all the more.

East was largely made up of such monologues, that were then linked together through the device of a fictionalised 'family'. They were by no means my family, but the stock characters of the typical English working-class family with all their frustrations and prejudices but seen through the eyes of an outsider or an immigrant.

'Mum' was a simple character I had observed in my East End early life. And was more of a caricature. As I recall the mums in our East End street, they were after a while almost sexless. Brutalised by indifferent husbands, with poor wages and drugged by a constant watch of brain-numbing TV. There was not the faintest vestige of feminism about them with their headscarves and clod-hopping shoes. Mum was a pitiful sight and yet at the same time she did have an imagination and keenly observed a life out in the wider world which was denied her.

A scene where Mum is 'sleeping' with her husband and reflecting on her 'lot'.

MUM: *'Sometimes I get gorged in my throat when I see him sleeping … Lump sweaty, beer-gutted, farty, no hope, thick brained and me, the other half of nothing fed with electric media swill … Consumer me … Hawaii Five-O, Z-Cars, Coronation Street, Beat The Clock, University Challenge, Sunday night at The London Palladium … On The Busses, play of the month, play of the week, Watch with Mother, tea, fags, light and bitter. Ha! Ha! And Ho! Ho! Bingo, eyes down, clickety click … What the papers say … Reg Varney, The Golden Shot, Live Letters, tits, Green Shield Stamps (hallo dear, how are you? Turn over shut up and let me sleep … Fart, belch the music of the spheres … Got a clean shirt? Who's running at Epsom, The Pill is safe, abortions rise … I would like to practise today … Tippett's sonata number three, six hours of it, I must be ready for my BBC recital on Wednesday … Then I may pair it with Mozart's 'Concerto in C' … Terry Riley, mind you needs dextrous finger work … I'll leave that for now and pick up my percolator at the Green Shield shop … Wall's pork sausages for supper and Fray Bentos peas … MacDougal flour for a smooth pastry … So I smell? Does my mouth taste like an ashtray? Will my lover meet me after I play Brünnhilde in 'The Ring' at the stage door to Covent Garden and buy me a filet mignon in Rules café or The Savoy? Will we drink Champagne and discuss our next production of Verdi's Otello but wants Bernstein to direct … I'd be happy with Visconti really … Maria is coming to tea … Must get some Lyons jam tarts … I met Hemmingway in the brasserie Lipp today, he said my poetry soars to heaven … Come and have some wine with Gertrud, there will be some very nice people there.'*

DAD: (Waking up) *'Shut ya gob, can't you let me bleeding sleep?'*
(Blackout)

So out pour all the bits and bobs, all the waffle from her experience-starved brain. She is pathetic but at the same time has a vivid imagination that has not quite been numbed. Her info on the world may come from an old TV set, but it had had an effect on her. I remember in our council flat in Manor House N4 the programmes that we used to watch and I got used to viewing the backs of their heads as they gazed upon the goings on in the world. I was mostly out and leading the life of a teenager, which provided most of the material for the two boys in the play, Mike and Les. When casting *East*, I decided to cast a male actor as Mum for no other reason than my theory that East End women gradually turned into men by middle age.

Paradoxically, the men who played Mum were nearly all utterly brilliant and almost stole the show. The first actor was Robert Longden, who played Mum to perfection. Of course, all the men who played the role were gay, and they gave the part of Mum a sweetness that rounded her off. They were not only playing a woman but 'commenting' on the role of womanhood. It would have been hard for a woman to have captured that particular quality. For whatever reason men seem to have the ability to make themselves look absurd and ridiculously comic on the stage. The grotesque impersonations of 'Mother Riley' by Arthur Lucan or Les Dawson's seaside landladies would be well nigh impossible played by an actress, given the satiric comments they make about the female sex.

When I first wrote *East*, my mandate to myself was that it should have no holds barred, no restriction but to speak freely. Without restraint as might a teenager to his closest filth-raking, 'chinas' or 'mates' ... To be bold to write in a way that has seldom if ever been done before. Seeing that my raison d'être for this piece was to let out the most exciting moments, the most savage times, the most glorious times, the most, the most, and I let it all pour out.

Then I took a good hard look at what I had written and decided that it needed to change. With all its vulgarity it needed some elegance, and so I started to rewrite much of it in a free verse style, which I felt gave it more of a savage wit since writing in verse invites you to play with language, to let it strut about a bit. At the beginning I needed to start with a clear purpose to introduce the players and show the background whence they hailed.

I was thinking of my own environment where I used to hang out with the lads of Stamford Hill. There was a cinema just round the corner from an amusement arcade. There was an alleyway just before the cinema called the 'Super', and this is where the lads would go to settle their differences. My cousin Sid had one almighty punch up there with a well-known 'tearaway' from Stamford Hill. I was privy to this. I have never forgotten it. It was heroic and of course my cousin, although young, thoroughly vanquished the enemy.

To my young mind Sidney was heroic since he was a mere stripling of sixteen and his opponent was a well-known 'bullyboy' of eighteen or nineteen. He had assaulted Sid as he was taking his jacket off to prepare for a challenge. It took him several weeks for his face to heal. Sid then challenged Harry for an equaliser. I don't believe anyone had ever challenged him before. Sid's older brother Willy, who was a ju-jitsu expert, trained him, since this would be the only way of beating his opponent Harry, who had a monstrous punch. Every night Sid and Willy bussed to Stamford Hill, where the battle was going to be, and waited in a shop doorway for Harry to turn up. I believe Sid would have waited forever. Well, eventually Harry was obliged to face the music and accept the challenge, and a group of us went round the back of the 'Super' cinema at Stamford Hill – this was the traditional place to settle conflicts.

Never had my young heart beat so fast. Sid was my adorable cousin and I loved him, never more so than now. Sid thrashed him. Ronny Mitchel, another Stamford Hill tearaway, actually stepped forward to stop it, but Willy quickly interjected with 'Don't interfere Ronny!' Sid had been avenged. That night is seared upon my brain forever.

Probably this was in my mind when I wrote the beginning.

LES: *'Bung us a snout Mike ...'*

MIKE: *'OK, I'll bung thee a snout Les.'*

LES: *'Now you know our names.'*

Mike: *'Mike's OK. After the holy saint ... Mike with a hard K. Like a kick ... Swift ... Not mad about Les.'*

LES: *'It's soft. It's gooey ... But choose it I did not ... In my mother's hot womb did she curse this name on me. It's my handle ... Under the soft it's spikey, under the pillow it's sharp ... Concealed instrument ... Offensive weapon lies waiting.'*

MIKE: *'Oh, he doth bestride Commercial Road like a colossus ... That's my manor ... Where we two first set our minces on each other ...And those Irish yobs walk under our huge legs and peep about for dishonourable bother ... He's my mucker, chin or mate.'*

LES: *'And he mine since those days at least twelve moons ago when sailing out The Black Raven pub in Whitechapel, the self same street where blessed Jack did rip and tear in cold thick nights so long ago ...Those muffled screams and slicing flesh no more than sweetest memories of him who went so humble 'bout his nightly graft. Tell how it chanced that we, sworn mates was once the deadly poison of each other's eye.'*

MIKE: *'He clocked the bird I happened to be fianced to, my darling Sylv (of legendary knockers) and I doth take it double strong that this short git in suede and rubber, pimples sprouting forth like buttercups on sunny days from of his greasy boat: That he should dare to lay upon her svelte and tidy form his horror leering jellies ... So I said to him ... "Fuck off, thou discharge from thy mother's womb before with honed and sweetened razor I do trouble to remove thy balls from thee."'*

And so the play, or rather the scene, continues, broken up and encouraged by the 'chorus', who are just Sylv, Mum and Dad seated upstage and throwing in the odd piece of aggressive encouragement.

Chorus: *'Destroy him Mike … For fuck's sake don't just stand there. Nut him in the nose, and part his skull for him, the greasy turd.'*

Now for some reason these interpolations were very funny, since they spoke the lines in perfect unison and with a sense of exaggerated outrage …

In the original production I chose to play Mike, and Barry Philips acted the role of Les, and was perfect in it. Barry was a natural actor, born of the British working class and yet aspiring to be a classical actor. Added to this he was an astounding mimic. The style of the play, or what evolved during rehearsal, was to play the two yobs with a certain manner that was closer in some scenes to a classical actor's approach. Certainly not yobby, which is unfortunately the way I nearly always see it played. We were really commenting on our wayward youth, our maniacal teenage hormone-charged wildness. Yet we were both hardly teenagers. I was thirty-seven and trying to display the bravura of a seventeen-year-old. So the performance would have to be highly demonstrated, satiric, comic. And I do believe we managed to achieve that slightly 'Brechtian' form to it.

In fact, I got so carried away by my obsession about the 'style' of the piece that I thought it would be a betrayal to have such a thing as a table and chair for the family's eating scene. By now we were fortunate enough to have acquired the services of the great comic actor and RSC player Barry Stanton. While I was dithering and struggling in my head to find the appropriate way to stage the scene, Barry just grabbed a small wooden table in the rehearsal room, dragged it centre stage. We grabbed four chairs and suddenly, with his spontaneous energy, it was like a stick of dynamite had exploded, and the scene eventually became the most outrageously funny in the whole play.

In fact it was so raw and alive that we rehearsed it only once. I felt that by some miracle we had found it, and didn't want to test it until we reached Edinburgh. A piano accompanied much of the action, and sometimes it sounded like one of those pianos one heard accompanying silent movies. We had two different pianists during *East*'s run. The first was Neil Hansford, and then we had John Prior, who stayed with the play for the entire run. We were blessed with the most talented bunch of actors I could have wished for. Once the beautiful Australian Anna Nigh had auditioned I knew she was Sylv to a 'T'. Anna Nigh was also a combo of many talents, part dancer, part singer, and she had that wonderful classless Australian verve and played cockney as if to the manor born. Mum was played by Robert Longden, who really could not have been better, but, as I said, when it was necessary to change casts, each actor who took on Mum was quite marvellous. Eventually Mum was played for the duration by Roy McCarthy, who was equally brilliant.

During the first dinner scene, for which we used 'real' food, baked beans on toast, Barry Stanton would suddenly take off on an adlib which was absolutely brilliant and it became part of the play. I never even commented on it, but took it to be a natural response to the spirit of the play … So, when dad expostulates on his 'great moment' when the Nazi Oswald Mosely marched down to the East End, the baked beans really flew.

FIGURE 9.1 The Australian tour of *East*, 1978. L–R: Roy McCarthy, Barry Philips, Matthew Scurfield, Sylvia Mason, Steven Berkoff.

Apart from that scene, we had no props since 'we' were the props. When Mike talks about the fantasy of his life ... a motorbike, Les has to be the bike, which I leapt on using his arms as handlebars and our voices for the growling of the machine. Now, curiously, I had never once ridden a motorbike. I could barely drive a car. And so I went into a motorbike shop and bought a manual from which I freely borrowed.

Because Barry was able to enter the spirit of the machine, the scene became one of the highlights of the play. In fact, a would-be New York producer, having seen the production in London, wished to take us to New York. Some months after he had seen the production, he asked me whether I could use an American bike for the scene instead of transporting it!!

I became so enamoured of the motorbike scene that I felt I had to at least learn how to ride one of those beasts. My dear friend, the actor John Joyce, now sadly passed on, always rode a motorbike, and kindly gave me a few lessons, which encouraged me to take it a step further and buy a second-hand 'trail' bike which was continually breaking down. Then one day I went out and bought a new one, a Japanese Suzuki. Oh my god, I felt like a real biker!!

I took it for regular servicing at Highbury Corner, and one day I traded it in for a 650cc. Now I really was becoming Mike in the play. I was growing into my role outside the stage. I started driving my motorbike through England. When I eventually got to California, I just had to buy a Gold Wing, a Honda 1,000cc.

In fact all I really wanted was to be able to drive a car and get a licence, which I eventually did in Los Angeles.

Since I felt that the play had to take us far beyond what anyone had really seen or heard on the British stage, I had to have one even more outrageous scene. It was my 'cunt' speech. While I wrote it so effortlessly, and it simply concerns a juvenile fantasy of sexual obsession, I found it difficult to even think of playing, and during rehearsal I would often skip the scene and get on to the end ... Not a great idea.

Anyway, the time came to play it. We were at the Edinburgh Festival in 1975. The play had gone really well on our first night and we were getting to the 'cunt' speech. I had to do it alone. It could not be done to 'Les' since he didn't even want to share the stage with me for that particular scene ... Well I just stepped centre stage and said the words but at too great a speed, the speed of a coward. But the next night I slowed down, the audience were stunned and just sat silently. By the end of the week I had relaxed and found my body acting out the shape and contours of the female 'pudenda'.

After a month it became the most outrageous scene in the entire play. So it shows you that it takes experimenting in performance to discover how to do a scene, and no matter how it may daunt you, just be brave.

Three years later we were invited to do a sixteen-week tour to Australia, which we were so very happy to do. For all of us ageing juveniles Australia became our great and promised land, and we were feted and celebrated from city to city. Matthew Scurfield had taken over from Barry Stanton, who had other work, and Matthew was perfect for it since he was not just an actor, but a yoga master, and his movement was extraordinary. We could never work with just an actor unless they had something really special, like Barry Stanton or Matthew Scurfield.

Sadly we never took our team to the USA, which is a real shame since I feel that *East* would have shown the New Yorkers a different side to the English theatre. Too late now. From time to time I am asked to watch a group of actors try to do *East*, but they never can They are always too enslaved to naturalism. However, one day I will direct it again. Although I did so once to celebrate its twenty-fifth anniversary with a very good team led by Matt Cullum, who was really rather special. Damn it, he was good, and seldom acted again. Such a shame.

Sometimes an actor will come into your life and it's as if a powerful light is suddenly switched on. Matt had this. A cherubic young man with a shock of red hair which seemed to suit his spirit perfectly. I believe that actors who possess this light have an inner power that charges everything they do. He then became in later years a production manager and was equally good in that direction. And so, he earned more, which was necessary since he now had a family, but I hope to see him act again.

10

HAMLET, SHAKESPEARE

The Roundhouse, Chalk Farm 1980

Now it was time for the big one. *Hamlet.* Time was running out for me. I was forty and on the edge of the planet Hamlet but now was determined to explore it. I even wrote a working memoir of the whole process called *I Am Hamlet*, which was published by Faber & Faber. It all started as did almost everything in those days with me. I had to instigate and push the whole thing up a very steep hill. However, I had a great team of colleagues, who by now had been working with me for several years. They were actors to the skin of their teeth and would be able to put it together.

I was sitting in our little tenement flat in Edinburgh, which I had bought courtesy of a decent pay packet in Düsseldorf. It was a simple, beautiful thick granite-walled tenement typical for Scotland's working classes. I bought it since I already had knowledge of it when it was rented to us during one Edinburgh Festival. Rick Clutchey, the ex-convict maverick who staged Beckett's plays in San Quentin Prison and called his team of actors The San Quentin Theatre Group, had rented it the year before. When Shelley, my dearest wife at the time, who was running a small dance company called Basic Space, wrote to me in Düsseldorf to tell me about it, I was sorely tempted. It was only £6,000. So I just threw caution to the wind and bought it. Stripped it bare and we moved in. I would be able to go just for a few weeks from time to time, but Shelley would have a great 'pad'.

I hadn't been working for a month or two and was feeling suddenly deeply depressed, and like many actors was envious of the way dancers could just throw their leotards in a bag and head off to dance classes each day. Anyway, I got so down in the dumps I almost wept. I whined 'My life means nothing to me.' I felt utterly depressed and worthless. Shelley said 'Tell you what, just go to my studio and start working on Hamlet … Just go in and practise some of the text. You've been talking about doing it for years and now's the chance … just start!'

She gave me the key to the studios not far from where we were living in the sweet and beloved Dean Park Street in Stockbridge. I went into the room. It was spacious and warm. I just liked being in there. I love rehearsal rooms. It's where you give birth and so it's a womb for creation. I took a chair and placed it in front of me … I imagined Claudius, the evil King kneeling before it … I began:

> *Now he is a praying*
> *And so I'll do it …*
> *And so am I revenged.*
> *And so he goes to heaven.*

The language swept through me as if an electric current had revived my tired, depressed and underused brain cells. Suddenly, I was alive, I was living, breathing, existing for a purpose. I ran through the lines of the entire speech. I saw Claudius kneeling in front of me. I felt from that moment *Hamlet* was in my veins and my blood was feeding it. I did it a few more times and then felt satisfied that it was within my grasp and that I would do it at last and no longer prevaricate.

In doing that small scene I began from then onwards to start directing it. As I said the words 'And so he goes to heaven and so I am revenged' I stopped for a moment, a split second, and mimed stabbing him to death. Claudius falls forward mortally wounded. I then say 'This must be scanned' and then we do a reverse video trick when the action is reversed. Claudius in slow motion gathers himself up again to the position he was in before I stabbed him. We have shown my passionate desire and then my doubts and acted them out. Brilliant. I was exalted, and all this came from that morning in the little church hall used as a rehearsal room for my wife's dance company.

I then continue the speech,

> *A villain kills my father; and for that,*
> *I, his sole son, do this same villain send*
> *To heaven.*
> *O, this is hire and salary, not revenge.*

I walked back to our tenement in Dean Park feeling exalted. The working on one's craft, enlarging it, examining it, imbibing it brings the soul to life. So, now that I was determined to go ahead with it, I managed to find an excellent school gymnasium in Edinburgh which was perfect for our production since the audience would be sat on four sides. We would play in the round. This was going to be for The Roundhouse, that magnificent theatre in Camden that was the brainchild of Arnold Wesker.

We would work on it very slowly with just my usual very determined and committed group of actors, Matthew Scurfield and Barry Philips. Those two actors were capable of doing anything. And so the three of us started blocking it in a wonderful church hall we had found in Holborn. We would block out the other characters and get a rough sketch of the character of the production. A few days later we added Gertrude, who was Linda Marlowe, then others came in gradually, testing them out, until we felt that we had the right actors for a revolutionary *Hamlet*. Then the twins David and Tony Meyer came in to play Rosencrantz and Guildenstern, as twins!!

They were perfect and slowly the company grew. I was as proud as I could be with them while still trying to play Hamlet at the same time. This gave me one or two problems. I did need some help, but I took advice from some of the actors who would react to my performance. I had worked with most of my cast for years and we had merged into a harmonious group. I had no problem getting or even seeking advice from my fellow actors. After all, we were a team and it made them also more involved and responsible.

I recently had the misfortune of working for a maniacal director in Los Angeles, who started screaming at me when I made a simple comment about one line to a fellow actor, which I felt wasn't as clear as it could be. He started screaming 'Don't you dare give notes to another actor!' I was so astounded at this Neanderthal response that I walked out. Under his misguided direction, the play never even got to see the life of day. It collapsed under the weight of the director's insane bullying and incompetence.

Ophelia then joined us, played at the time by the lovely young actress Chloe Solomon. We were joined by Roy McCarthy, who had played Mum in *East* and was just too perfect as Osric. Roy, sadly no longer with us, was a very witty, dry, acerbic actor. He was proudly gay and made no bones about openly floating his gay credentials. He was also a superb actor.

We were well on our way, and finally we found an actor for Polonius who was physically as far away from the conventional Polonius as you could imagine, but was perfect. It was a relief to be as far away as possible from the benign, doddering old cliché we usually expect from the role. Our Polonius was more of a cunning henchman to King Claudius. He was stocky, comic and even rather dangerous, and yet that combination seemed to work extremely well.

Then a tall young actor joined us called Rory Edwards, who was to be a stalwart comrade for many years and do many productions with me. We were a team. Of course we needed the musicians and used our brilliant percussionist John Prior. The church hall was quite long and frequently used as a basketball court and had white lines demarcating the playing areas on the floor. This I decided would demarcate the walls and rooms of the castle; and so when the actors made entrances they would walk along the white lines, turn left or turn right and in some cases, as at the beginning when Horatio arrives to question the guards and mimes, climb up a staircase to reach them on the battlements.

We were creating the bricks and mortar of the building, or the flesh and blood of the production. Our set, a roll of white masking tape and two dozen cane-backed chairs. The old familiar ones that used to be seen in old public houses. For the audience most especially half the excitement is not only witnessing the actor close up in the round but also being able to 'see' the walls and corridors of the castle as acted by the players. This is the thrill for us. So each scene as performed by the 'team', the

FIGURE 10.1 *Hamlet.* L–R: Linda Marlowe, Steven Berkoff.

ensemble, can be brought to life by human beings, and this stimulates the imagination of the audience. The last thing we need is a set. And of course the more set, the more props, the less the actor. This is just my view, but it is one that has not only served us but helped us be creative as actors.

We did our first run through at the Almeida Theatre in Islington in a large rehearsal area we had rented for two nights. Now a curious thing happened to my concerned and anxious mind, since each scene presented a problem to me as an actor. Was my confrontational scene with Ophelia working? Or 'To be or not to be'? But I knew all would be revealed on our first run through. We would not be finishing until late and so I went out shopping for supper and had invited Terry McGinity, who was then playing Laertes, and Linda Marlowe, who was playing Gertrude, to dinner. It was to be spaghetti bolognese since I could keep the sauce in a pot. So I went out and bought the meat and some veg to go with it, and in the afternoon prepared a beautiful bolognese with tomatoes, onions and herbs. I half cooked the pasta, drained it and left it in the pot. So when we came back we could be stuffing ourselves within minutes. I was living in Islington at the time. My beloved wife Shelley was working in Edinburgh. We were to start around 7pm and I walked along Upper Street to the Almeida.

We all met, briefly chatted and then began the run through. We start with the cane-backed chairs in a straight line on the top side of the rectangle. The cast were all wearing elegant second-hand dinner jackets. The reason for this being that I felt like we might be an orchestra, performing our separate and several instruments. Also it looked so elegant. I as Hamlet merely wore a smart double-breasted jacket and white unbuttoned shirt, or tieless as I should say. John Prior begins by a loud drum beat for the lights to snap on. We are a frozen group like Madame Tussauds. The excellent German actor Wolf Kahler played the ghost. He too sat on the last chair. After a few seconds the first actors, playing Marcellus and Bernardo, rise and, very slowly, take opposite diagonal lines, until they meet in the centre. As they do, one of them shouts 'Who's there!' and is then relieved when he sees that it is a comrade. They have been moving with a spear (mimed, of course) cradled in their arms, twisting their bodies from side to side as they vigilantly keep watch.

Horacio says 'Has this thing appeared again tonight?,' referring to the ghost. As he says this, we observe a grey-haired tall man slowly rise and move along the back of the stage. It is eerie and the two soldiers react, striking at it as if it were made of air.

The performers are like an orchestra and the chairs that they occupy are set on four sides, and so, depending on the scene, they can be used flexibly and most conveniently for the next scene. The next scene is set in the court with all the courtiers and King Claudius, Queen Gertrude, Polonius, Laertes and of course Hamlet. As the last scene ends with the two guards anxious to inform Hamlet, a drum beat signals the next scene, which is achieved by simply creating a circle of chairs set on the circle of the basketball court where we rehearsed. Claudius begins his opened peroration. I sit with my back to the audience. My first few lines are

> *Seems, madam! nay it is; I know not 'seems.'*
> *'Tis not alone my inky cloak, good mother,*
> *Nor customary suits of solemn black,*
> *Nor windy suspiration of forced breath,*
> *No, nor the fruitful river in the eye,*
> *Nor the dejected 'haviour of the visage,*
> *Together with all forms, moods, shapes of grief,*

That can denote me truly: these indeed seem,
For they are actions that a man might play:
But I have that within which passeth show;
These but the trappings and the suits of woe.

It's quite a wonderful opening speech for Hamlet, and the whole audience has been waiting for the legendary, most famous character in the whole of Shakespeare to open his mouth. I sometimes wondered, as I sat there listening to all of them spouting off, whether a voice would even come out of my mouth. But this night, this night of our very first run through, this so special night in the large rehearsal room at the Almeida, my voice just flowed out of me, simple, elegant and without nerves or concern. I had never been so relaxed. It was if I had taken a drug. Every scene just flowed through me without effort, without stress. As I was acting I felt that it was almost too perfect. I had rarely, if ever, felt like this before in my entire acting life. I even felt that I should stumble over the lines a bit since this was all too perfect, and would it last until we get to Edinburgh? I simply could not go wrong.

We finished our run and we were all quite happy with ourselves for having got through it. Linda and Terry came back for supper since, in those dark old days in Islington, there were few, if any, cafés open. The supper tasted divine and the wine heavenly as we celebrated our efforts and chatted happily, as all actors do after a performance.

All the kinks got ironed out. I didn't force or overdramatise, nor did I shout or rave. I had prepared myself. By preparing the supper, by shopping for all the ingredients, by cooking our future supper carefully and calmly I had put my mind into a process of 'settlement'. You can't cook or prepare a meal in anxiety or stress. And even if you do have some qualms at the beginning, these qualms will dissolve since you will soon be in a state of balance. Preparing the spaghetti bolognese had without doubt settled me. I could think of no other explanation for my clear and careful performance. Of course, when on tour I won't be preparing a meal in my digs each night. It would not even be possible, but suppose there was something that one could do to settle one's mind. As if you were fine-tuning an instrument. Meditation perhaps, something to straighten out the tangled knots of the brain.

I've rarely found it. Once in Australia I had the same feeling after I had jogged to the theatre. I arrived sweaty and purged, and the performance was as calm as ever. Eventually we opened in Edinburgh to some really excellent reviews, and I was beginning to look forward to our London opening at The Roundhouse. I had spoken to the producer (who should remain nameless), and they had promised to hold the space open. I never promise my cast anything like future dates until I am certain not only of the success of the play, but reviews etc. So I did say that I was not sure to one or two of them just in case it went no further. One of our charming actors told the aforementioned producer that we weren't going anywhere after. I suppose he knew no better. But the 'producer' with whom I had spoken, and for whom I was deliberately putting the play in the round, chose not even to come and see us!!!

I was utterly choked and shocked when I asked why she hadn't been in and why she didn't even think of talking to me for fuck's sake, the producer, conceiver and actor. Realising that she had made a gaffe, the charming producer then found a few weeks for us and all was well again. We were rescheduled for the following year after we had secured an exciting tour of Israel for a really splendid Israeli producer, and this was one of the most exciting tours of our lives.

We were never so happy. We arrived in Israel, and I was so proud of being invited to this amazing country and playing in Haifa, where the previous year I had directed *Agamemnon*. But then they knew me as a director and now I had to prove myself as an actor. I was certainly on edge, but we got through successfully on our first night, if a little sweatily. We all celebrated in a typical Palestinian restaurant a few doors away and we were a bunch of exhausted, happy bunnies. Now we were all set to play in Jerusalem.

In Jerusalem we were given digs in a quite beautiful and ancient part of the old city. The show went well and the audiences were deeply appreciative. After a week in the main Jerusalem theatre we were all put on a bus and toured some of the kibbutzim around Israel. Each had a well-equipped theatre and a most receptive audience. In some kibbutzim we were given rooms. It was now the Jewish Passover and we were all invited to share the Feast of Passover with the kibbutzniks, and the management of the kibbutz took all of our actors to one side and expressed a strong wish that each of the actors sit at a different table so that we could be shared among the workers and staff. What a smart idea, and so they could be grilled by the Israelis who were longing to know all about us. They were all curious about London and our working habits and how we became actors and what we thought of Israel.

It was a wonderful day, and every actor had a story to tell. On our last gig we played in the open air and at first it was still light, but, as the evening drew in, the audience, whom at first we could clearly see, became shadows in the dark. Our longish production finally came to an end. The lights came on and the world was alive again. The ovation we received was the most enthusiastic yet. Since the kibbutz theatre was full to bursting, the producer made a speech to the audience asking them whether some of them could give accommodation to the actors for one night. We gathered our little cases and all stood in the foyer on one side while our kindly benefactors stood on the other. At least a dozen, or more, people were waiting. And then to our both shock and amusement we were put on offer! Hands shot up. 'Who would like Laertes?' Many hands. 'Who would like Ophelia?' Many hands. 'Gertrude?' Many hands. 'Claudius?' One or two hands. 'Hamlet?' Many hands.

And so it went on until all of us were housed for the night. It was the first time I had ever felt like I was in an ancient slave market. But it was great fun and then we all departed into the night to our various hosts. That was the last performance. The following day we all stopped off at Masada before returning to Jerusalem. As we reached the top, one of the tour guides told us the story of the last day of the brave zealots before the might of the Romans, who used a battering ram mounted on a recently constructed hill. Knowing there was little chance of survival or an appalling life as a slave, the head of the community made a speech telling them what they must do. Which of course was the ultimate act of self-sacrifice. She then looked at all of us and asked, as was usual, whether anyone would volunteer to read that very moving and yet stirring speech. I could not miss the opportunity and put my hand out. I read it as movingly as I possibly could. I was never so proud in my life. The other actors had already returned down the steep slope to get the bus. I was the last one left. And then I too raced down the long, steep slope of Masada. We returned to Jerusalem.

The Roundhouse – continued

We now returned for the final act in the *Hamlet* saga at The Roundhouse. The contrast between how we were treated there and in Israel could not have been greater, but we managed and had a good advance and were all hopeful. The reviews in Israel had been highly supportive and glowing. After three or four previews we opened. The reviews could not have been worse!! We were shocked, not just by the negativity of the reviews but by the gross ignorance of what we were attempting. It was quite shocking. All were spiteful, petty, childish and almost infantile, though the reviews have long been consigned to the garbage bin where they belonged. We soldiered on. In the first week I happened to see Dustin Hoffman in the audience. Since it was in the round I chose to do some speeches slowly, turning on my axis. I felt like I was appealing to the whole audience. On my last turn I saw the 'famous' movie actor. I then went into overdrive and acted as I had never done before. Of course he came back stage and we all had the great pleasure of chatting to him when we stood on the steps outside The Roundhouse, since our nice producer had made sure the bar was closed after the interval. He told us all that ours was the best *Hamlet* he had seen. We were all as proud as Punch.

A week or two later, when the savage reviews had decimated our audience to a few scattered bodies around that large area, I saw Hoffman again! He had come a second time, but, although it was no fault of ours, I felt ashamed for him to have seen how the audience had dwindled. I again went into full overdrive. A smattering of applause. I waited in my dressing room for him to come again. There was no knock on the door this time. Now, as it so happens, I had met up with one of the last of the grand European producers, called Jan de Blik, from Holland. He booked us for a grand tour of Europe ending up in the studio theatre that was run by Jean-Louis Barrault, the ultimate master of French theatre, at his theatre ironically called Le Rond-Point. Back in Europe all spirits revived. In every theatre we played at we received standing ovations. We did at least six cities in Germany, including Frankfurt, Düsseldorf and Hamburg, also Basle, Antwerp and then Paris. The diffe-rence between European theatre and British at times is immense. Not that the highly realistic, 1960s–1980s theatre is not highly admired. However, there seemed to be far more tolerance in Europe for more adventurous theatre that strays away from the formal and traditional. Ideas are much admired, as is movement and mime, or telling the old familiar story in a unique and unfamiliar way.

In Paris Jean-Louis Barrault, Master of the Théâtre du Rond-Point off the Champs Élysées, came to see us on our last night. Naturally enough, since we were playing in his theatre. I have always deeply admired this remarkable actor/writer/ director/mime. Of course his brilliant talents as a mime drew me to him, and I really felt he was my French spiritual cousin. There is no acting more remarkable than his opening performance of the white-faced mime in the wartime classic *Les Enfants du Paradis* directed by Marcel Carné. So I could not have been more proud playing in his theatre, and he has left an indelible impression on me.

11

DECADENCE

Arts Theatre 1981

As it so happens, *Greek* was out on tour in the British provinces, and naturally I was touring with it. We had opened in the beautiful little Half Moon Theatre in Alie Street, East London. It had been in past years a synagogue and therefore still had the balcony for the ladies, lest we so vulnerable men be swayed from our devotion by the unguent perfumes of our beautiful wives! Bob Walker had made a small, dynamic theatre out of this space, and it was thriving. We had a really splendid first night there, which I shall never forget. I was so proud since it was such a verbally adventurous play, yet, I hoped, daring and rather explicit.

Part of me wanted to play Eddy, and another part felt that it was so autobiographical it felt like indecent exposure. So I cast Barry Philips, a very bold and dynamic actor who had by now worked with me in several productions. A brilliant, even breathtaking Messenger in *Agamemnon*, Les in *East* and now Eddy in *Greek*. I have to admit that he was almost perfect in it. Dad was played by Matthew Scurfield, who was also a stalwart long-term player, who played an amazingly explosive Dad in *East*. And Linda Marlowe played Mum on tour. The reviews were middling, and one idiot, a critic who had also had slim fame as a poet, gave it one word. 'Yuk.' Anyway, the poor man has virtually faded into obscurity.

Well, while on tour I could not help but reflect on the fact that I might have been playing it and giving it the full welly. But I knew I was really too old for the role. I was sitting in a café on one of the tour dates and began doodling as was my wont. Just letting ideas dribble out of me and see where they led me. In fact, I thought I was being awfully literary since I had in my possession postcard-sized pink cards. I must have read that the Russian writer Nabokov would write on small filing cards. I began to doodle. The preciousness of the small cards, coupled with sitting in a small, charming café in the open air, meant that it had to be somewhat lyrical. So I started. I was determined to write a large role for myself. I had watched my marvellous actors sweating and roaring each night, while I just sat, watched and gave the odd note. Or fussed about the lights. I was deeply frustrated.

So I wrote, and the first line just oozed out of me. The main characters were called Helen and Steven, a couple of upper-class toffs, and their nemeses were lower-class Sybil and Les.

> HELEN: *'How sweet of you to come on time ... bastard, sweet darling ... my you do look divine. Have a drink ... what? Cinzano and bitter lemon and a dash of ice. Oh darling, you do look nice ...'*

And so it continued and I just let it go wherever it wished. I had her sitting on a luscious white leather sofa ... After she finished her opening salvo I responded, but it had to be somewhat gloomy, and what could be gloomier than a man confessing to his lover that his wife has rumbled his little secret. And, of course, it all had to be written in verse. This gave me so much more scope to invent and be playful, scintillating and sometimes even absurd.

> STEVE: *'So bleeding dextrous, wouldn't you know,*
> *Too much bloody ice love, taste like a crow,*
> *You ask me the cause of my down face,*
> *Wait till you hear what I have to say,*
> *Unzip your ears and let me flood them with verbs*
> *And make your mind a jangle of nerves ...*
> *The bloody bitch got cute*
> *Decided for a hunch to hire a dick with a nose like a Jew*
> *A private detective in case you're not yet clued.*
> *The bloody bitch got wise*
> *When too many spunkless nights rolled by*
> *Made her think I was not emptying my teapot*
> *In her old kitchen sink!'*
> HELEN: *'Oh fuck darling.'*
> STEVE: *'Yes, you've said a mouthful there ...'*
> HELEN: *'Don't worry darling, there's nothing to fear,*
> *Say your hard-on's taking a small holiday this year.*
> *The stress and pain of conning your way in this world*
> *sends the cock to the brain.'*

And so it went on in this fashion, all in verse, and it stretched our vocal chords as well as our minds, we became smarter, wittier, cleverer, our tongues became elasticised. Also it fertilised my brain cells. By writing in verse one's imagination is stretched and your invention far more witty than when one is writing in plain prose. This was just pouring out of me without too much reason, although there was plenty of rhyme. Eventually a theme started to wrap itself around the skeleton, as it is wont to. I had created the scaffold and my imagination had to weave itself around it. Simply, it was about an affair that Steve is having with an upper-class party girl. Steve himself is an upper-class, rather sneaky dandy who has married, of course for dosh, a working-class but super-rich daughter of a builder.

Steve is now being spied on by a very working-class private dick called Les. He is employed by Steve's rather vulgar but stinking-rich wife. So far, so simple. However, the catch in all this is that, when the scene changes to the lower-class couple, the same actors play the other two roles!!

This affords great fun and games.

Now, how bloody original is that? And how challenging for an actor, since the actor has to change in a split second from one character to its opposite on the chromatic scale. The point being that there but for the grace of God go I. Just an accident of birth, parents, district, school. Just by virtue of having an educated or comfortably off parent you could be a Steve or a Les, or a Helen or a dumbo Sybil.

But also underlying this was the subconscious desire to do something so demanding I would make up for the last year's dearth of performing and having to watch my brave and bold actors galloping home and feeling that extraordinary and wonderful feeling of accomplishment each night. That is truly wonderful. But of course I did have the satisfaction of having written it, not to mention directed it, but the truth is that, after seeing it a few times and nursing it, it starts very much to pale. So now I was in my element with *Decadence*. As usual when writing a play, I aim to focus on what draws the best or the worst out of the characters. What do they truly live for, what makes them happy or even what disgusts them, what horrifies them?

Curiously, in the end I seemed to show that the upper-class couple had by far the most fun and excitement. I started to rehearse with Linda Marlowe. I had worked with her for some years by then, and we knew each other well enough to feel free and unselfconscious. I usually get certain phobic reactions when starting a new production. In this one I started to get vocal paranoia. Since Helen, my partner in the play, begins with a long excitable speech where all her stops are pulled out and the audience really get to know who she is. I am still, like a wax statue, coldly listening and then I have to start like a greyhound in the slips. After listening to my inamorata in the play, I suddenly have to speak, brightly and clearly. As she reaches the end of the speech I feel my throat slowly start to clamp up, and then I might even have to clear my throat. This was terrible and went on for a few days. Suddenly I had had enough. 'I think I must find another actor,' I sadly declared. 'I've had enough.' My nerves are doing funny things to me. I even mentioned a few actors whom I admired. But she wasn't having any of it. 'No,' she broadly exclaimed, 'It's your role and you have to do it! We all get the "funnies" at the beginning and I get them too.' From then on I decided to just concentrate and be calm when she does her opening speech, and it all came out well.

And then it just poured out of us like a tap pouring alcoholic language and we were away. Our speeches were vast torrents and then we semi-improvised links

FIGURE 11.1 *Decadence*. L–R: Linda Marlowe, Steven Berkoff.

between us and I could invent very cheeky improvisations, and the great quality about Linda was that it never for a second fazed her. Sometimes we played together doing all that soppy little baby talk that the Chelsea set or upper classes engage in and it was supah funny!!

It took quite a few weeks to learn, but then we were ready and decided to do a try out at a charming little theatre in Hampstead, and I invited only a couple of critics. I trusted a few critics and, not wishing to blow the play out of the water at first exposure, I invited just two. I believe one was Nick de Jongh from the *Guardian* and the other was the *Times'* Irving Wardle, who I always thought was very fair and could even make a negative review sound vaguely interesting. After six really happy weeks there we booked ourselves in at the Edinburgh Festival, where we played in the converted left-luggage room of the splendid Caledonian Hotel for three weeks. We got splendid reviews and I was now flowing along quite happily. After the show each lunch time, I was really quite content to find a nice café to relax and sit and write my journal, and this I did most days. One lunchtime Paul Scofield came in, and he wrote a most charming postcard spiced up with the sweetest compliments, which of course I have kept ever since.

After *Decadence* in Edinburgh, I was able to deposit our inexpensive show into the Arts Theatre, that beautiful little theatre off Leicester Square, and I booked it for eight weeks. How did I happen to write a two-handed play? I began by working on large-ensemble plays, which I actually felt more comfortable doing than small works. But I could not help but notice that I was getting the most cruddy reviews for works like *Macbeth*, *Agamemnon*, *The Trial* and *Hamlet*, so I thought that I would write a play with a cast so small that even if the critics tried to kill it I would always be able just to pay the rent.

The longer we played together, the more Linda and I could play, improvise and generally clown around, but the beauty in all of this was that Linda simply ignored my antics when she wished, as if too 'haughty' to get involved, which was perfect, except when we improvised together. The clowning actually helped prevent the 'characters' from being merely mouthpieces for large chunks of opinionated verse.

The eight weeks simply flew past, and then I had a twelve-week tour of Australia, which did drive me a little crazy, since I was playing the insane Roderick Usher. But, when we came back, by chance the Arts was vacant again, and this time I said I want to play for as long as the play can run. So I was in for sixteen weeks!! It was a little tough, so I cancelled Mondays since I was the producer and did two shows on Saturday, and that was more than enough. Six shows a week and I was on the peak of my form. Many nights Linda and I would go to Joe Allen, and in these days it was a simple and fantastic restaurant and we were so happy.

As fate would have it, we got invited to perform in LA at the small Pilot Theater high up Santa Monica Boulevard. Susan Albert Lowenberg, the producer who invited me to direct *Greek* at The Matrix a year earlier, had seen *Decadence* at the Arts in London, where we played happily to nearly 300 laughing faces a night. Now we were in a ninety-nine-seat theatre which even then we had trouble filling, but we received rave reviews and stumbled along for eight weeks. I don't think I had been so happy in my life. I was now living and working in LA. I had a second-hand massive Honda Gold Wing and at the end of the show and after a few drinks and some delightful sushi we would drive all the way back to Venice Beach. The grim, seedy and colourful hippy enclave. My room and kitchenette was $250 per week and I saved my salary or as much as I could. The life was good and friends were plentiful, amongst whom was Georgia Brown, another East Ender who loved collecting fellow cockneys like me and making us part of her gang. It was then that I got cast by Martin Brest for his film *Beverly Hills Cop*, my first movie in LA!

I had by now flitted across the pond several times to see my beloved New Zealand lady, also to absorb the sheer wildness of LA. For some reason I could not seem to connect with the film industry, but oddly enough I did with a small but dynamic theatre world. A young lady had seen my play *Greek* in London and had persuaded a small Hollywood theatre on Melrose Boulevard to stage it. I flew over after a long tour of Oz and directed it. Strangely enough, my Oedipal fantasy set in a dystopic East End won best production, best ensemble and best play! I now had an agent. A lovely man called Martin Gage. Within a few weeks I was called to an audition for *Beverly Hills Cop*; as I entered the huge gates of Warner Brothers, I felt I was walking into a dream.

I met Sylvester Stallone at the audition and indeed he seemed to take to me. Martin came to see me on stage and it was then confirmed. Stallone left the movie after some minor disagreements and Eddie Murphy took over. The rest is history, but then Stallone, remembering me, cast me in his next film, *Rambo*, and I was flown into a storm-swept Acapulco to play a Russian officer who tortures Stallone.

I never was so lonely in my life as I was among all those stuntmen and fellow actors, but I made it through to the end and never was happier than when I left.

We shot *Rambo* in and around Acapulco, Mexico. I was flown in and ensconced in a five-star hotel, fitted for my Russian uniform and all was well. Unfortunately, filming on location is subject to the temperament of the weather, and Acapulco was in the middle of storms. Everything depended on a hundred different elements melding together to make shooting possible. We did some studio work, but then 'Sly,' as he was known, didn't like the photography, so days were spent waiting for a replacement. Then the director was replaced. And so it went on. Film actors don't quite have the same need for each other as stage actors. On stage you are thoroughly dependent on your fellow actors – you almost feed off each other. On film you can in fact be shot separately … The compelling need for each other is far less acute. The stuntmen all stick together in their group and the major stars in theirs. The leading actors rarely deign to fraternise with the lower orders, so I found myself alone quite a lot. Eventually I found much nourishment and human society with the actors playing the POWs; they were a great team of guys and eventually I wrote a play about all of us. It is called *Acapulco*. I did, however, like Stallone quite a bit. He was friendly and built like an Adonis.

The film was a huge hit, my second major movie in a year! I later staged *Acapulco* at the Odyssey Theatre, which then became my LA home for try-outs.

12

RANDOM THOUGHT

Vsevolod Meyerhold

Biomechanics. Making the body tell the story. Emphasise the story, comment on the story.

The term biomechanics was first conceived by Russian theatre directors, principally Vsevolod Meyerhold, probably in the twenties in that heady time post-revolution. Oh, what a relief to no longer cater to those boring audiences slathering over endless Chekhovian revivals. Now with freedom came the unleashing of the worker's imaginations, and theatre of endless possibilities.

Put simply, biomechanics is the fusion of biomechanical life and industrial life and how this fusion heightens and intensifies the theatrical experience. I was already experimenting with biomechanics before I was even aware that it was a movement expressing itself with great force across Russia.

Having had the great advantage of studying Jacques Lecoq's technique, I was already primed to discover the extraordinary possibilities of the human skeleton. As I had earlier mentioned regarding my adaptation of Kafka's 'Metamorphosis', the creation of the beetle was a perfect challenge in which to explore those techniques. The unfortunate man/insect has become more mechanical than human. His soul is still very human, but his body is mechanical. He lay there quite still in his room, moving only suddenly and of course shockingly. His six legs represented by the actor's hands, knees and feet. No extensions or props are needed since the body does it all.

The family are seen at breakfast agitated that their 'breadwinner' has not yet surfaced. They are eating their breakfast, their morning routine, somewhat smug and satisfied that their able and idealistic son will never let them down and soon will rise to begin his endless scurrying round the city … I chose to have the family sit with some distance between them, each isolated in their own small spot. Since we did not wish to merely act 'eating', I encouraged the actors to perform to a metronome. Gradually they mastered the movement, breaking their body down into small sections, even to the movement of their mouths. The effect was fascinating, it was family life almost surgically anatomised and strangely as mechanical as their son's. This was mainly used at the beginning and sometimes during the play, and when it was used the performance came startlingly to life. Over the years I have directed many productions and in many languages, and I have never once been disappointed by the actor playing the insect. It seemed that by eschewing the 'human' element they had paradoxically become more than human.

13

WEST

Donmar Warehouse 1983

West was actually my first play for the Donmar. It's strange how plays start. The wonderfully charismatic director Bob Walker who ran the renowned Half Moon Theatre in a converted synagogue in Alie Street in the East End was really quite a loveable friend. Effervescent, cheeky and strictly competitive. And we were always bantering on who was the best director. I worked for him only once in a ridiculous one-act play called *Hot Pants* which is best forgotten about, but it was a lot of fun working with Bob. As far as I was concerned we were from different planets. I had just completed my first workshop at The Oval House of Kafka's *The Trial* which I had also adapted, and this kind of work made my life seem worthwhile, so when he offered me the lead in this silly one-acter I felt it would be a jolly comedown and relaxer after the month of work we had just done on *The Trial*.

Shortly after, I learned that he had managed to get a job at the BBC and he was looking for plays for their drama slot. He rang me one morning and asked whether I had anything that might be suitable, something strong, dramatic and different from the usual fare. I said I would have a go. As soon as we put the phone down I slid a piece of A4 paper in my typewriter and began. Since I had written a play called *East* I decided to write a play called *West*.

East was a highly symbolic play about the energy and imagination locked inside the minds of unfulfilled, wild teenagers, also about the explosive energy in the working-class kids unrefined by the forced manners of the upper class. Also it was a fantasy.

As kids we always talked about going 'up West' as a kind of very special treat since the West End in those days was a glorious wonderland. To go up West meant wearing a smart suit, dining in the famous and elegant Lyons corner house where my mum would take me from time to time, bless her. She always wanted to give me a treat. She took me to the salad bar, where for a fixed price, three shillings and sixpence as it was then, you could fill your plate to the brim, which I did. And of course could never finish it.

So *West* was just a term almost for a mysterious wonderland where beautiful women strolled down the streets of Soho offering their wares … And the smart cafés were far beyond our reach. *West* took this a stage further since I hadn't a clue in my head of how to start the play or what it should be about, and even as I was writing it the plot came into being.

Now, each really vital working-class area had its leaders, tough guys, also called 'Shtarkers', and there was one who fascinated me above all others. His name as I knew it was 'Curly King'. I met him one day in the Stamford Hill amusement arcade where one played pinball and put two pence in the jukebox. He had just wandered in with a couple of hangers-on, I presumed, since they didn't say much. Curly was a shortish, compact alpha male with startling dark eyes and a mop of curly hair, hence his *nom de guerre*. But the total effect simply mesmerised me. He was like a Gorgon, a wizard, a male predatory beast. He was to haunt my life for years to come. I felt he was like the monster in *Beowulf*, and at the same time he was dazzling and menacingly attractive.

The term 'Shtarker' comes from the German word for strong. Hence a strong man, tough guy, or bully boy. Its origin is Yiddish. I believe Curly was half Jewish, brought up in the ghettoes of the East End. He was a minder for the Krays at one time, and yet his reputation when I was a teenager was legend. Everybody had heard of him. He was fearless and, I think, something of a psychopath. His main haunt seems to have been the Lyceum Dance Hall in The Strand, where he would appear with his team of bully boy mates every Sunday night. Invariably there would be a punch-up at the end of the evening. They'd gather in a nest at the far end of the dance hall like it was their hang out. Where the beasts lurk. As a raw teenager whose main interest was jiving and finding young girls to take home if they didn't live too far, the Lyceum was my favoured haunt. A magical world full of mystery, exotic cheap perfume and the dizzying proximity of the glorious bodies of young women as you danced with them. Sometimes I saw Curly at the famous jazz haunt called The 51 Club off Leicester Square. I rarely spoke to him but would keep my distance. The last time I saw Curly was in Israel on Dizzengorf Street. He had actually opened a furniture module shop. I believe it was a skill that he had learned in prison. I crossed the road and he greeted me like an old pal. I was playing Hamlet on a British Council tour. He was accompanied by a huge dog. When by chance I met him on the beach a couple of days later, I was with some of my cast. I felt both proud and nervous introducing this ex-London gangster, and as I was talking his dog started to dig up the sand beneath my feet! I wasn't safe even from his dog!

So I began writing *West*, and it had to be a revenge story based on an almighty battle that took place in Stamford Hill where most of the action takes place. Mike was alias parts of me and parts of my heroic cousin Sydney Bennet. Sydney actually fought a young hoodlum who had attacked him totally unprovoked one afternoon in the cinema. I was just fifteen at the time and I watched the revenge fight. I have never forgotten it. Syd's courage was quite matchless. My cousin was a hero, he was everything that I wished I could be, but certainly was not. I suppose I may have had other talents. I hope so.

So I began writing, and as usual had no idea of how it would turn out, but in my usual manner let the web of my imagination slowly unravel itself. Also I wrote most of it in verse. An East End play in verse was something a little original in those days, since one didn't write in a poetic form unless it was something rather grand and elevated.

I began with a line from one of my short stories:

> Breathless, I was aghast, when I saw,
> Standing beneath the blinking lamplight,
> This geezer, all armed, a certain aim he took,
> And felled the swarthy git from Hoxton
> With a deft and subtle chop.

Mike, our hero, is surrounded by his coevals, four of them, who all chip in from time to time. They are dressed very elegantly in fifties-style suits. Their gestures parody the movement of the smart working-class kids of the period until it almost becomes a dance style. Mum and Dad are seated upstage and are revealed as the lads strut off. Then there is Sylv, Mike's girlfriend who shimmers so sexily between the two groups. Basically again it's autobiographical. The parents, like all those simple hard-working members of the lower class, are tormented by the antics of highly testosteroned youth. Of course the Mother, like my own mother, bewails their stranded son, and yet she confesses her deep love for him, while Dad, like my dad, whines that their son is a deadbeat with no hope of redemption. A 'stinking low life'.

I put everything about my own misbegotten youth in the play. But also there were lively and comedic turns, and we see them in the gym working out, all mimed of course, and then in the dance hall doing the jive, which was a delightful sequence in the eventual production.

Now we have to see the other gang, Curly's mob, and the gang was played by exactly the same actors as Mike's gang. To do this they doffed caps, chokers (scarves) tucked in their waistcoats and strutted on, uttering a strange cockney argot that basically made no sense except for the first two verses.

> CURLY: *'I'm known as The Avenger*
> *When they see me, they run pell-mell!*
> *For they see before their runny eyes*
> *A short pathway to ultra-violence*
> *And a swift descent to hell*
> *So come on boy I'm waiting*
> *I hear you're on your way*
> *I'm hungry for the blood of victims*
> *I need another jerk like you*
> *A mama's boy to slay.'*

A drum beat accompanied their strutting walk while they intoned a mock lingo after the above words.

Their chests thrust out, this small gang circled the stage, and it was the funniest thing to see and the audience howled at their ridiculous antics, but at the same time it told you everything about them. The cockney neck thrust, the shoulder pulled or jerked back, the perpetual cigarette poking the air.

Mike and Sylv are having the kind of problems that all late teenagers have, and Sylv is always waiting for him. However, a challenge has been issued by Curly to meet his 'nemesis' Mike at the Hackney Marshes one week from now. A battle to the death. When I was seventeen I had a girlfriend called Sylv, and we used to go out together and end up at the Hackney Marshes, where our relationship was consummated. She lived in a grim old council flat nearby with a semi-delinquent brother and her unfortunate mum who suffered unfairly with extreme elephantitis. It was not the most favourable environment to be in.

Mike travels to work each day by tube train, which we also put in the play, along with him entertaining us all with the description of a young man selling 'three-string diamante pearls' from a suitcase and then dashing into an ABC café when there was a sign of the law coming. I believe the letters ABC stood for 'Aerated Bread Company'. The ABC was one of the most dreadful chain cafés in London. I know since I used to go to them. There is nothing on God's earth worse than an ABC. One day during the Xmas period my smart and canny streetwise friend called Barry Wise, who hailed from Hackney, asked me whether I would act as a 'watcher'

FIGURE 13.1 *West*. 'Preparing for night out'. Photo: Roger Morton.

when he was doing his street spiel, and he offered me a pound a day, which was quite generous in those times. Barry had such a flair for doing the street spiel while selling his 'three-string diamante pearls', and I envied him for it. For his sheer effrontery and bezazz. So I borrowed some of that bezazz for Mike.

Eventually the time came for the battle, but there was no opponent on stage since Mike would be describing the fight as he was doing it. It was quite a *tour de force*, since Rory Edwards, who played Mike, had the most marvellous moves and was able to suggest being hit by an invisible foe. This young actor's fortitude and imagination were formidable.

But I run before my horse to market. I am describing the production as I did it at the Donmar Warehouse. What actually happened was that I finished the play for Bob Walker, who was at The Beeb as we called it. He sent it in and the poor fools rejected it!! Some little time passed, and I was paid nevertheless and went on my way to do other things.

A couple of years later Bob asked whether he could direct it at the Donmar. I was happy for Bob Walker to direct it, since he had introduced the producer to my play, but Ian Albery decided, once he knew I was on the scene, that I must direct it, since I had already directed *East*, my other East End play. Bob was not at all put out, but I was grateful to him for having introduced the play.

It was very successful, and I had a splendid cast that could not possibly be bettered. We set up thorough casting sessions and I found my team. It was an exciting rehearsal period, and many of us bonded for many years. The main good news was that Limehouse Films wanted to film it for Channel Four and so it was filmed, and very successfully too, by Cyril Frankel

I could not have been more proud. The reviews were excellent, but I never heard from the producers again, unfortunately.

However, I think the positive critical response might have been due to the fact that it was a very physical production, using East End argot written paradoxically in verse. I think this tickled their fancy. But, having done it, there was no great passion at the time to discover whether I had any similar works up my sleeve.

It was a successful run of sixteen weeks. So I dedicate this piece to Ken Sharock, who played Curly, to John Joyce, who played Dad, Syd and the lovely Stella Tanner who played Pearl (Mum).

I miss them all, they were wonderful and so was the Donmar in those days.

P.S. My beloved cousin Sydney Bennet, who inspired much of *West*, sadly passed away just a few months ago. I do miss him, but his spirit still survives, I hope, in *West*.

14

HARRY'S XMAS

Donmar Warehouse 1985

I wrote this weird, sad and self-pitying play sometime in 1983. A rather melancholic tale about a young to middle-aged man who hurtles into the depths of depression one Xmas when, newly divorced, he finds himself alone. I remember having spent Xmas with my sister and her family in her home in the northern suburbs of Britain. It was not the happiest of experiences for either of us. Well, this became the rather rancid material for a play about loneliness. The set was totally bare except for a small desk downstage. On the stage floor I had drawn out with white tape the outlines of 'bed', 'toilet', 'kitchen' as if for rehearsals in a TV studio. On the desk were a rather mournful collection of Xmas cards by which Harry, the protagonist, measured his popularity. It's a long monologue, basically, which shows Harry at the countdown towards Xmas.

There are still a few days to go and yes, he might even now get an invite to some old friends' Xmas do. As the days slowly tick down, and in spite of his real and brave efforts to try to rekindle some past romances, he finds himself bereft. The last day comes and then it is here. Old songs by Bing Crosby and Sinatra welcome in Xmas day. From his basement flat he can hear the odd joyful yelp as happy voices repair to the pub for pre-Xmas dinner drinks and happy chatter. Their voices are like nails piercing his flesh.

He decides to brave it out, have a good few gulps of anesthetising alcohol and drift through it. There is a phone on the desk and he does make an effort to contact some human support, but the lame responses he gets drive him deeper into his swamp of worthlessness.

Somehow his life has been a failure. A failure in the sense that he has no close mate, no human being with whom he could share his agony, his joys. Although once there was. He starts taking his 'pills', no doubt tranquilisers prescribed by his doctor. He takes more and more until finally he is solemnly content. Now he begins to feel that he need only continue, just slowly continue to be eventually rid of all this. I started rehearsing and as usual all props bar the phone and Xmas cards were mimed. I actually liked playing Harry. The audience were quiet and attentive and in the end rather moved. I loved so much the sheer freedom of working alone, and not only working alone but being free to do just about anything I wished. Mime allows you that without the vulgarity of realism.

When one is alone on stage, one is terribly exposed, and so you rely on your technique, partly as a mask and partly to illustrate your private life to an audience. I took great care to detail precisely all those personal moments when one is alone in one's home, even to sitting on the toilet. I felt miming it 'normalised' the situation.

I accompanied myself with vocal sound effects for boiling kettles, tea, washing etc. There was one armchair centre stage near the front where I would sometimes sit to watch what we call 'The Box'. When I gulp the last few pills after having taken them all day, I die in front of the TV, which is happily playing *I'm Dreaming of a White Christmas.*

I slowly give up the ghost. As the lights go out on me, the phone on the desk bursts into life. Who was it? A friend? A saviour? An equally lonely woman? We will never know. I did actually make a TV version for Limehouse Films, which was at that time run by Mark Chivas. A most benign gentleman who was a successful BBC drama producer. Now what makes this all the more interesting is that he was the son of my English teacher, Mr Chivas, whom I adored when he taught me at Raines Foundation Grammar school in London's East End. How very bizarre. I was incidentally the head of my class in English. I loved the way Mr Chivas smiled with such elegance, titling his chin up as if he were thanking the heavens for the beneficence of his mood. He kept a large handkerchief in his sleeve, which I thought so very smart.

Following this play, I then came on to perform *The Tell-Tale Heart*, a perfect evening you might say.

The Donmar charged me a reasonable rent and, since some of the reviews were quite supportive, I played to a nearly full house most nights. I was really happy. I had returned to my first love, the theatre.

15

ACAPULCO

The King's Head Theatre, Islington 1986

I began this play in Acapulco when acting in the film *Rambo II*, and I think writing it helped to keep me sane. The film was basically good Hollywood shlock divided chiefly between the American POWs kept behind barbed wire and in cages. These were precious booty for the Vietnamese clients of the 'Russkies'. Stallone is of course there to rescue them and to prove that the 'establishment' were hiding the fact that there were still our boys out there and being forgotten about. A really worthy subject.

Of course I found that I bonded more with the 'lower orders', and when I did venture out in the evening it was usually with them. Acapulco is a tourist seaside on the Mexican coast that is a combination between abject poverty and gloating consumerism. Many of the hotels that line the sea front were built in a pseudo-Aztec style that appealed mightily to their mainly American tourists, who did not have to travel too far for a taste of foreign exotica. The lower orders, the actors who were kept in the 'pen' mainly as background, had little to do during their odd days off filming. They were a mixed bunch of people, part-time actors, some of whom were adventurers who lived in Mexico City picking up odd jobs in films or TV. My main companion of choice was a man called Voyo, a Serbian giant who was my bodyguard or assistant, since I was after all a general. General Orloff. Voyo acted as a complete beast of a man who also had the most charming innocence about him that was most endearing.

He was excited to be cast as a Russian heavy in a major action movie and somehow allowed his excitement to get the better of his sense. In the film he has a fierce battle with Stallone, which, obviously, the hero wins. That's what action movies are about, defeating the enemy no matter how strong they seem to be. Voyo was becoming rather 'mouthy' at the lunch table – boasting that he was so very powerful, how could Stallone possibly beat him! The audience won't believe it! Word got back to Stallone and he wanted to fire him immediately. I went straight to Stallone, begged him to give Voyo another chance and promised to keep him in check.

This obviously reminded Stallone of the poor brute Lenny in Steinbeck's master-piece *Of Mice and Men*. So Stallone 'cast' me as Lenny's minder and I promised 'Sly' that I would certainly keep him in order. I was actually prepared to walk off the picture and my $60,000 job if Voyo was sacked.

So Voyo was my one stalwart buddy. There were others in the prisoner gang whom I also bonded with, particularly one Jewish New Yorker who related a story of how as a young man he was picked up in New York by Salvador Dalí's wife. He may have reminded her of Dalí as a young man. He was a man just at the edge of his youth and had quite a charisma and ability to tell great yarns, but I knew that the Dalí story was true since I also had it confirmed in a biography I had read about her and how they actually took him to their home in Portlligat as a kind of gigolo for her.

Then there was a young Scot who had somehow ended up in the 'Zona Roja' (the red-light district in Mexico City). So some nights we would sit in the bar and spew out our life and adventures, such as they were. I had little to say to these guys since I was so miserably out of it and just longing to go home and do something useful in the theatre again. But oddly enough it was here in the hotel that I read a most astonishing book called *The Conquest of New Spain* by Bernal Díaz. One of the greatest books on the conquest of the Aztecs and the killing of Montezuma, the Aztec king, that has ever been written. I believe it was also a favourite book of the great French theatrical madman and visionary Antonin Artaud.

I always kept a journal, especially when travelling and working, but now it dawned on me to write down these bar room stories that I was hearing most nights. There was such vitality in these poor down and out small-part underdogs. Here was such a passion, a desire for adventure, such unspoilt vigorous enthusiasm that put all the other actors, stuntmen and Sly's gang in the shade. So I did. I wrote every-thing that I could remember and called the play *Acapulco*. I even gave myself a role as Steve, the watcher, the listener, the sad older actor in the background. How we would roar with laughter at Voyo's highly elaborate stories of his sexual conquests and his boasting of his 'prick like horse' as the Mexican women, the staff, maids and waitresses fell at his feet. Years later, but not too many years later, I actually cast the play in Los Angeles at the Odyssey Theatre. Voyo even came to see it very proudly to hear his life played out on a stage. He also brought his wife!!

'Oh, Berkoff makes all that up, of course he does ... He's a writer, that's what they do.'

The Odyssey built a magnificent steel bar, which was the entire set, and I had a great team of actors and quite a marvellous one playing me, called John Horne. He captured me perfectly. So God bless you John, for he is now in the great green room in the sky. I even had the interest of Brad Davis, but he couldn't make a week of rehearsals that I knew was vital for the ensemble. That is a decision I'll regret the rest of my life. I knew and loved Brad since he played in my LA production of *Metamorphosis* some years earlier. Acapulco did not get the best of reviews, although

I loved it and thought the actors did a fantastic job. It ran its allocated six weeks and John Horne was quite marvellous.

I began *Acapulco* with music that exploded onto the stage as hands shot out for drinks, nuts, cigarettes. It was a splendid beginning and I thought it worked well.

Starting with an explosion of sound, gesture and action immediately concentrates the attention of the audience – it's also very exciting.

We even had a young lady called Chandra Lee at the bar who became part of the action. She was great, gamely and funny, thank you Chandra.

Eventually we did the play in England at The King's Head, Islington when my friend Dan Crawford was there, and this time I actually played myself in it. We also had a very good cast, easily as good as the LA cast, who were superb.

I was more than a trifle anxious on the very first preview, but once we got into it the story seized us all in its great muddy paws and we flew through it. There was not a night when we did not receive cheering ovations at the end of the show and then we tumbled out onto the warm summer pavements of Upper Street, chatting to our friendly and enthusiastic audience. I had listened so carefully to the bizarre stories of our gang in Acapulco – they were bizarre indeed, and I am so grateful to them all for sharing their lives with me. Good guys! We mimed all the drinks but used the empty bottles. It was inventive all the way through until the very end when the barman, who is Mexican, tells us all a story of the horrible invasion of the white barbarians from Spain. It was originally written for myself as a kind of finale for Steve, the 'loner', but I believe it was Alex Cox, the film director, who suggested that it should be the local barman who tells us all the story, and it worked brilliantly, especially as played by Paul Bentall.

It felt like a logical conclusion for the 'loner' Steve to not only have this information, but to be committed to the telling of it as a good-hearted liberal. However, when the barman spoke those lines with his beautifully observed Spanish accent, the story becomes very moving, since he's talking about his nation, and I was grateful to Alex Cox for suggesting it

Those were happy days.

So many thanks Hilton McRae, Joe Mantana, Paul Bentall, Connie Hyde and the funny scene stealer Terry Beesley. In the LA production, Tom Flynn, John Horne, Chandra Lee, Rickey Pardon, Michael Sollenberger, Richard Vidan and Sam Vlahos.

P.S. I recently learned that Terry Beesley had left us at a terribly young age. He was such a lively, loving soul as everyone who saw him perform or met him will testify. R.I.P. Terry

16

CORIOLANUS

The Public Theater, New York 1988

And so another Shakespeare. And this time it's actually an offer from New York, from no less than Joe Papp, the CEO of The Public Theater, also called the Shakespeare Festival Theater, in Lafayette Street on New York's East Side.

I had never read *Coriolanus*, although I had seen a production some years ago at the National with Ian McKellen, who gave a very good performance in a rather dull production. Some years before, in the days when great foreign companies used to be invited here with some regularity, I did see the Berliner Ensemble with the remarkable actor Ekkehard Schall as the protagonist, which was superb. I was acting in my play *Greek* at the time at the beautiful Wyndham's Theatre and used to go on stage with *Coriolanus* nagging at the back of my mind.

I tried reading it and it was hard to stay awake, since there were just too many subplots and just too many generals to keep apace with it all. But eventually I found myself in New York for the first reading. The principal roles had fortunately been chosen by Joe Papp, and I cast what I would call the 'ensemble' or chorus, which suited me quite well, since I knew as always that the ensemble would be the backbone of the play.

With an astute, imaginative and fit ensemble, all problems become immediately solvable. The ensemble become the core of the play. In *Coriolanus*, they could change in a split second from grumbling, whining rogues, to tough, hardened fighters. A swift shedding of a jacket, then adding sunglasses, and the impression is of a completely new group of people. Suddenly they become the gang of Aufidius. Not only is this vital to the strength of the production, it also elevates the smaller players into a high-powered team.

Joe does love 'stars' like a typical East End Jew, for whom the glory of stardom blows the ghetto dust out of their eyes. He chose, for Coriolanus, Christopher Walken, who apart from a burgeoning film career had a strong background as a stage actor. A few weeks earlier, Walken rang me from New York to case the situation and to reassure himself that I was not going to put them into togas and miniskirts. 'No,' I replied, 'modern dress, in fact New York style.' He was then reassured. Aufidius was to be played by a powerful black actor called Keith David and Volumnia by no less than the internationally celebrated actress Irene Worth!

I had my work cut out, especially since Irene had played Volumnia twice already. I hardly ever make plans before I have all the actors on stage in front of me. This is my mode of operation. I wait for the chemistry of the actors to ignite, and they would tell me what I would need to create the production, aided I must say by a gifted musician, and this I had in spades with the talented percussionist and composer Larry Spivack.

This prevents me from anticipating the production and commissioning huge, expensive and defunct sets before we had even begun. The company would tell the story using, as usual, their bodies and their energy. This is the most creative way to go. Also it inspires the actors' imagination and stimulates their imagination. Neither should the set reduce the power of the actors' ensemble work. In the western theatre world, the director is obliged to work with the designer and anticipate the set, since in the commercial logic of theatre costs it will take several weeks to make the set and create the costumes. That is not to say that this way cannot work, but it severely hampers innovation and the organic flow of the production.

Joe Papp, having to run a complex theatre operation with five different acting areas, had to keep his eye on the logistics and was frequently requesting me to come up with something. I had to give him something and so the first thing I could think of was to set the play in a New York mafia Italian setting. So I told him that. Modern sharp suits for the Roman generals, sleazy suits for the plotting tribunes and a dozen cane-backed chairs.

The first read through was predictably boring, with everyone self-conscious reading in front of each other, but I knew that the actors needed it to break the ice. The next day we began in earnest. The first scene opens with the riots as the deprived citizens are marching on the senate to demand their rights. A very familiar scene. I felt that the scene should begin with an explosion from the ensemble as they rush in, armed with rough, crude weapons, including of course baseball bats. They wear beaten up trilbies and caps. They look sturdy and dangerous. The smart stage management have already brought these props in, and I am grateful to them because they already looked like the real deal. Actors appreciate any aid to getting into character, one almost sees them transform before one's eyes. Once they had the 'accoutrement' they were ready to rock and roll.

The guys are ready to start. We read the first couple of pages and appoint the first citizen, the leader and agitator. I look up to the podium where Larry Spivack, our musician, sits and waits. Now, the first moment. 'OK Larry, give us some sound just to get it going?' Larry replies, quite naturally, 'What kind of sound do you want?' Now I don't want to get into a discussion about this, since the percussionist will see what's going on and respond instinctively. 'Just try anything ... OK ... go.' Larry then hits the drums with a resounding tattoo that has us all frozen and made our hair stand on end. It was sensational. 'OK guys, now we run on to this and when we get to centre stage we freeze.' So we tried that. Larry hit the drums one more time, the gang came racing on with cries and shrieks and, as the drum stopped, so did they. An active group suddenly freezing on a dime is an exciting thing to watch. I must confess that I was happy and even somewhat thrilled. This showed the way I was going. We were not going to be a group who sit around feebly and listlessly as the director discusses the play with them. Not us. As soon as the first freeze occurs, they are rock still, like a massive Rodin sculpture.

Roger Smith as First Citizen: 'Before we go any further, hear me speak.' He has shot to the front of the gang and faces all of them. The mob now cry in unison a voice to wake the devil. 'Speak! Speak!' Before they move further he sets out his plans. They answer in unison. The mob is a mighty force, a giant fist ready to do damage if their demands aren't met. Then, as if by chance, a Senator comes on the scene. He is Menenius, a liberal and friendly to the people, and he begs them to air their grievances.

They do, although somewhat reluctantly since their forward motion has been temporarily halted. Now they are obliged to hear Menenius' attempts to calm them down by preaching to them a somewhat stale parable about the belly and how the Senate is the belly, which needs the people to supply the viands to help it function and which in turn sends nourishment to feed the people. I found the

FIGURE 16.1 *Coriolanus.*

story somewhat tedious, but it does its job, which is to take the steam and passion out of the mob.

Just as he finishes his pithy tale and the mob pull themselves together to continue, who should appear on the scene but the volatile dictator, Coriolanus.

Menenius has taken the wind out of the mob's sails, merely by the trick of distracting them and slowing their progress, forcing them, through his elevated status, to listen to his twaddle. Their excitement at the beginning is diffused.

The guvnor strides on. Larry's drum once more sets the scene. The mob feels exposed. I think of a billiard table. All the balls comfortable together and then smashed by one cue ball. He comes on and smashes them to the four corners. The mob, having been first preached at by Menenius with his tedious 'belly' speech, are now unprepared for the shock of seeing Coriolanus.

They are no longer a tight mob but scattered into twos and threes. He gives them a mouthful as if he were lashing them. I remember reading about Olivier's opening speech being described by one critic as seeming as if the lynch mob were being lynched by one man!

Walken liked this. He approves of this style, working instinctively, spontaneously. He is flushed, excited. He tastes blood. So of course I now say 'Let's run that' ... He demurs ...'I wanna see it through, just get an overview.' If I listen to him it means we don't rehearse what we have just discovered. He wants an overview. This is the old world where directors just block it crudely. The leads being paid full attention while 'others' are just serfs standing around just like every single production I have seen in London. I don't like it but I give in. I will work with the ensemble and bring him in later and so work this way. Walken's power was good in the opening scene and so we carry on. I don't wish to have any conflict with this actor and so will block it at speed. I'm glad about what we have already found and hope that the impetus continues.

And now his first scene with Irene Worth as Volumnia, his doting mother. I am slightly apprehensive but I have a simple idea, for here we will create an imaginary garden. While her daughter-in-law sits and sews, very deliberately Irene will trim the hedges, but softly, deliberately taking in the whole space.

Arboreal. Tranquil as she realises the battle to come and even brays with delight at the blood to be shed since it betokens 'honour'. Eventually, I shed this idea and have the two of them sewing in unison, which looked like a Victorian painting. By changing to the sewing 'in unison', it became a highly elegant statement of two high-ranking ladies and therefore most symbolic. A touch of Kabuki!

Now as they speak I have Coriolanus enter with his troops, slowly, gradually at the same time as the ladies are in the garden, and so we are able to see one scene dissolve as the other takes its place and the battle commences. The things that one can accomplish with a physically first-rate group of actors are indeed wondrous. The leading actors had no problem working with such a talented ensemble, they even enhanced their performance.

We worked on these scenes for many weeks until we had explored every possible variation. One of the scenes was to allow the troop to disappear off stage. Then, with the wonderful accompanying music, watch as single soldiers entered the stage, moving very slowly and cautiously as if in a deep mist. Next, unseen by them and from behind a second soldier, the enemy slowly enters. Swiftly the second soldier kills the first, who then rolls off the stage. During this another soldier has entered and just as swiftly cuts the throat of the other, who also slowly rolls off the stage. Now another soldier is seen, silently making his way to the last soldier who also succumbs.

This now goes on and on as one soldier is slaughtered only to be replaced by his enemy. It was a frightening and bizarre scene and can be made to last as long as one wishes. It makes the point of the savagery of war without endless battle rehearsal and bruised and battered actors.

Now, another rather significant point in the play is when Coriolanus, still known as Marcius, reaches the gates of the city. Usually this is a major part of the play, since the gates lead to the Volscian territory. Well, I decided that we do not need the gates, but we need to demonstrate the power of the gates by pitching our power against them. Again gratitude to Jacques Lecoq. As a group we stood in a line and hurled ourselves against the invisible gates, first with our shoulders, heaving and howling, and then with our hands flat out against the gates we withdrew our bodies. We now had sixteen strong arms outstretched against the gates. Next once again we charged the gates and slowly, very slowly the giant doors opened. All done by the actors 'acting' out the gates. Coriolanus utters 'The gates are ope,' and in we go.

I felt this to me a most significant moment since it not only provided an exciting moment for the audience, but also demonstrated how very vital the actors are, and not just the few leading roles but the backbone of the ensemble.

We win the battle, with what I thought were far too many self-deprecatory comments from Coriolanus, which in a way demonstrated less his supposed modesty but rather his monstrous arrogance. Shakespeare seems to enjoy Coriolanus' fairly frequent comments on his alleged 'modesty', so when he explodes we can judge for ourselves how skin deep his modesty is!

However, his enemies, the tribunes, wish to provoke his pride and arrogance and thereby demonstrate to the people how unfit he is to rule and thus in a most dramatic scene engineer his exile. This backfires, since in his exile he bonds with his old enemy Aufidius and plans now to take revenge on the ungrateful Romans and make war on them with his new partner.

Volumnia, his doting, proud mother, makes the arduous, terrifying journey to his camp and persuades her son not to do this. He is so moved he actually weeps. This I found most difficult to elicit from the actors who have played it, excellent as they were in other scenes. However, Coriolanus is persuaded, and, in a scene of sublime celebration, Volumnia, played by the remarkable Irene Worth, returns to Rome proudly waving the peace treaty.

I like working on the scene where his mother goads, persuades, begs, pleads with her son not to punish Rome, but to try to forgive the Romans. This is a rather wordy and difficult scene as his partner Aufidius cynically watches. When I directed it in Munich, I decided that Virgilia, the wife of Coriolanus, played perfectly by

Sona MacDonald, rather than just be a silent, docile observer standing motionless while her powerful mother-in-law makes her case, should also be begging and pleading, but mutely and only using her body. This she did by slowly sinking to her knees and even more slowly kissing his boots, and even more slowly crawling between his thighs as if she were like a snake, but an adoring one. So as Volumnia is cunningly wrapping him in a web of the most persuasive words, his wife is wrapping a skein of devoted sensuality, and lo and behold he is broken down and gives in to those two powerful female forces.

We now see his erstwhile enemy in his chamber with his 'men'. They sit in the cane-backed chairs. They look an impressive line-up of actors until we realise that they are exactly the same army as serve Coriolanus. This was achieved by such a simple effect I am loath to mention it! In London it was a black actor, Colin McFarlane, who played Aufidius, and played him well. Colin is blessed with such a great sonorous voice. His expressive face gave immense power to the role. Of course it was Joe Papp, the New York Public Theater's director, who by casting Keith David, a well-known black actor, inspired me to keep Aufidius as a black warrior.

The cast now simply shed their 'street clothes', which reveal them in smart black uniforms. They put on their sunglasses and become the black-shirted soldiers of Aufidius, all in seconds. Meanwhile, Aufidius is seething while he discusses with them the betrayal he has felt from his ex-partner Coriolanus. However, they wait for him to enter with his 'peace treaty'.

Coriolanus enters the camp and offers his peace treaty. He has taken it out of his black, narrow briefcase. It had to be a hard case so that when it was slammed shut it made a strong 'thwack', i.e. end of all future negotiation. Aufidius now excoriates him. He had fought and shed much blood of his countrymen for nothing. Their voices are raised to fever pitch. Coriolanus is challenged to a battle he cannot hope to win. He is surrounded and impaled like a butterfly to the floor. He is thoroughly destroyed in a very dramatic killing, Aufidius finishes him off with a final blow, whilst Coriolanus is pinned helplessly to the floor. The play is nearly over. His lieutenant picks up the now discarded paper which contains the peace treaty. He kneels, places the paper back in its 'coffin', slams the case shut. It shuts with a giant drum beat. Blackout.

17

RANDOM THOUGHT

Directors and intendants

For the umpteenth time I received a note of rejection for one of my plays. Now, there is nothing unusual about this, since I've been receiving these rejection notes for most of my adult life, but, not looking on the gloomy side, these billets-doux *have revved up my willpower to put my plays on myself. This I have been doing and have toured the world with them. On a rare occasion a theatre director might just take a chance on me, but it's been less than a handful in fifty years. And I have been most grateful since it has spared me the always daunting task of casting actors, raising money and searching for theatres and often financing the plays myself.*

Now it occurs to me that most directors in Britain perform two tasks, which are basically in opposition to each other. They are both the leading director and change hats and look for other directors who might keep the theatre reasonably exciting to theatre-goers, and there's the rub. Whilst there is no doubt that they wish to employ sound, experienced and talented people, there also exists the little germ of caution that the invited guest might have a taste for work completely opposite to their own, after all a resident director has spent years honing his craft and life choice of work, and, like acting, it is highly competitive and directors, no matter how pleasant and self-assured, do not broach the subject of an outsider changing the formula.

I know this way of thinking is highly dangerous since it might afford the second-rate talent an opportunity to camouflage the rejections they've suffered as sour grapes or the myopic world of the establishment who did not deign to recognise their formidable gifts.

So one must be especially cautious not to fall into that tumbril. I have been fortunate enough to be employed in the past by producers in the USA and in Germany, where they are called 'intendants'. Now, these intendants have zero qualms about employing a challenging director, since they are not being challenged and are free to explore the world's theatre as Joe Papp, New York's great and late impresario did; they are concerned with bringing the most exciting talents to their theatre. When I visited New York, Joe Papp agreed to see me within twenty-four hours and, after a brief chat, offered me a job on the spot. Producers are searchers, always on the lookout for the next new flavour. In order just to see the latest director at the

.... *I had to wait months since he was 'in rehearsal' or just preparing for a rehearsal, and when I did eventually see .... I had to wait another couple of months for his expected rejection.*

When my ever-earnest and battling agent wrote to see whether there might be a way forward, since the good director did confess he liked the play, he replied that unfortunately he was busy again in rehearsal for the next few months. This man is not doing his job. His job is to find the greatest art he can, but he evades all responsibility by stating that he is in rehearsal and so he's let off the hook. I repeat, he is not doing his job. This is the British way of theatre. My old ally in Germany, Günther Beelitz of the Düsseldorfer Schauspielhaus, flew to London to see me and immediately booked my version of Kafka's The Trial. *This I directed successfully in that magnificent theatre, and I followed it with* Metamorphosis *and a while later* Coriolanus, *at the Residenztheater in Munich. In German, of course.*

I had already directed the play for Joe Papp in New York, where it was the success of the season and inspired long debates in the New York Times. Joe Papp was like a father figure, and he had the patience to encourage and support. By combining the two jobs of director and producer you are also effectively robbing the new applicant of work. I recently had a meeting with Mr ...., and when I told him I wanted to direct a classic that I had recently tried out at the Edinburgh Festival, he replied 'Oh, I might be doing that myself, not sure, won't know for a while yet.' A f.....g outrage!

He certainly has no time either to travel outside of the UK, scour the world for other work, nor give any opportunity to innovative directors from the UK.

Joe Papp was one of the greatest impresarios in America and he was constantly touring the world, hoping to find the best talent to fill his theatre. I was proud to be employed by him. Those doing double duty as director and producer also will only fulfil part of the job, but they will manage to get away with it most of the time. Let a director direct and not be responsible for hiring, firing and working out the budget. We will be in a better situation and you'll see a far better theatre.

18

GREEK

Wyndham's Theatre 1988

Oedipus by Sophocles has inspired me for as long as I can remember, although I had only seen it once. That was Ted Hughes' savage adaptation, directed less savagely by Peter Brook in the late sixties. John Gielgud was painfully miscast as *Oedipus*, but valiantly and uncomfortably waded through it. Gielgud, while possessing flute-like vocal chords, was most successful in expressing the torments of the wounded, rather that the howls of a fighter

I had an *Oedipus* within me, and one fine day I heaved it out of my system with the utmost relief and I called it *Greek*. In common vernacular, *Greek* was meant to be at the edge, extreme, carnal, and in brothels the word 'Greek' had even another interpretation, which was said to be anal sex. I decided to write my modern version and, once I had begun, it just poured out of me without stopping.

I found a relevant commonality to life in London. Nothing seemed to fit as well as the city I was living in at the time. The Greek plague that had extended its poisonous roots into the Greek city in my play was for me, symbolically, London. It wasn't too hard a stretch of the imagination to see that we were living in a state of chaos, being blitzed out by the IRA every few weeks, endless strikes, massive unemployment and garbage piling up in the streets. It was 'the plague', and in my youthful enthusiasm I saw myself as an aspiring Oedipus ready to combat the plague and all its filthy adherents. I would do it, I, Eddy, the title character. I naturally thought of myself as Eddy, but knew that regrettably I was a little bit old for the role.

It came to me as a bolt of inspiration right out of the blue. My play began quite simply with a brief description of my neighbourhood, which was in fact early Islington, which for reasons of poetic elegance I renamed 'Tufnell Park'. The name seemed to be perfectly nasty.

So I was spawned in Tufnell Park.
That's no more than a stone's throw from The Angel.
A monkey's fart from Tottenham
or a bolt of phlegm from Stamford Hill.
It's a cesspit right,
A scumhole dense with drabs
that prop up the corner pubs.
The kind of pubs where ye olde arseholes assemble
The boring turds who save for Xmas with clubs
My mum did that, save all year for her slaggy Xmas party
of boozy old relatives in Marks and Sparks
cardigans, who stand all year doing
as little as they can
With one hand in the bosses' till
and the other scratching their balls.
Rage against the blacks, envying their cocks,
Loathe the yids envying their gelt,
Hate everything that walks under thirty
and fall asleep in front of the telly.

This is only a short extract, but what I was describing was my rancid neighbours in the seedier streets of Islington, and no area could have given me more background material. I thrived on it. My mum and dad in the play were of course nothing like my quite elegant working-class mum, but were the neighbours all around us. Dad, one day, calls me into the kitchen and reveals a strange story about a fortune teller at a fairground who forewarned him that his son would one day 'kill his old dad' and he also sees something worse than death and that's 'a bunkup with his mum'.

So Eddy decides to leave and try his fortune. My cockney argot was a perfect simulacrum for the Greek language, since it substituted a real environment for the original and on top of that gave it the rich humour and irony of working-class Brits, or more importantly Londoners.

There is something about cockney, with its cheeky mixing of words and idioms that gave language a more 'foreign' feel, for example 'SHIT GIVE UP THE GEN/ SPILL YOUR GUTS/ OPEN YOUR NORTH AND SOUTH AND LET ROLL THE TURDS BEFORE I PONEY MY Y-FRONTS. IN OTHER VERBS OPEN YOUR CAKE HOLE AND UTTER. LET ME EARWIG YOUR HOBSONS. NOT YOUR SON? OH BOLLOCKS AND CRACKLOCK.'

Basically Eddy, Oedipus, cannot escape his fate, and in fact the more he tries to escape, the more he tightens the noose around him. It is such a cruel play. For the first phase, when Eddy slays his father, I substituted a conflict in a cheap greasy spoon café, where Eddy is assaulted and bullied by the owner. This results in an almighty punch up, which is fought with words. An idea that I borrowed from a Sam Shepard play, *True West*. It worked beautifully, and we worked out some splendid moves for it. In the end Eddy slays him. One of the waitresses, the wife of the café owner, justly says 'I didn't know that words could kill.' Very apposite. This fulfils the second part of the oracle's dreadful prophesy, when by unintentionally slaying the café owner, he was in fact slaying his own father.

They immediately fall in love, and this gives me the opportunity to write some of the most passionate language I had ever written in a play. This they spoke simply to each other holding hands across a table. The table and four cane-backed chairs were the entire set, and it could not have worked better.

I approached this in quite a different way from my usual method of writing. I actually filched it from the love letters I wrote to my beloved, when we were momentarily parted. They seemed to work perfectly, especially when spoken by that wonderful actress Gillian Eaton.

The waitress, in fact Eddy's real mother, now tells her new lover (her son) how she once had a child, but lost it in a terrible boating disaster during the war, when their Sunday pleasure boat at Southend was hit. She even kept the little bear that her child once possessed. It was fished out of the water. He is much moved by this story and wishes to see the little bear, which of course she has never let out of her sight. Eddy glances at it and feels a very strange sense of familiarity.

In London, meanwhile the rats are on the march and there are a few swift scenes of murder and mayhem, which the cast play with skill and abandon, especially the bombing of an Irish Loyalist pub. Eddy is sick to death of this and wants badly to do something. He vows to kill the Sphinx, who is apparently responsible for much of the mayhem, so he bravely volunteers to solve her riddle.

The Sphinx is played by Eddy's stepmum, actress Georgia Brown. To demonstrate that there is a powerful sphinx in all women, we had her wiping down the table with what appears to be an old rag. Suddenly, as she is singing some old cockney song, the sound changes, the lights go out, she puts on the thing she had been using for a dish mop. It is her black wig. The lights come up and the soft, familiar mum has suddenly become this horrendous creature. She speaks what is her credo on the pathetic nature of men, which is of course the most feminist speech I have ever written.

The Sphinx distilled every offence committed against the earth and human kind, and undiluted spew of bile. This is a feminist tract where the Sphinx traces most of the world's ills and perhaps quite justifiably to the mindless greed of men. I have read many of the accusations levelled against the male doctrine of superiority for years. I took it to the extreme in the Sphinx's passionate speech.

You make me laugh, you fool man/ you should know about brothels, they exist for you to prop up your last fading shreds/ men need killing off before they kill off the world/ louse, you pollute the earth/ every footstep you take rots what's underneath/ you turn the seas to dead lakes and the crops are dying from the plague that is man/ you are the plague/ where are you looking when you should be looking at the ghastly vision in the mirror/ the plague is inside you. You enslave, whip, beat and oppress, use your guns, chains, bombs, jets, napalm, you are so alone and pathetic. Love from you means enslavement, love is fucking, helping is exploiting, you need your mothers you

FIGURE 18.1 *Greek,* London, 1988. L–R: Steven Berkoff, Bruce Payne, Gillian Eaton, Georgia Brown.

motherfucker. To love is to enslave a woman, to turn her into a bearing cow to produce cannon fodder to go on killing/ can you ever stop your plague/ you're pathetic, unfinished, not like me, never like us, a woman, a Sphinx. Women are all Sphinx. I have taken the power for all, I am the power/ I could eat you alive and blow you out in bubbles/ I devour stuff like you … You punk hero/ flaccid man/ macho pig/ rapist filth and shit/ oh, nature's mistake in the ghastly dawn of time.

After this blistering diatribe against the male sex and mindless violence, she puts the riddle to him. 'What walks on four legs in the morning, two legs in the afternoon and three legs in the evening?' Eddy almost instinctively knows the answer, and it is 'Man! … As a baby in arms he walks on four legs, in the afternoon as a young man he walks on two legs and in the evening when he is erect for his woman he sprouts the third leg.'

It's perfect and he solves the riddle. Of course in the original text Oedipus says 'In the evening when he is old he walks with a stick,' but mine, the Berkovian version, is very suited to young Eddy.

So now Oedipus is promised the hand of the queen for ridding the city of the Sphinx and therefore marries his own mother. Meanwhile, Creon has returned from a consultation with the oracle, who presents Creon with yet another conundrum to solve. That unless the city finds and punishes the killer of the late king Laius, the corruption of the state will continue. Therefore Oedipus puts everything into solving the crime, unbeknown of course that he is the culprit.

However, in my version Eddy becomes the great entrepreneur, successfully becoming a rich and powerful man. Now he decides to visit his old mum and dad, where he proudly recounts his great achievements. Dad now feels it's safe to recount the reason he was thrown out of the house and how he was found in the River Thames after the pleasure ship they were on hit an old World War Two mine. Now Eddy's wife, hearing all this, remembers how she lost her 'little Eddy' and of course concludes that the baby was hers. There is a grand denouement as his old mum and dad reveal for the first time that Eddy was not theirs. Eddy is shocked beyond words.

> So the man I verballed to death was my real pop, the man to whom my words like hard-edged schrapnel razed his brain, was the source of me. Oh stink warlock and eyes break shatter, cracker and splatter!
>
> Who laughs? Me who wants to clean up the city, stop the plague, destroy the Sphinx, he was the source of all the stink, the man of principle is a motherfucker, oh no more will I taste the sweetness of my dear wife's pillow.

But then Eddy has a change of heart, which is the main change I made to the original. He decides not to tear his eyes out.

> Oedipus how could you have done it? Never to see your golden wife's face again, never again to cast your eyes on her, and hers on your eyes.
>
> What a foul thing I have done, I am, the rotten plague, tear them out Eddy, rip them out, scoop them out like ice cream, just push the thumb behind the orb and pull, pull them out and stretch them to the end of their string and then snap! Darkness falls. Bollocks to all that!
>
> So I run back. I run and run and pulse hard and feet pound, it's love and I feel, it's love, what matter what form it takes? It's love and I feel for your breast, for your nipple twice sucked, for your breath twice smelled, for your thighs, for your cunt twice known, once head first, once cock first, loving cunt, holy mother wife, loving source of my being, exit from paradise, entrance to heaven!

During this passionate outburst of Eddy, he is running on the spot, running dynamically as he can't wait to get back to his wife/mother. The drum is beating and the last word ends with a grand crescendo. And of course, it's quite ironic since Barry Philips did a very similar and dramatic run as the Messenger in *Agamemnon*!

This is one of the most dramatic ends for a play I have created and because it was so positive and so life affirming the audience were on their feet.

The switch I made from the original classic play, where Oedipus tears his eyes out, is in mine reversed, because Eddy is really innocent of the crime, since the fates 'manipulated' him into it. In consequence, his run is a triumphant and passionate affirmation of the life force – joyful and guiltless.

Barry Philips played the part as if he had been born to play it, and he truly lived it. By some fortunate circumstances the play was translated into French and directed by Argentinian opera director Jorge Lavelli. It was also blessed by a talented actor on loan from the Comédie Française, who was also utterly brilliant. So I was indeed very proud to hear my modest play being spoken in that most beautiful of languages.

P.S. But years later I heard it in yet another language, the language of music, in the Mark-Anthony Turnage opera of *Greek* at the London Coliseum no less!

19

SALOME

The National Theatre 1989

This extraordinary play came to my attention decades ago when I went to The Roundhouse. This beautiful, rather bizarre building was used as a turnaround for British rail. The large central area served as a platform for spinning the trains that would be either stored or put on 'bays' to be sent in other directions.

That version of *Salome* was a curious production by Lindsay Kemp. While there were flashes of Kemp's mimetic style, I felt it didn't really capture what I then read in Oscar Wilde's masterpiece. Wilde's play had an awesome lyricism and daring, which went beyond anything I had read in Victorian drama. It was closer to the kind of literature in *fin-de-siècle* Paris. However, I was really grateful to Lindsay for having introduced me to it. Lindsay of course was playing Salome in his own inimitable style.

I thought the play was quite erotic, beautifully written and incredibly sensual. I just had to do it, but, like most obsessions I have, I brood on it for years until at last I found an opportunity to do it. I knew that I had to play Herod. It seemed to have been written for me. The language just drooled off the page. I loved the brilliantly clotted sentences, with their descriptive and sensual depictions of peacocks, jewels and even apples in a hypnotic overload – it was almost … narcotic. I had to do it.

I had always wanted to stage *Salome* since I first read it way back in the seventies. The text is luscious and in fact almost super-luscious as if it were an ornate piece of art-nouveau jewellery but in words. In fact it is so exotic it might be called rather pretentious, but as a theatre piece that very duality is what theatre feeds on. But the role was one that I craved. It was a luscious overripe fruit. It was a drug, an opiate shot to the senses. A hallucinogenic feast of words. Who could resist? Only the cold-blooded English who rarely if ever performed it. Not too surprisingly, it was written in Wilde's favourite language, French. But I also loved it since in Herod I had the opportunity to be all those things I secretly craved. A part of me, anyway, since I am anything but decadent, but don't we all wish to fulfil those buried and secret desires? Thus we become actors.

I discovered the manner in which I would direct the piece when I was working in Paris directing a French production of *Metamorphosis*. In one of the main open spaces by the Pompidou Centre – the dazzling piece of architecture designed by Richard Rogers – I saw a small group of mime artists enacting a scene from a western in ultra-slow motion. They wore light silk blouses and the wind flowed through them, which added to the eeriness and beauty of their movements. They mime the bullets slowly making their way to each other, and frankly I had seldom seen anything remotely as beautiful in the theatre.

I knew that the preciousness of Wilde's text had to be delicately conveyed as if it were almost a religious text. Delicate, precise and perfect, shimmering like a dream. As it so happens, the year before I had been performing *Decadence* at The Gate Theatre Dublin for the producer Michael Colgan. He happened to mention that they were going to celebrate the opening season of The Gate, which was in 1928, with the programme that was then chosen.

FIGURE 19.1 *Salome*, Brooklyn, 1995. L–R: Carmen du Sautoy, Imogen Claire, Russell Layton, Victoria Davar, Maria Pastel, Reginald Tsiboe, Steven Berkoff, Christopher Brand, Zigi Ellison.

That programme was quite revolutionary for the time, since it included Eugene O'Neill's *The Hairy Ape*, Wilde's *Salome* and Ibsen's *Peer Gynt*. Well, two of my favourite plays on earth were in that bunch, *The Hairy Ape* and *Salome*. He asked whether I would like to direct *Salome*! Which of course I leapt at. He also asked whether I would like to play Herod, since I had mentioned my great desire to play that role, but I felt that I should start just by directing it and once I had the blue print that is exactly what I did.

We had assembled a first-rate cast in Dublin, and on first rehearsal I explained to the cast that we would be preparing this all in slow motion. Though it took a while, it gradually came together, but it was not quite gelling. It was only when Irish actress Rosaleen Linehan came in and accompanied the action with just a few selected notes on the piano that it started to make sense. Music from the piano is almost like a light shone on a piece of sculpture, it reveals and enriches the language. Even adds shades of meaning that heighten the listener's senses. Also a piano adds a certain mystery.

Alan Stanford as Herod was quite magnificent, since he seemed to epitomise Herod. With his tall, heavy build, his large, florid face and deep bass voice he perfectly matched Oscar Wilde, who in turn was probably the model for Herod. Olwen Fouéré played Salome with exquisite finesse and so all in all we had a first-division team and I was proud of them.

Whilst I was working in Dublin, I happened to notice a street performer in the beautiful Grafton Street. A pedestrianised area where also sits the magnificent Bewley's tea shop. The performer's shtick was to turn himself into a living statue, and when he moved he did it in super-slow motion. Now there is an executioner in the play, and it occurred to me that this man would be perfect for the role, so I asked The Gate Theatre whether we could employ him, which we did. He remained silent on stage for the whole period of the play and the audience could never see him when he moved. But a few moments later when he caught their eye again he was on the other side of the stage! The execution was exact. He slowly entered the cistern by perfectly miming a set of stairs, very gently touched Jokaanan to have him kneel. He then drew out his large sabre and 'beheaded' him.

The light on the scene goes out on the execution and immediately comes up on Salome, who begins her piteous lamentation. She will have what she desires. She cradles the head in her arms, and kisses his lips. She kisses his lips and triumphantly gloats 'I have kissed thy lips Jokaanan, I have kissed thy lips.' 'They had a bitter taste, but they say love has a bitter taste.' Salome is then executed on Herod's demand. 'Kill that woman.'

We opened to the most extraordinary reviews The Gate had had in years, and soon we were invited to the Edinburgh Festival. This was a mixed blessing, since it was to be performed in the main festival and therefore would be reviewed, and thus I would be upstaged by my own production when and if I eventually chose to play Herod. However, in Edinburgh the play was sold out, it was a *succès d'estime*, and the cast swam in the delirium of approval.

Well, since coincidences were piling up and invites flowing, it just so happened that my mentor, hero and idol Laurence Olivier died in 1989. Therefore his bereaved widow, the actress Joan Plowright, who was scheduled to perform in a play by a Spanish playwright and directed by the great Spanish actress and director Núria Espert, dropped out of the show. Since she was then obliged to cancel, a long space of two or three months became available at the Littleton Theatre.

I, of course, was chosen to fill it. One of the conditions was that I play Herod and recast it in London with local actors. This did understandably cause a bit of grief within the splendid Irish company. However, I did have a firm commitment from the very beginning from The Gate's producer Michael Colgan that this was to be a try-out since it had been my life's ambition to play Herod and direct it. London is the world centre of theatre and I was invited to take it to the National Theatre by Richard Eyre, an offer I could not refuse.

I began casting once I reached London, since the National Theatre beckoned. I was so surprised at the sheer lack of young talent around to play Salome, but eventually we did find a virginal sweet thing in the shape and person of Katherine Schlesinger, niece of the brilliant film director John Schlesinger. This was a quality I was desperately looking for.

Katherine had an almost childlike quality, so sexually innocent that she could 'play' the provocative young temptress. Even her demanding the head of the prophet simply because he refused to kiss her is a supreme act of childish petulance. Which is also in keeping with her tormented regret as she cradles the decapitated head after she has commissioned the ugly deed. Alas, she cannot put it back!

I then began the rather daunting task of fitting into the role of Herod, and did my very best to erase the great shadow cast over the play by Alan Stanford's performance. Deciding to make it an innovative production in slow motion helped me as an actor to absorb the language more easily. This is far more challenging than the usual 'real-time' movement you see in most theatres. Also, I had an intense love of relating movement to language.

The audience seemed to love what we were doing, since it was my passion to give Oscar Wilde and his brilliant play the most delicate structure to see it in. I had a very strong instinct that the text was so precious that it had to be carried like a fragile parchment. The slow motion that we used seemed to intensify the language; every moment was highlighted, even down to the most mundane. Coupled with Roger Doyle's atmospheric music, the combination of movement, language and music in perfect synchronicity with each other produced a very heady effect.

The play received excellent reviews, and I had one of the greatest triumphs of my life. We then transferred to the West End after the run concluded.

It was the Phoenix Theatre in Charing Cross Road. We enjoyed a further run of about ten weeks as far as I remember, and we were very happy there. For a short time I was riding the crest of a wave. *Salome* was playing at the National, *Metamorphosis* was playing in Paris and *Greek* was due to open at Wyndham's Theatre. Of all the many people who visited the theatre, one was the American movie actor Al Pacino. He said he was so taken by the play that he immediately asked me to direct him in it on Broadway. Of course he wanted to play Herod, and I had to very politely turn it down since this was a part I wanted to play in New York.

Normally, I'd have been agog to direct the great Pacino on Broadway. What an opportunity to enter an entirely new world. However, I had to be sure of the 'ensemble', which for me is always the key to any production I do. When I said this to the producer, however, he somewhat dismissed my overriding concern when I said it was necessary to have a few days to cast and workshop the actors. This in fact helped me to dump it.

Although up to that time I had no offers, lo and behold about four years later when Pacino had performed in his own production of *Salome* on Broadway (which apparently was not too successful), I had an invite to play my version at the Brooklyn Academy, New York! We played for only one week in 1995 and were sold out, and had been for over a month before we opened. We then toured it through Europe and Australia, it was quite a journey.

P.S. There is something about the very last performance, something you wish to mark as a unique occasion. I was desperately keen to have a farewell do for all of us. I found a stunning Art Deco restaurant in Manhattan called Captain America. Ah, this is perfect, I thought, and booked a long table running right down the centre. The huge cocktail bar was like an altar on a rostrum at the very far end. After the matinee that day, I went round the dressing rooms and invited all the cast for a fare-well do. To my astonishment, they all thanked me so much for the suggestion, but seeing as it was their last night in the big city, each wanted to do something quite different. I sat in my dressing room, applying my white makeup, despairing of actors. But just before curtain up and the final performance, the SM came to my room and informed me that the cast had decided to come after all! The night was in fact splendid, I felt like King Herod.

20

ONE MAN

The Garrick Theatre 1991

The following year I thought I would have a go at a one-man show just to demon-strate how versatile I thought I was and to have a change from the fairly demanding task of casting actors and working with them night after night, as pleasant as that may be. But just to do your own thing is very exciting as well as even more demanding.

It had to be tried out at the Edinburgh Festival. I thought I would do my com-pellingly sinister and frighteningly comic Poe's *The Tell-Tale Heart*, followed by a piece I wrote years earlier called *The Actor*. *The Actor* was very special to me, since it was in a way a condensed story of my life. The third piece, called *Dog*, was based on a number of horrific incidents where American pitbulls were causing terrible injuries to young children until they were eventually banned.

Reading about these ghastly maulings in the papers, I started to imagine the kind of loathsome yobs who possess them, and this put me in a stirring mood. I had to write it out in a one-act play, which I called *Dog*. I made my character a combo of every revolting and debased habit of those we like to call the working class. A football yob whose true love of his life is his adored pet pitbull. Now, as is my wont, I gave lines to the dog …

> *Stop pulling my lead, you cunt, or I'll bite your fucking leg off!*

Oh what joy in letting go of myself, letting it all hang out, being bold and brazen and bad. A right bad Cockney, although a bit more Romford.

> *Nah, 'e's awrite, gets a bit excited that's all, 'e's gotta bad press … 's not his fault that some kid stuck his nut between 'is jaws …*

And so in the true nature of theatre you can do and be anything, and so I played the heavily panting, tongue-lolling beast as well as his owner. Simply moving from

FIGURE 20.1 Steven Berkoff in *Dog*.

one to another. Wonderful!! I really loved playing it even though it was the most exhausting thing I had ever done. It has to be played absolutely full on. The man actually became quite touching at times. The complete antidote to Eton. His spirit was manic and robust, hilarious and explosive. I naturally put in lots of business when he goes to his local pub and knocks back ten pints of lager ... goes outside the pub to heave up and suddenly Roy, the dog starts picking through some of the meatier heavings. And then the bloke slithers around ... 'Right skating rink it was' ... I then perform a mime of a skater.

But for me as an actor the *coup de théâtre* was at the football match, when Roy in his excitement suddenly pulls the leash from his owner's hand and leaps after the ball. The consequence was that Roy's owner says to him that he's gotta go. I, now as Roy, whimper rather pathetically, but the dog's whimpering does become too much for his owner, and I confess that

> *I was jokin', I wouldn't do that to you, would I? 'Course I luv ya … I do, 'ere give us a kiss.*

I mime pulling around the dog's jaw, which he has sulkily turned away from me. And mime giving him a big wet tongue-lolling kiss. This used to more or less conclude the piece, but after playing it for some weeks it occurred to me to put my head in its mouth. In homage to Marcel Marceau, who used to do an act called *The Circus*. He plays a lion tamer, which of course means Marcel Marceau sticking his head in the lion's mouth.

The audience by this time are roaring with laughter. But then mime allows you to go wherever your imagination wishes to lead you and so, gripping the dog with both hands around his middle, I lift him up and gradually thread my head through his body, pulling the dog's body right over me and then from the darkness of the dog's interior my arm reaches out for its anus. My finger 'finds' it and then my other hand comes over and I gradually pull its anus over my head and then actually mime climbing out.

> *You liked that dincha!!*

Massive laugh, end of piece. I played this on and off for many years, the last time in Australia on tour in around 2008.

I had been playing *The Tell-Tale Heart* as part of a one-man show since 1985, when I did it with a one-man play called *Harry's Xmas*, which I played at the Donmar Warehouse in the days when other playwrights and actors had the opportunity to play there. In earlier days it was run by Ian Albery, for whom I directed *West* in 1983. That was a production I was so proud of, and it was well received.

'The Tell-Tale Heart' is a marvellously macabre and brilliant short story by the highly literate Edgar Allen Poe. The play version, which is really just the short story with a few tweaks, suited me down to the ground.

It also made the greatest use of all my movement training, since I could physically create the room of the old man whom I am obsessed by on account of the infirmity of the old man's eye. This eye so disturbs the character whom I played that he becomes fixated by it. So much so in fact that he feels he cannot exist until he has rid himself of the old man. This story is, one might say, a perfect interpretation of what is now called obsessive compulsive disorder. One's life is somewhat held in stasis, forever ruminating about the same bloody thing. A true actor's disease. Perhaps that's why it attracted me so much. It's very rewarding for an actor to use voice and body in equal measure, and my training in mime made this a perfect

FIGURE 20.2 Steven Berkoff in *The Tell-Tale Heart*.

vehicle for me. When the madman, which was me, enacted his deed one could not only follow every second of the action, but equally hear his innermost thoughts. After I had smothered the old man, I lifted my saw from its hook and began sawing up the body. But first I started with the head, for which I used an axe. As I brought it swiftly down, a spurt of blood shot out, which I also enacted as it sprayed all over my face. After wiping myself clean I sawed the legs off, accompanied by my own sound effects of a saw rasping through the flesh. One sound. And then it reaches the bone, a second harsher sound, and then as it goes through the bone a third sound as it tears away at the outer flesh once more. This is tiring on the voice and so for the arms I just used the axe for two swift cuts.

Of course the gist of this macabre tale is that the obsessed madman hears the heartbeat of the victim, beating so loudly he imagines that the sound will actually penetrate the very walls of the house and alert the neighbours. After having disposed of the old man's body beneath the floorboards, he hears a knock on the front door. It is the police, who have been alerted to the scene by a neighbour who heard the old man scream 'once, once only'. However, being a man who exchanges one obsession for another when a second obsession comes to replace the first, he imagines hearing the heartbeat of the chopped-up victim beneath the floorboards. He can take no more and blurts out his crime. I naturally entertained the police in the very room in which I had committed the murder, even down to impersonating the police in swift flashes from murderer to police.

The satisfaction of playing this story is being able to act out not only the sumptuous and deeply expressive language but also the very fabric of the building and everything pertaining to it. It was very satisfying to play, and I performed it for five weeks at the Donmar Warehouse along with a short dystopic piece about a lone suicidal man who attempts to deal with yet another solitary Xmas.

Harry's Xmas and *The Tell-Tale Heart* shared a common theme of the main character's terrible sense of isolation and even rejection, and therefore tended to obsess about the most simple things. And the rejection of Harry during the Christmas season seemed to compound his loneliness with that of the insane killer in *The Tell-Tale Heart*. This manifested itself in his morbid obsession with the flaw in the old tenant's eye.

21

KVETCH

The Garrick Theatre 1991

Still digging inside the compost heap of my own struggles, madness, obsession, compulsions, I suddenly found that they all come from the same weird source, a mind slightly warped by some childhood need that perhaps had not been satisfied ... or maybe it's something to do with it. But I nearly always make my works or write my plays as a form of exorcism.

My mother, when troubled by something that was not easily solved since there were always two sides to the same story, would say 'I've got a "Kvetch".' And I was always around to help her solve it.

So I wrote this play whose first words are 'I'm afraid.'

It was a family saga with the ageing mother-in-law and the guest. But in this play everybody in it suffers from Kvetching. My autobiographical character, Frank, suffers most of all, but all share a high degree of the Kvetch disease. Although known as a Yiddish word, its roots are German, where it means to pinch or to squeeze. This makes a kind of sense, since it is you, the victim, who is being pinched. Pinched between choices, decisions, wishes, guilts. My mother was a giant Kvetcher, and I believe I may have carried this from some kind of contamination. Of course acting also helps to spread it, since there is not a day when you don't have to make a decision. But don't Kvetch about it. Sometimes the Kvetches can turn on a hair when it gets really serious. In one play I had to count how many times I used the word 'that,' and whether I could permit myself to omit a couple of them.

Most humans do suffer from this bizarre stress to a greater or lesser extent. But the way I manifested this traumatic symptom in the play was by giving voice to the two sides, the Janus face. So as we say one thing we immediately contradict ourselves.

> FRANK: *'Hal, do yourself a favour, come to my place, why should you go home to an empty apartment? What life is that? You go home and who welcomes you? The cat? So*

come for a nosh. Listen, Gordon Bloom it's not, you know what I'm saying … We'll have a homely meal and put our feet up and watch a movie, sure we got cable … have a beer.'

HAL: *'You sure it's ok?'*

FRANK: *'Of course I'm sure … I'm positive … I'd like you to … why not … you'd like her … it'll make a change … a new face spices the evening … we'll exchange Kvetches … I mean stories about our anxieties … ha! ha! then we'll watch Paul Newman killing a few people, wadya say?'*

> (Aside) *'Oh God, I hope he says no, I don't know what we'll talk about … suppose the bitch hasn't enough food … suppose she's overcooked it 'cause we're late … or even worse gone to bed cause her ulcers are playing up … gavalt or shit … or maybe her mother's there who belches … of course, it's a Friday! … Her fucking mother will be there belching, the food will be overcooked and I can smell the stinking cabbage twenty floors down.'*

HAL: *'You sure you want me to come?'*

FRANK: *'Look, I'm not forcing you, you're your own man, so make it another night, when you're free … you say "Frank, how about tonight?"'*

And so it goes on. I had this idea that what people really feel and think is said almost as an afterthought … what they are really thinking deep in their head, the things we are too civilised even to breathe. So throughout the play all the characters are speaking in two voices, the sociable public voice and then the deep, interior Kvetch-blasted voice which comes up from the broiling, steaming depths of their real selves.

The horrors of a divided mind are too painful to think about, since one is caught on the horns of a dilemma. Where you believe one way is bold, fearless and courageous and the other wretchedly cowardly, miserably weak. It's awful, and what is the most awful is that as soon as you come down on one side then the other is pulling you on its opposite with just as much force as the first. And so these poor wretched humans go about their lives as bi-persons. And of course, like the best self-portrait painters, one uses oneself rigorously as the pathetic material.

As usual I staged it simply. A table shaped in perspective spreading out from the back and widening at the front so the actors did not mask each other.

Hal, Frank's friend who is invited for a cosy but painful dinner one night, finds that gradually he is, to his great surprise, beginning to relax and enjoy the company. As he is relishing the moment, his other self springs into life. As he does so, the rest of the cast continue their meal silently. He then develops a severe Kvetch as he starts to imagine that it would be appropriate to one evening return the favour. Now he imagines his rather humble abode and slowly begins to Kvetch. Would his modest home be suitable? Where would they eat, in the kitchen or in the dining room? All the ramifications come into play, becoming more and more complex as they increase. The music centre is in the living room and so it would be better to dine in the living room, but there is not much convenience in the living room since he

FIGURE 21.1 *Kvetch* at the Garrick Theatre, 1991. L–R: Henry Goodman, Stanley Lebor, Steven Berkoff, Thelma Ruby, Anita Dobson.

would have to shlep the food in and out, whereas if they ate in the kitchen, everything would be more convenient, but without the music.

So this goes on, and while he is describing his torment as to whether he drags the music centre into the kitchen, the other members of the cast become involved as his surrogate props. We see the interior of his mind as they all gather round shifting the table backwards and forwards. It's so very sad that the tormented person's most awful 'Kvetches' arouse the audience's most hysterical laughter, since is it not true that we all suffer from this to a certain extent? We are all so much alike, except in this family's case it does seem more intense. I was able to discharge all my Kvetches in one go. Everything, all those most painful ones, the ones that give you stomach ulcers. And it won the Evening Standard Award for comedy of the year!

So even one's agony provides one's most interesting work.

I actually first staged this play in the Odyssey Theatre in Los Angeles. I had a first-rate cast with a dynamic comedian called Kurt Fuller as Frank, Mitch Kreindel as Hal, Laura Esterman as Donna, Marcia Mohr as the mother-in-law and Ken Tigar as the businessman Donna eventually runs off with, as does Frank with Hal once he overcomes his Kvetch, a devious subplot.

I loved directing this play, as movement was the second part of the creative effort. It seems to gel when I put the two elements together. And once again ideas that were gleaned after spending years studying the wonderful opportunities that movement gives you to create so many ingenious short cuts. When Frank and his wife Donna go to bed and when he fantasises of a beautiful woman he nearly met on a beach and whose vision he stirs up as he makes love to Donna, she equally, as she is being made love to, fantasises about the muscly garbage collectors. For the bed we simply threw a huge eiderdown over the table and had it spread out, a stage manager held two cushions behind them and *voilà*!

The play was hugely successful in LA and ran for a couple of years, and then they kept it in their repertoire for another couple of years. Sometime later I decided to play it in London and was blessed with Anita Dobson for Donna and Henry Goodman for Hal, and I played Frank. We opened at The King's Head, Islington, famous for its one dressing room and the one loo. Then of course the Edinburgh Festival, and at last we opened at the Garrick Theatre in the West End. The whole thing was a quite wonderful experience and just shows how you can turn your quirky demons into your slaves.

Kvetch has been done all over the world, including Paris, where it entertained the audience in French. I was so proud to hear my play spoken in that wonderful and exotic language.

The French cast, so used to all explanations and actions being served purely by the language, perhaps failed to understand how important the movement was. The director, Jorge Lavelli, a reputable Argentinian more successful with opera, was not so familiar with the movement which made the play so successful in London.

22

RANDOM THOUGHT

A lunch in Brooklyn with the *Salome* cast

One of my cherished places happened to be the world-renowned deli not too far from us. It was called Junior's. I wanted so much to impress my lovely limey cast with the wonders of this city, and this was one of them and an ideal place to go after our matinee day on Saturday, so that's what we did. After the house came down, some of us dashed to Junior's and ordered a corned beef sandwich. The table already had a large bowl of delicious pickled cucumbers, an absolute must for every run-down, grimy ghetto in ancient Warsaw or Łódź in Poland. We ordered a sandwich to share since there were only two of us so far.

It was one of their famous corned beef ones. Two slices of rye bread between which was a giant smile of pink corned beef. When it came, I of course had to share it and so, raising the lid of one half, I gently prised the corned beef off onto another slice of bread the waiter thoughtfully brought me. It was beyond delicious even if I infrequently ate meat … Ah! Now the rest of the cast are turning up, gazing, turning and gawking as one does when the appetite's aflame for adventure. Well, no need to order more, just at the moment, since we still have plenty here.

And I gently prised yet another couple of slices from my gargantuan half, as did my first partner from his half, and soon we were all munching away and absorbing America as only Brits can when seeing, smelling and hearing the noise and bustle of a city made famous only by movies. So we munched and crunched and slurped and burped until we were full as monkeys. What a shame some of the cast chose to stay at the theatre and have a kip, we said, for they missed not just the grub, but the whole electric experiment of the deli and all who came to eat there. There were some reasonable scraps left and so we asked the nice waitress for a doggy bag and gathered them up alongside a couple of handfuls of pickles. We returned to the theatre and passed our 'haul' back to one or two of the cast who didn't make it to Junior's, and they were indeed extremely grateful.

It is said that Jesus fed the hundred who came to hear him preach with just seven loaves and seven fish. And the crowds were indeed fed and not only fed but left scraps behind, since they were full. The secret is that if you believe something enough, with enough passion and heart, it will manifest itself before you … Alternatively, Jesus may have bought his fish and rolls from Junior's!

23

BRIGHTON BEACH SCUMBAGS

Riverside Studios, Hammersmith 1995

I was walking along the Brighton seafront some years ago on one of those sunny seaside days. A day when the coast draws all the working classes from South London for a day of frolic by the sea, when, from one of the deckchairs lining the beach and facing the sea, I heard the dulcet tones of a rather large lady ring out: 'So wadya want on your bleedin' burger?'

She was standing, about to purchase the said item from the pier a few yards away. Her voice was Wagnerian, threatening, expressing insane frustration and sourness from a relationship long gone belly up. There were two blokes in two deckchairs and one other woman and all their heads were turned towards the 'Screecher'.

That was enough for me. The seed had been planted and it became *Brighton Beach Scumbags*. Even the title was a small act of rebellion against the more nostalgic and saccharine tales of New York, called *Brighton Beach Memoirs* by the renowned playwright Neil Simon.

My story followed the lives of two couples now in their fifties but still faithful to the emblems of their youth, i.e. a large Tony Curtis quiff on Derek and jeans and punk braces on Les, plus billowing floral dresses for the two women. But most of all and intrinsic to their tribe, the values were totally unchanged since the fifties. In their eyes, the working class were heroes, gays were pooftahs and all foreigners, wogs. A simple and straightforward interpretation of life that was not too complicated by any notes of 'liberalism'.

Derek, a self-styled leader of the small group, has returned to Brighton on a nostalgic visit with Dinah. Since this is where they courted thirty years ago, and of course they expected Brighton to be more or less the same as they remembered it so fondly. The two friends, Dave and Doreen, are their best friends, come along for the ride, although the two couples travelled there in separate cars. Their separate journeys and routes become quite an important topic of conversation once they meet up. Cockneys are masters of the road and endlessly quote the best routes!

Before they have met up, Derek and his missus Dinah have visited one of those old-fashioned beer and sherry houses, which were built in a deliberately Victorian style and are recalled as being very charming. What they find to their immense shock and utter discomfort is that the pub has now been monopolised by the gay fraternity, after all this is Brighton. This was not the cosy watering hole of the past but something intensely sinister and even in their eyes threatening, since they have nothing whatsoever in common with the new clientele.

Dinah even feels somewhat threatened by their svelte looks and snappy outfits, plus their slim, gym-trained bodies. She is a fat tub of lard, having borne a child a few months earlier and carried for rather too long layers of blubber which both she and Derek are keenly self-conscious of in front of the gay community. Derek and Dinah are convinced that people are staring at them in a rather contemptuous way. They don't stay long at the pub, but meet up with Dave and Doreen and occupy four deckchairs on the front. This is how the play opens and perhaps why at the outset of the play Dinah is so on edge. They're now happily ensconced in their chairs facing the rolling surf, safe from the toxic atmos of the 'pooftahs' and now can happily let loose all their opinions, jokes, sarcasm, prejudices etc. while slowly getting pissed with a steady stream of canned lager.

The stage is bare and we only hear the steady sound of the surf and some muted cries of holidaymakers, children and seagulls. We all know that Brighton is one long carpet of round pebbles and so every time Dinah (brilliantly played by Annette Badland) walked to get burgers or beer she'd make wonderfully crunching sounds vocally which was also terribly funny.

They chatter about this and that, their journey, the things they liked when they used to come to Brighton and other nostalgic memories. The day passes pleasantly, and of course Derek and Dave, being real self-centred and narcissistic blokes, have a whale of a time. Burgers and beers are brought in frequently, mostly fetched by Dinah. I suppose she wants the exercise, to lose weight at every opportunity. Of course the burgers are mimed exquisitely by the actors, especially Mike Jenn, who really made a meal of it. Even the hiss as a tab was pulled off the can was perfectly reproduced.

They decide to split up for a while, the boys stay together and explore the pier and the women go for a stroll and agree to meet back there in an hour. In the meantime two of the gays from the pub have come on to the beach and are sitting in the vacated chairs. On their return, Derek and Dave spot them immediately and thus begins a small confrontation which ends as a semi-drunken Derek boots one of the gays viciously up the backside. The gays beat a hasty retreat. Their large commotion on the beach has momentarily attracted a lot of attention. Then it all quietens down. Derek and Dave go back to the chatter and the women have gone off to get some more beers. Suddenly they see in the near distance a long line of gays, pointing them out as the culprits and heading slowly and menacingly towards them. This is not looking good, and Dave pleads with Derek to split and fast, but drunken Derek won't have it …

But they're poofs, they're not blokes, you don't run away from poofs.

But Dave wisely runs, leaving Derek to face them alone. There is a blackout during which we hear the horrible noise of a body being beaten. When the lights eventually come up, we see Derek covered in scores of empty beer cans and blood. He is semi-conscious … He pulls out a cigarette, lights it and says … 'Bollocks.' Blackout.

I was very happy with this production, because I was able to show two random couples desperately trying to take nourishment from a nostalgic visit to Brighton, as I myself have done many times. There is something about the innocent British habit of seeing the seaside as a pure childhood escape, as they reflect on life sitting in four deck chairs facing the audience. They cannot see that times have changed, and one has to change with them or be seriously wounded in the attempt to preserve old values. I think all the actors carried the play off very well, and their movement of eating and drinking was immaculate, since we didn't eat or drink anything. And Derek's comeuppance at the end was a rather harsh lesson to learn.

24

RANDOM THOUGHT

Mechanicals

You gotta larf, because if you didn't you'd have to cry. Read in the papers last week of the disaster at one of London's newest theatres. Apparently the electrics got all mucked up and the revolving stage got stuck and the performance had to be cancelled. That's a disaster. Not cancelled because of the frailty of an actor, or an unlucky accident during the performance, cancelled because the electrics are not up to the demands of the staging. Oh my, the bloody, bungling stupid revolving stage. The stupidest piece of mechanics yet invented, which totally absolves the director of using their creative resource, in other words their head, to shift the action by the dexterity of the actors. How often I have sat and watched as the revolving stage bumbles round with the actors for the approaching scene just standing there like lemmings. How many times have I seen the blasted thing get stuck, the result of which brings on the company manager with a sickly apologetic grin over his face as he confesses that the show has to be cancelled! Appalling. Apparently on this occasion, the lead actor came on and apologised to the sold-out house.

Theatre is an empty magic box and there is nothing you cannot do if you have the imagination to do it. In fact, the very limitation of theatre stimulates and encourages the imagination. I did enjoy another mechanical disaster at The Old Vic during the first night of Hamlet *with Peter O'Toole, since this time Laurence Olivier entered the stage and made the most eloquent speech, begging forgiveness and pleading for our patience. When the play actually did continue it was something of an anti-climax.*

But if I am to think of the worst 'inventions' that have been introduced upon our stages I would be loath to blame the poor director for their total lack of physical skill to conjure magic out of the actor. After all, they can't do everything and they usually hire a 'movement' expert to help them out, and there's nothing wrong with that if it will improve the total performance. But I might draw the line at using a hologram to represent Ariel in a recent production of The Tempest. *As I didn't see it, I can only hope that it fulfilled the desires of the director. But where I have to draw the line is when he boldly states that Shakespeare, if he were alive today, would certainly not shrink from using such bold and new techniques.*

I am sorry mister, but he would not, he would definitely not, since he uses language to take us into ethereal worlds, not stage tricks. He would not need to use some mechanical ephemera.

I'm sure that there could be a place for all the technical genius of engineers to enhance and excite, particularly in musicals, for example Julie Taymor's The Lion King *... However, in the end there is nothing more aesthetically exciting than to see the magic of theatre created solely by the skill and imagination of the actor.*

25

MASSAGE

The Odyssey Theatre, Edinburgh Festival 1997

Massage. A strange subject to be sure, and what on earth would lead me to this? Sometime in the late sixties or early seventies there crept into our safe, tolerant and dull suburbs a most curious manifestation of sexual behaviour ... the 'massage parlour'. A phenomenon that, along with many other quixotic tastes and habits, originated from China or Thailand.

Little neon signs went up announcing that here one could be actually massaged by a member of the opposite sex, usually a young lady, and the very fact that a woman would massage a male body was a uniquely exciting concept, it almost beggared belief. The idea was simply wonderful. Not a lurid prostitute's den in some dirty back alley in Soho or Paddington, sex the British way. But a perfectly wholesome, clean, legal and upfront massage parlour where you might also avail yourself of various other treatments like foot massage or even just head massage if that's all you desired. I always remember, when working in Soho, seeing the poor ladies for hire, leaning their worn-out bodies against the wall, and did feel very sorry for them.

London was becoming civilised. Naturally, after a while the temptation became too great for me to resist, and so one day I actually decided to overcome my fears and, during a fallow period in my relationships with women, decided to enter one of the said establishments. Unlike a brothel, there is no talk or even possibility of penetrative sex. On the contrary, you enter a cubicle and shortly a young woman will ask you to disrobe, giving you time to do it. Now, for a lonely young, or middle-aged, man, the opportunity to have a gentle woman's hands massaging your body is a delight the like of which I had never before experienced. You are given a choice of oil or powder, and soon you are floating in a soothing world of delirious sensations and there is simply nothing on earth like it, especially if the masseuse is from the Far East.

Once having experienced it, I felt no need to repeat it, since I had now found a girlfriend and had no need, but I never forgot it.

Then I wrote *Massage*. It had been floating around my head for years and I thought the subject raw, passionate, sexy, dirty, carnal, and so it lit up all those zones in my brain. I wanted to write something bold, sexual, raunchy and even political. When I had finished it I felt it was far too shamefully filthy for an actress to sully herself by putting those disgusting words in her mouth, let alone the action, so I decided to play it myself in drag. My desire was to 'symbolise' a women in the way that we see in pantomime, or Kabuki theatre. The plot was basically quite simple as it was also quite cunning. A boring married couple are living in the suburbs. The wife goes out daily to what the husband believes is an ordinary office job in some remote part of London. It's a job so boring that the husband can barely even bother to ask her what she actually does. The wife travels daily to a remote part of London, where she happily works in a massage parlour. Her husband has recently retired from work and is quite content to rely on his wife's 'modest income', most of which she saves for a rainy day.

The play deals with the day to day comings and goings of the trade. The wife actually massages the customers, and any sexual preferences are actually mimed by the actor/wife and of course mime perfectly performed not only tells the story, but also allows one to satirise and exaggerate all the elements of sexual shenanigans and actually reduces any vulgarity.

If one wishes, mime tends to make action exceedingly comic and sometimes outrageous, but can also make some very valid points about society.

I decided to open the play at the Odyssey Theatre in LA, a small theatre I have had the pleasure of working in many times. I knew that the costume I would wear was all-important, but initially the person responsible for my wardrobe didn't have a clue in hell. But one day I was walking along Venice Beach, LA when I saw a seaside boutique, where in the window was a very cute one-piece stretch dress in a kind of leopard print. I actually went inside the shop and tried it on. It looked so good that I was emboldened to step into the main shopping area to express my pleasure at my new find. After all, I was an actor and therefore the impersonation of a woman was only one of the tools of my trade, which is to crawl inside the multitudinous personalities that exist in our society. I had found the one-piece stretch leopard print dress and I was happy. I had found the outer skin of the character. Each day I rehearsed with my co-actor Barry Philips, an Englishman who had made his home in LA. He played the husband excellently and completely captured the stolid British worker in a beautiful comic style. He couldn't have been better in the part. I had auditioned other American actors but none could come even near a solid, tough, imaginative Brit. Especially one from the working class with that legacy of humour and wild cynicism that is second nature to a London Cockney.

Barry then introduced me to a great wig maker in Hollywood, where I bought two cheap off-the-peg wigs and I was halfway there. When I rehearsed the part I felt more and more the feminine side of me begin to grow, and it was not a struggle to find that part of me, since we all have an opposite within us. I started to feel a strange sensation of relief as if I had been at last released from the responsibility of having to prove my masculinity, the tough guy, the Coriolanus, the Macbeth, the hard bloke. With feminine feelings now seething within me I could be lithe, soft, serpentine, playful, sexually precocious. What fun! I found a good pair of high heels and then found the walk. Soon after, a young woman gave me the makeup kit, but it was the eyelashes that seemed to soften and glamorise my face. A little blue eye shadow, and then the lipstick and I was there. Also I found the gestures coming to me so readily for what I saw from keen observation over the years. Oh it was heavenly to play. There was no intensity, no force and certainly no strain.

The Odyssey Theatre helped by creating a perfect set containing a giant massage table plus other quite clever phallic appurtenances, like a pipe for the old man in the shape of a curled penis. However, I had written a play that was distinctly bawdy, filthy and I think very funny. Now I have become female, and while once I would have been boiling with embarrassment to have even considered playing a female, now I wholeheartedly embraced the female within me. I feel within every male actor there is a female dying to get out. The reason could be that actors do love to express characters totally opposite to their main personality. So, by playing a female character, I was able to explore and play with my feminine side, and found that it was a totally liberating experience. One was no longer obliged to be a strutting peacock of a male and for many, including me, that was quite a relief.

The play begins with some cheeky and sensual cabaret-style music. The door opened, and first of all I showed a well-trimmed leg waving at the audience. That was of course followed by me as I introduce myself and the play:

> *So many years have passed since first I found the way to honest toil by doing what I like, that is to squeeze those miles of cock that sausage-like have passed between these walls. So many cocks, some small, some large, some tall and thin have strutted and have heaved their silver pearls upon this well-worn slab. They stand up to attention, ready and alert and pass themselves to me in hope that I might shed their load and send them back into the world all light and fresh, and ready now to face the thing in semi-detached bliss*
>
> *With me their fantasies are fulfilled … I am the shepherdess who tends the sheep and milks the cows … Squeeze out the nectar and the pain … I'll rent my hands and voice … My subtle touch to their world-weary aching ends of flesh, just aided by the finest oil … I'll baste their swollen joints, caress and soothe, tickle and pinch and faster now and faster doth my hand like a pneumatic pump explore the riches down below and bore and drill until the hit, the target, bull's-eye, whoosh! The spray ascends like showers on an April morn. Some Kleenex doth remove the clues, then off they go, these noble and gallant men of England, to return to their dull wives who frame their dried-up lips into a ring of woe, doldrums and demands of married life.*

Much fun and silly entertainment is to be had from this play, and it was not really dirty or disgusting for a moment. What it was, might be called outrageous or

FIGURE 25.1 *Massage.* L–R: Steven Berkoff, Barry Philips.

satirical. We played a short eight-week season and it was a happy time for both of us. I recall now twenty years later how relieved I was at the end of the play driving down to the San Francisco Bar/Pub a mile down the road and sharing a heavenly panini and a first-class margarita. I thought of London, where they were still being pushed out of their dreary pubs at 11pm. Once I got to my motel on Venice Beach I even gave up a prayer of thanks.

Barry and I did do it just one more time at the Edinburgh Festival in August of that year, and then for some reason we or I put it to sleep. Such a shame, but I think

I was getting tired of all the preparations like wig, eyelashes and nails before going on. But I still missed it, and about ten years later I managed to revive it with another actor, Johnny Coyne, who was equally good, but this time I added another male since playing all the other parts was far too much for one actor. So I had Michael Jenn play the massage parlour's clients, and this he did quite brilliantly. We played in Tunbridge Wells of all places and a few times in Winchester, then no more. I believe it's one of my best works and it ain't been seen in London, but I am not sure I wish to get the stockings on again. I'll find someone else ...

26

DECADENCE

Wyndham's Theatre 1997

In the interceding years much had happened. I stuck to my game plan of doing theatre and not remaining in LA to drift my life away in movies and even fight to obtain those mind-numbing roles. From time to time, movies were a good break and fun to do, but my objective was to find the reason God put me on this planet. I had other plans and nothing excited me more than the theatre, since I was now a writer and felt there was so much I wanted to say.

Decadence had a slow, but painstaking build up. When I rehearsed the play with Linda Marlowe, we did a try-out at the small Hampstead Theatre, which was called the New End Theatre and was once a morgue. I deliberately asked just two trusted critics to come, since I wanted to have a long try-out before exposing it too fully. Fortunately the critics gave very positive reviews. From there we went to the Edinburgh Festival and played in the left-luggage room of The Caledonian Hotel. In Edinburgh at festival time you will play just about anywhere, Following this, we did secure an eight-week season at the Arts Theatre in the West End, which also had a very healthy response. I then had a pre-booked tour of Australia, but when I returned I managed to secure a fifteen-week season at the Arts. Linda and I were both very happy there, and played to good audiences for the whole run.

In London I found the producer Chris Malcolm and we became a partnership. From time to time he would find West End theatres that had some 'dark patches' while waiting for the next 'biggie'. Five years later Christopher did say that Wyndham's might be available for eight weeks and would I like to go there? 'I would,' I replied, and we opened for our fourth run in London and now the audiences were really building. This was my very first West End theatre and I could not have been happier …

I had just returned from New York where I staged my play *Kvetch* with American actors in an off-Broadway theatre on the previous Monday, so now I had two premieres in one week! But alas the Broadway critics didn't quite get *Kvetch*.

27

SHAKESPEARE'S VILLAINS

Theatre Royal, Haymarket 1998

I've always had the notion that an actor is tested to their limits by tackling, at some stage in their acting lives, the Bard. Shakespeare's complexity is also his thoroughness and utter dexterity in examining the human soul in the most finite detail. But not only does he do that, he also plays with the mind's complexity, juggling several thoughts in the air simultaneously. Sadly, few actors now can capture that same effervescent quality in their acting. Shakespeare challenges the best of us. When the actor is matched to the role he or she is playing then an electric glow emanates from the stage. In my extensive play-going life I have seen a rare few times when that has happened, and how very grateful I am to have seen it!

The late Alec McCowen had this quality in spades, for he really did seem to live the text throughout his body and voice. He didn't so much seem to play the role but actually appeared to operate on it with a scalpel-like precision, peeling it off layer by layer.

When I saw that Paul Scofield was to attempt King Lear with Alec as the Fool, I actually felt a certain amount of concern for Scofield, fearing the imp by his side would innocently emasculate the great Paul, but I need not have worried since Scofield's Lear was a monument carved out of rock and the Fool made no dent in it but merely acquired his rightful place as a sounding board. There were very few voices like Scofield's on the stage in those times. It was unique in that it seemed to travel from infernal depths, and so when it surfaced it came with added tonal hints that became strange journeys. He gave the art of acting a supreme lustre that so enchanted young ears to throw themselves headlong into the melee of the profession.

While he was on the stage you were glad to be in the audience sharing those precious minutes with him. You felt privileged to be there and indeed most fortunate to be alive and bear witness to a theatre marvel, alas now departed.

Scofield was quite brilliant in *Amadeus*, but the great man could also be flawed if he was not in the right hands, and I did chance to see his Prospero in a rather lame production of *The Tempest*. Such a shame, since this was a role where he ought to have been able to reveal those glorious depths. Sadly not. I did, however, catch him acting with Irish actor Patrick Magee in Charles Dyer's *Staircase*. Both actors were brilliant, and Scofield especially so, with such a wry gift for comedy.

I must now boast that I had the great privilege of hearing from him when he sent me a postcard congratulating Linda Marlowe and myself for our performance in *Decadence*, which was playing in the left-luggage room of The Caledonian Hotel at the Edinburgh Festival. Thus all of a sudden I became an ally of the great man, and we continued to communicate with each other almost up to his death.

Sometimes, a great performance will just pop out of the blue and stagger you with its sheer brilliance and daring. Then, for some inexplicable reason, the actor will disappear off the face of the earth.

Such an actor came into my life when I saw Peter Wyngarde's magnificent performance in Christopher Fry's *Duel of Angels*, an adaptation of Giraudoux's *Pour Lucrèce* (with Vivien Leigh and Claire Bloom). I was stunned by Wyngarde's bravura performance, his posture and his electrifying delivery. Here was a master actor. By some wonderful act of chance I saw him being advertised on TV playing Petruchio in *The Taming of the Shrew*. Again, a performance of pure, stunning genius.

Such a great shame that he fell into the deadly maw of TV soaps and then we lost him forever. But that was a voice that, once heard, could never be forgotten.

I was also proud to call him my friend during the few brief times that we met. But I was deeply sorry that he never returned to the stage, where his real magic could be revealed.

Olivier was my first introduction to Shakespeare when the world was introduced to his remarkable film of *Henry V*. I was far too young to be affected by it, but over the years it has grown as I have. To hear him embody Henry is even more remarkable today since his style has not aged in the least. In fact, it thrills me even to hear that musical, metallic voice ring out in a way that no actor in the world could possibly replicate. Olivier is the master. The high priest of Shakespeare, as if born to play him. Olivier's father was a man of the church and the young Sir Laurence used to recount how much he felt a spiritual resonance inside churches.

So, for Olivier, Shakespeare became the holy scripture and with such a voice, with such amazing vocal dexterity one might say that his sound was suited for nothing else but Shakespeare, yet paradoxically he was able to capture the flat, end of the pier, tones of a down and out entertainer like Archie Rice.

Some classical actors have a ready-made musical instrument in their vocal chords that lends a transcendent quality to whatever role they play, almost as if it 'spiritualises' the very part they are playing. Ian Richardson was one such actor. Christopher Plummer is another. Chris has a voice of incredible power and elegance. I had the great fortune to perform alongside him in a production of *Hamlet* that was televised for the BBC. Consequently I was able to see him rehearse every day for four weeks. What a lesson in acting and stagecraft! I had, I have, never forgotten it. What a talent that man possessed and, if that were not enough for one human being, in the evening he would sit at the piano and dazzle us with his pianistic skills!

Damn it. How can one even begin to compete? My modest role was Lucianus, the murderer in the players' scene. I was first cast by Phillip Saville as the Player Queen, but I suggested to Phillip that, since they had not yet cast Lucianus, I had a friend who was a killer mime who would be perfect for the Player Queen. Hence Lindsey Kemp joined the company and in fact choreographed the scene perfectly, and the Canadian producer Sid Newman was mightily impressed.

That production was one of the major events of my slowly evolving acting life. It was such an event, largely because I was surrounded by some of the most exciting actors in the British theatre. It could not possibly be better. Christopher Plummer as Hamlet, Robert Shaw as Claudius, Alec Clunes as Polonius, Michael Caine as Horatio, etc. and TV director Phillip Saville directed it superbly. And to finish, of course, Donald Sutherland was a youthful Fortinbras. Since time was of the essence, the players' scene was replaced by a mime, which lost nothing of the power of the language since Lindsay Kemp's choreography was spellbinding and I was proud to be part of it.

I absorbed Plummer like a drug and so when I next had a major role I was mighty successful in it. I felt that Plummer had liberated me, taught me to be daring and do the unexpected. So thanks, Chris.

It was 1964, the four hundredth anniversary of Shakespeare's birth, and to celebrate this momentous occasion, Olivier was preparing to play Othello. The big one. He had been appointed the Artistic Head of the National Theatre, which occupied The Old Vic until the new building was ready.

I remember a very ordinary Hamlet, surprisingly from Peter O'Toole, which suffered by comparison with Plummer's Hamlet which was still very fresh in my mind. No doubt the fact that Plummer had been directed by the great Scottish director Tyrone Guthrie made all the difference in the world.

Olivier was now taking on Othello. An astonishing choice for him, since one would not have said he was ideally cast for such a role. But Olivier typically was determined to overcome all perceived handicaps, and worked both body and voice ruthlessly. He even managed to lower his voice by a whole octave. Olivier was distinguished for his high tenor voice, even when used like an oxy-acetylene blow torch. But not a deep bass normally associated with playing Othello.

I managed to get tickets for the first night at Chichester, and went with my girlfriend by train from Victoria station. We did have a sense that history was going to be made this night. Olivier's dulcet tones were first heard when a voice on the theatre's tannoy implored us to take our seats as the curtain was about rise in three minutes' time.

I need add little more to the mountains of commentary that have been written except to say this: it was a night like no other night. It made me not only proud to be an actor but also honoured that I chose such a profession. I was exalted to represent where possible the great poets of our nation.

The Chichester Theatre thrust into the auditorium and our seats were perfect. The lights faded and we sat in intense anticipation and not without a certain amount of fear for this actor, with so much riding on his back, with such high expectations. Soon, he strode on.

A spectre dressed in a pure white robe which glistened against his highly polished dark skin, a long stem of a rose was in his hand, which he gently waved from side to side. His voice was low and lustrous, as if bathed in honey. When he spoke no one in the house moved. We scarcely breathed. Gradually, as the play commenced, we became first of all seduced by this magnificent actor with his enlarged lips and African vocal patterns. Then we became alarmed for him. Actually, his facial makeup was quite brilliant and, with dextrous shading, managed to make even his lips appear large.

During his torment perpetuated by Iago, a superb Frank Finlay, Othello's power was growing as he was being provoked by Iago's cunning, but he could do little except howl and rage in deep frustration. But what howls. What rages. We had never witnessed anything like it. Olivier had reached deep down and pulled out of himself satanic forces that can only be unleashed in times of stress, the like of which we had never seen. His body writhed as his thoughts began almost to chew him up from within like a plague of ants eating away at his innards. I can still see him vividly in my mind's eye over fifty years hence. It was probably one of the greatest nights of my life.

I decided a while ago, after having directed and played in a production of *Coriolanus*, that it was time to go it alone. After all, I thought, pianists frequently perform solo, as do singers and various cabaret performers, and so do actors. I had the great pleasure of seeing Sir John Gielgud doing his one-man Shakespeare performance entitled *The Ages of Man*, and it was quite unforgettable. It ran for about two hours, and I recall it to this day.

No more arduous back-breaking work of casting and producing, raising money and dealing with a whole bunch of differing temperaments. Just yourself, on the stage, unhindered, free, able to tap into whatever mood wafts your way. I felt that I could give the Bard a good run for his money, although my experience was limited to fewer than half a dozen productions. I had played a rather young Macbeth, which I had also directed. *Hamlet* in the eighties, which we toured around Europe, *Coriolanus*, which we took to Japan, and a *Richard II*, which we played in New York at The Public Theater to sizzling reviews. Quite a contrast when I directed it for the Ludlow Festival in a rainy summer, although being set against a castle gave it a tremendous atmosphere. In both productions of *Richard II* I was happy just to be the director.

So, I put my favourite speeches together and began. Oh, how liberating it felt, how exciting just to be paddling up just one stream. Also, it would become a lecture demonstration. After all, I would introduce the speech I was about to act out and then comment on it when I reached the conclusion. The entire show would, I thought, be adequate for just over an hour ...

Now a curious thought entered my mind. I found that I was more interested in giving the show a theme, and I also found I was being drawn to play the 'villains'. They were far more complex and in a way deeply divided. They were having to wear the mask of innocence Janus-like while breeding blood-curdling themes within their jaded souls.

I then found that they all shared certain characteristics. As if a vein of discontent ran through all of them, which somehow linked them all, and one of the most familiar themes was their 'defence' for their crimes. That they felt unloved, neglected, unwanted and, most of all, unrewarded.

As Richard III says, 'Why love foreswore me in my mother's womb, she did corrupt frail nature with some bribe to shrink mine arm up like a withered shrub.'

Iago's justification that Othello has had his way with his wife, 'I hate the Moor. I know not if 't be true, but I, for mere suspicion of that kind will do as if for surety.'

In all, I ran through key speeches of Iago, Richard III, Macbeth, Lady Macbeth, Shylock, Hamlet, Coriolanus, Oberon. Now, whilst Hamlet is by no means considered a villain, having once played him in my early days, I sense in him an aptitude for villainy and revenge above and beyond the passionate desire he has to avenge his father's death. He drives his beloved Ophelia to suicide, and is completely indifferent to the death, though accidental, of Polonius, casting him off with the rather cold utterance 'thou finds to be too busy is some danger' after he has skewered him through the guts and has little or no regret for the act. However, he has mind enough to counsel his mother Gertrude on the wisdom of sexual abstinence that night – and concludes with 'I will lug the guts into the neighbour room.'

I had played Coriolanus and found no problem in casting him as a villain, though with reason. As for Oberon, I felt that a man who secretly applies an aphrodisiac drug to his beloved was certainly not a saint.

Of course, some of the performance was tongue in cheek, and I did make a case for all of them to be among my cast of villains. I began simply wishing to try and demonstrate my versatility as an actor in Shakespeare. I had never been offered a role for the RSC or the National, although I had auditioned for the directors of the day, and while part of me really ached to step on those great and historic stages and to develop my stage muscles in Shakespeare, it was not to be. I would have to do it myself, and do it I would.

So, I began learning some of the roles I had not played, and slowly the show came together. The next step was to now show what I had achieved, and I managed to get a two-night gig in Utrecht. The performance went as well as could have been expected and lasted just under an hour. I then organised a short tour of one- or two-night stands in Cyprus and then a week's run at the Everyman Theatre in Liverpool.

Now, by whatever means information percolated down the grapevine, it came to the attention of Arnold Crook, the Managing Director of the Haymarket Theatre in London. He informed me that he was coming all the way up to see me since he was looking to replace the brilliant Barry Humphreys, whose show was unusually not selling. I did my best that night and was informed with all haste that he wished me to open with *Shakespeare's Villains* at the glorious Theatre Royal in three weeks! The show was still comparatively new and I had not yet even worked out my opening speech before getting into the Shakespeare. I was both nervous and elated, but knew I had only a short time to try to bring the show to fruition.

It was the summer of 1998. I entered the magnificent historic theatre and put my simple costume in the star dressing room on the ground floor, the number one room. The number one dressing room was probably given to me since I was the only actor in the building. It was a large, very comfortable room, and I could almost feel the ghosts of some of the greats who had stared into this same mirror over the last decades. They were civil enough to engrave my name on a brass plate nailed to the door. I was rather in awe of this position and hoped so much that I could live up to it. Once I had lit the show as carefully as I could, giving a different lighting state for each of the characters, I was ready to begin a week of previews. My company manager Nick Mattingly calls me for the 'half'. The 'half' is actually thirty-five minutes before the off, when the curtain rises. When the stage manager knocks on the door and announces the 'half', on a first night especially, this might be the most terrifying sound you'll ever hear! I dress in an elegant black shirt and trousers and highly polished black shoes. I leave my room and open the door for the stage. I'm on the right-hand side and step on to it. The curtain is down and the membrane of the curtain is all that separates me from the audience whom I can hear clearly.

The curtain slowly rises, my top light exposing me in a suitably villainous 'stance'. I begin.

> *What's he then that says I play the villain, when this advice is free I give and honest, probal to thinking and indeed the course to win the Moor again?*

Suddenly, I stop and the full lights come on. I very casually stroll down and speak to the audience … totally out of 'villain' mode. The following is just an excerpt from my introductory speech.

> *What is a villain?* (I smile at them. I am calm, benign even.) *A villain is a person who is motivated purely by their own lust, desire and greed, irrespective of the pain they may cause you, or even inspired by the pain they may cause you. A villain is someone who (according to psychologists) had little love in their early life and therefore has no pattern of love to pass on; like an unnourished tree that can only give off bad fruit, a villain can only give off bad deeds, the milk of human kindness does not run through their veins. Now, for the purposes of tonight's lecture I have decided to categorise villains into various types, for example we have clever villains, insane villains, genius villains, satanic villains and mediocre villains. And Iago is a mediocre villain, small-minded, petty, jealous of everything you possess, jealous of your skills, jealous of your treasures but most of all, he's jealous of love that you inspire. Since no one can love a villain … you might fear them, you might even admire them, but you can never love them, and this love that Othello has for Desdemona is like a great sun in the sky, exposing Iago in all his mediocrity. It hurts his eyes …*

This speech goes on for some time until I come back to the speech of Iago where I stopped before. The audience are now certainly warmed up to the kind of performance they are about to see. Although, it did take me many months before I had really worked out the commentary.

As I was 'improvising' the commentary, I relied on my own intuition to power its way through the debris and clutter of my brain. Suddenly, a perfectly apposite thought will pop up. It feels so right, that I will store it for further use. But this can take some time, days and even weeks, if not months. But then it is set and will remain. When some commentary feels a little forced or even tired, I will drop it, and that will benefit the piece. Sometimes I even surprise myself by the pithiness of my commentary, though others may not think so. Eventually I felt really comfortable, satisfied with what had just surfaced, almost without thinking. The brain's unconscious is a formidable and quite startling tool. It will not let you down.

The review night came and went, and it took me many weeks before I could stand before that curtain and be sure of how I would start the show. The reviews were either praiseworthy or just plain insulting, but we soldiered on for the full six weeks. However, word got round and invites were coming in to perform all over the world. Soon I was travelling to Edinburgh, Dublin, Jerusalem, Hong Kong, Australia, Tasmania, South Africa (both Cape Town and Durban), Argentina, Rio then finally Bogotá, Bulgaria, Mexico, Los Angeles, Portland, Oregon and eventually New York.

My very favourable responses abroad did make me feel at times that the British were a very conservative bunch, who were almost hostile to their precious theatre providing something a little out of the norm. I will always remember one of the greatest productions I'd ever seen, namely The Living Theatre's *The Brig*, getting almost insulting reviews from the daily press.

I was on a tour of the Eastern seaboard and had already been turned down by The Public Theater in New York when I decided just to pop in for a brief chat, since I had worked there twice before. Rosemary Tischler, the casting lady, made a suggestion that I might like to do a few gigs at Joe's Pub, a small cabaret room next door to the theatre. I saw it during the day and was most depressed, the stage was minuscule, but I decided to take a risk and get it on there for two weeks.

The show went well, although I had no high hopes for it; each night the barman treated me to a drink and I was extremely happy that it was over. They don't do that sort of thing in England.

I had expected people to be drinking or still eating, but to my pleasant surprise they were quiet and attentive. In the morning papers I had the best reviews of my life!

It was all the more pleasing to me after the crap reviews in London, and that wasn't because the New York critics are conditioned to expect less.

Sometimes one thanks God and, as Coriolanus says 'There is a world elsewhere.' Opening at the small Joe's Pub, was a revelation, in spite of my doubts of playing before an audience who had been eating and drinking. They seemed to hang on every word, and I felt that they appreciated it if the actor took risks and wasn't afraid to expose himself. The reviews could not have been more different from some of the sour and churlish comments I received in London. I was reborn, my life could begin anew! I feel American audiences have a keen eye for something that is either unusual or not seen before and are unafraid to express, quite volubly, their appreciation.

The result of this was of course that the present CEO felt he had to ask me back to play in the large Anspacher Theater for a six-week run from January, and I couldn't have been more pleased. I was happy, delighted, thrilled and felt, at last, respected. I was ensconced back at the traditional (no frills) Gramercy Park Hotel and was beginning to feel part of the New York landscape. Most of the reviews were very good, with the odd caveat from a whining critic in *The Village Voice*. *The Village Voice* is thought to support radical theatre, but seemed to be rather dismissive and sarcastic when it reared its head. So I binned the negative review. My pleasure came at the end of the evening when I was comped a delicious margarita from the barman, and then a slow walk back to my hotel through the winter slush.

Shakespeare's Villains was kept in my repertoire for at least fifteen years.

28

RANDOM THOUGHT

One-man show

There comes a time in an actor's life, whether through unemployment, or sheer curiosity, when a desire will manifest itself to consider performing in a one-man show.

An exciting prospect, if not also wrought with a formidable degree of terror. The nature of a one-person show demands in no uncertain manner that you are possessed of a more than reasonable amount of courage combined with fearlessness. But once in full flow it is possible that you will release insights with a bravura not so available to you in a play. For myself a one-man show is possibly the most exciting event I could hope to see on a stage. What I saw on the night I saw the legendary Marcel Marceau in the late fifties was close to what I might call 'magical'. He defied reason and logic as he seemed to walk on air and create invisible objects in space.

Unlike in a play, where any over-enthusiastic effort will usually be discouraged by the director since you must not tilt the careful balance of the play lest you stand out and the pull the play out of focus, in a one-man show you are obliged to stand out and you have no one whom your enthusiastic excesses might disturb.

The world is full of endless possibilities, and the decision regarding what material would best suit you will be based on how close you feel to the chosen subject. Naturally, now that you are the author or adapter as well as the interpreter, you will be sorely tempted to unlock that dark, remote room inside where the demons are kept in safe isolation. Merely thinking about them is liable to have them stirring in anticipation inside you. Now that you are preparing yourself for that solo journey, take care lest you plunge yourself into the pits of hell!

However, great one-man shows do not have to be hell, but they have to be exciting. I recall the late and great Alec McCowen doing a remarkable Gospel According to St Mark. *He performed it as if he himself were there as a witness, with all the enthusiasm of one newly converted. He was inspiring to watch.*

And yet we are tempted since at last free of the petty boundaries of the play to actually explore exotic works.

Diary of a Madman, *by Nikolai Gogol, is a firm favourite of actors whose reputation has been of treading the path that few are tempted to take.*

I believe it was a favourite of 'scene-chewer' Richard Harris in his youthful days. Most of all, once you begin that journey, you will be astounded by how liberating it can be. Your world is your oyster, it has no limits. Your body is the most incredible instrument with which you may do as you wish. For now you are the owner, the manipulator and devoted guardian. No director will have any right to pass comment unless invited to. You are now the sole creator. You are both Frankenstein and the beast he created. What wonderful opportunities! By attempting one-man shows there is no doubt that you will improve as an actor, providing of course that you are blessed with the talent to accompany it. But the fact that you are already choosing this course would certainly suggest that you are ...

29

THE SECRET LOVE LIFE OF OPHELIA

The King's Head Theatre 2001

Sometimes I haven't a clue where some ideas come from, from what ancient soil they first thrust out their shoots. An epistolary play. I do remember some time ago there existed a maudlin American play that was always doing the rounds and was not learned or acted but simply read. This enabled the 'producers' who purveyed this 'easy on the ear' stuff to hire 'movie actors' who never had the pain of studying or learning the bloody thing to drag in punters. My opus had to be learned. Learned very carefully and the movement blocked-out.

So I chose to tell the back story of Hamlet and Ophelia as a very sensitive tale of two people who gradually got to know each other through their letters which expressed their deepest feelings, but gradually, slowly behind the play so to speak, behind the scene. And it just seemed to flow out of me. Of course I had to write it in verse. I enjoyed writing it and tried very hard to delve far more deeply into those more exotic areas of my soul. The challenge was to be almost Elizabethan by writing the entire play in iambic pentameter. I remember it was difficult to cast, but I eventually found two talented young actors and they read the text well. It was only when I found the pianist that, once again, with music the play really came to life. He improvised to the language very carefully and created a kind of pastiche Chopin. We found a young male set designer who hit exactly on the perfect design, which consisted of a large open envelope which took up the whole stage. There were two chairs, one either side of the stage. They mimed writing the letters, it seemed to work well. Here's a letter from Hamlet:

> *My dear Ophelia, so many thanks*
> *For entertaining us so charmingly.*
> *'Twas indeed the rarest joy to me*
> *to speak to thee and hear thy graceful skills*
> *Manipulate the mysteries of the lute —*

and bringing forth such sweet idyllic sounds.
I swear the very birds did cease their chirp
and on their branches listened gratefully.
I pray you will be happy here in Denmark
within the environs of Elsinore,
For though it doth appear at first remote
there is much here I know will interest you.
I will anticipate another visit
where though I surely lack your sylph-like art
I may perchance beguile you with the flute
or else engage your senses in the wild
to demonstrate our native falconry.
So, my dear new friend, until we meet again,
welcome to Elsinore with all my heart
Hamlet.

So via these letters they expressed their passionate love which grew as the play progressed. Reaching its climax when Hamlet writes about his horrid discovery of the King's guilt confirmed by the play within the play. And then his appalling grief at the tragic death of her father Polonius caused in fact by Hamlet himself.

The letters become even more terrifying and frantic. She can barely write anymore. And then most tragically comes Ophelia's suicide. There are no more letters, only Gertrude's voice is now heard as she tells the sad and terrible moving story of her drowning:

There is a willow grow aslant a brook
That shows its hoar leaves in the glassy stream.
There with fantastic garlands did she come
Of crow flowers, nettles. Daisies and long purples
That liberal shepherds give a grosser name
But our cold maids do dead men's fingers call them.
There on the pendant bows her coronet weeds
clambering to hang, an envious sliver broke,
fell in the weeping brook. Her clothes spread wide
and mermaid-like a while they bore her up
which time she chanted snatches of old tunes
as one incapable of her own distress
.... but long it could not be,
Till that her garments heavy with their drink,
Pulled the poor wretch from her melodious lay
To muddy death.

As Hamlet hears this terrible memorial to his beloved ... he say nothing, but his mouth opens and makes a silent howl ...

The lights fade. How could I or any writer ever compare to that haunting dirge of Gertrude. It has to be one of the very finest pieces of verse on death in the whole of Shakespeare. The play was staged in one act without an interval. The grief at the end of the play was quite palpably felt by the audience. We played it for four weeks at The King's Head, then the Edinburgh Festival, and were even invited to play it at Elsinore, Hamlet's original castle, in Denmark.

The atmosphere in the great room of the castle was so palpable, you could almost smell it. It bought a haunting sense of the inner life of those two sadly fated people. Though it was halfway through the first performance that I realised that this was the very room in which the BBC televised much of the *Hamlet* production in which I had played thirty years earlier! Christopher Plummer was playing Hamlet. At first I had not recognised it, without all the cameramen, lighting, fixtures and staff.

Regrettably the play is rarely performed, which is a shame since they are such haunting and lyrical roles for two actors.

30

MESSIAH

Edinburgh Festival 2002 and The Old Vic 2003

Some years ago I was directing *Metamorphosis* in Hebrew in Haifa, having just directed it in Australia for the charming Nimrod Theatre in Sydney, but I never tired of it. However, it was in an English bookshop in Haifa that I came across a most remarkable book called *The Trial of Jesus* by Chaim Kaplan. A fascinating book which makes a very significant point since the writer was a highly respectable court judge. The theme of the book is that the Jews have never defended themselves from the charge of deicide, a term which in itself is an oxymoron, since how can you kill a god?

And so Chaim Kaplan, chief justice, decided to defend ancient Jewry, as if in high court, and assembled all the evidence available. The main thrust of the story being that not only did Romans crucify Jesus, but so did early Christians in their reporting of the event. It is a most fascinating book, and whether Christian or Jew you cannot be anything but impressed by it and will learn a great deal. For example, even Pilate's washing of his hands. This would not be possible since the washing of one's hands was a Jewish ritual performed by judges on the rare occasion when a citizen was sentenced to death. No Roman would possibly defile himself by appropriating a strictly Jewish custom.

Also the overturning of the money changers' table in the temple forecourt attributed to the disgust Jesus felt about people dealing with money on holy ground doesn't quite make sense since the money changers were necessary to change coins with 'images' such as the heads or profiles of emperors, since this would be blasphemous by showing and by definition worshipping a human. The coins exchanged would be the temple coin with a human face and replaced with a Hebrew image of plant or flower. So why did he throw over the money changers' stall? There is a theory that the temple coin had the image of Caesar on it.

Hence render unto Caesar what's Caesar's and render unto God what's God's.

Anyway these and so many other theories in the book stimulated me to write *The Murder of Jesus Christ*, which was its first title. It took me many years before I eventually got round to staging it, but also many years after writing it I did eventually stage it at the Edinburgh Festival, with a remarkable actor called Rory Edwards as Jesus.

I started with the crucifixion and then worked backwards. I loved directing it with a splendid British cast, and in its very first incarnation Satan was played by Greg Hicks and I recall being utterly astounded by the brilliance of his reading. Greg has a voice which is thrilling to hear, also matched with a shrewd intelligence which simply illuminates the text

Then we did a run through at the Three Mills Studio in Bow for an invited audience. The reaction was very encouraging. The last supper was especially beautiful, since we based the grouping on renaissance paintings, and the music by Mark Glentworth was superb. Having gone this far, I decided to risk it at the Edinburgh Festival. We staged it very simply using the disciples as the backbone of the ensemble. So as Jesus was being crucified they play the dicing soldiers, abusing and vilifying him as he dies in agony. When he slowly came down from the cross, he was cradled by his adoring mother and was now surrounded by his mournful disciples. My inspiration for the scene had to be Michelangelo's remarkable statue *Pietà*. We staged The Last Supper with inspiration from da Vinci's painting. But the genius of Mark Glentworth's ravishing music helped no end.

It won the best production of the festival award, which is given out weekly. This time a Scottish actor, Tam Dean Burn played Satan. Sadly, our Jesus had some problems, the sort that are familiar to many actors, and left the stage when there were still two nights left to perform.

And so I rushed up to Edinburgh and went on with the book, which still seemed to work, and we were all happy, since we never cancel a performance if we can help it. The New Testament is replete with the most beautiful passages and incidents and is a gift for any playwright who is in touch with his or her own feelings. Strangely, or perhaps not, while painters strew the renaissance with the most magnificent imagery, as did many playwrights, in our age there are hardly any takers. And yet what a subject! Johnny Coyne played John the Baptist with an emotional charge I had rarely seen in the theatre, and Caiaphas was played by Raymond Sawyer, who had the ability to make you actually 'feel' the words while celebrating the Catholic Church's obsession with incense and delicate choirboys. Though one of my best pieces in my opinion, it had a hard journey until it got to The Old Vic. Three of us, including Vidal Sassoon, put up £150,000 to put it on, this time with Greg Hicks taking over Jesus, myself doing Satan, and Michael Jenn doing Pontius Pilate. The reviews were not only unkind, they were utterly stupid even to the extent of criticising me for putting this passion play on at Xmas instead of Easter!

We struggled to get an audience, but we managed to limp through our scheduled six weeks. The new director, Kevin Spacey, had just begun his stewardship of The Old Vic, although sadly we did not see him once. He was probably very busy. We finished the run just after the New Year, and I remember my main concern was getting enough people round for New Year's Eve.

Nevertheless, I still believe it was one of my best productions ever. And one of my best plays if not the very best.

Without question, I chose the most powerful subject I could find – the death of Jesus Christ. Because it was such a powerful story, I felt it drew out of me the very best of my writing. At the same time, I had done a massive amount of research, including reading an extraordinary book on the subject called *The Passover Plot* by Hugh J. Schonfield. I was determined to bind myself to the subject until I finally felt satisfied. Eventually I did workshops in Nottingham and at the Edinburgh Festival, before revealing it in London at that beautiful theatre The Old Vic.

Vidal Sassoon had been a friend ever since he saw my early play *Greek* in a small fringe theatre in Los Angeles. From then on he made sure never to miss any of my shows, and I was very grateful for his friendship and his enthusiasm. One day I dared to suggest the idea of him becoming financially involved, in other words to help finance it, which he readily did, and I was extremely grateful; although I knew he must be rich as Croesus it is all the more difficult to raise the subject. But I did and he replied that he would on one condition, that was he was to become my assistant! He was fascinated to know how plays get formed, to be behind the scenes, and he even offered to make tea for us! Of course that wasn't necessary. But he came to my flat in London's East End where I first started to rehearse it with Greg Hicks since it was his first time as Jesus, although it was also my first time as Satan.

I loved Vidal being there. We were both East End boys so to speak, although he was about a decade older, but extremely fit. He moved into Docklands for the month of rehearsal and was there every day, not missing one. Sometimes I get paranoid about people dropping in to see rehearsals unless it's someone who has something to do with the play. Well, when one morning without forewarning me Vidal came up to our rehearsal room with his wife, I very stupidly said that she couldn't come in. Dumb bastard I could be at times.

However, he took it in his stride, but I still regret that moment every time I think about it. My real terror was that I would have to step outside the relative comfort of The Director's Chair and step into that ring of fire. I was in a state of terror for days before I had to do Satan's five-page monologue. But the time had to come and so I did it, with a gigantic 'phew' at the end.

I approached the role as a human beast, totally satisfied with himself. The voice has to be dominant, crushing and fearless. Jesus was calmly sitting cross-legged centre stage. I wove my speech around him and then I slowly approached the audience, castigating them for their pathetic weakness for not giving in to temptation. I had to be svelte and persuasive.

One does of course worry about performing and directing unless the two flow seamlessly into each other. Coming on stage suddenly at the very top of the second act felt fine and much less nerve-wracking than doing it in front of your colleagues in a rehearsal room … I remember that I could never seem to find the appropriate 'Satanic coat' and I went from one to another. It had to look Satanic and had to be right. However, I duly admit that during one of *Messiah*'s outings we did a week at Riverside Studios in Hammersmith and I found an amazing black actor called Cornell John. He was blessed with a magnificent physique and he came on half-naked and was utterly mesmerising. He needed no coat to help him out as I did. However, when we eventually made the transfer to The Old Vic, the other two producers were adamant that I performed.

The character that I invented called Satan runs a gamut through history and becomes a mirror for all times, and mirrors society from then until today, in our 'Trump' times.

When Jesus is carried off the cross and is just left, dead, on the stage, since we were starting the play from the execution, he slowly gets up, replaces his plimsolls on his bare feet, gets on one knee and first does one lace up and then another … Such a simple act of 'resurrection' was quite electrifying to watch. As he gets up and dons a simple shirt he begins the Sermon on the Mount … In fact I recall him starting as he was lacing up his shoe:

(Jesus gets up slowly. Disciples bring him his clothes and shoes … he dresses as he speaks)

'I came to set the earth on fire!' 'Do you suppose I came to bring peace to the world? Not peace but conflict! Father against son, son against father, mother against daughter, daughter against mother …'

As I said already, the effect was electrifying, since we naturally believed that this is a barnstorming speech from the beginning. But starting it this way as simple and quiet, it had an almost mesmerising effect and built as the speech goes on to a tremendous climax. Of course I used the Gospel for many of the play's speeches that Jesus makes. I could see during rehearsal how much they still have the power to move one. They are inspiring and led me to believe that they must have been taken down verbatim by his disciples, who would have been with him from one destination to another. The Sermon on the Mount might have been something that he preached over and over again, since it contains such vital and dynamic principles.

We closed early in January in 2003 and we lost every penny of our money but I didn't care about that, since I often lost money on shows I believed in. And what better way to spend your money than on a work that reaches out to the world. I was happy and proud to be at The Old Vic in spite of sometimes playing to very small houses. The critics really did crucify us. I even felt a little ashamed that Vidal should see how poorly I am treated in my own country.

Vidal would not miss the money, that's for sure, but I admired him greatly for his serious offer to be a stage manager, even make the tea, since he was so very keen to see how a production was put together. It was a privilege knowing him and I was honoured by his support,

'They really have it in for you!,' he once said with a certain amount of humour, mixed with just a tinge of compassion. And he was so right, they did … However, this had been Olivier's stage and I was proud to have been even a small part of its history.

31

SIT AND SHIVER

Hackney Empire 2007

There is, among the more orthodox of the Jewish race, a ritual which is carried out after a death in the immediate family. The ritual is a ceremony dedicated to respecting and mourning for the deceased. It entails clearing out a room so that mourners may visit and sit with the bereaved family for as long as they wish. Usually they sit on hard chairs, drink tea and chat about their memories of the person who has now passed on. It's natural to extoll the virtues of the deceased, how much the person meant to them, and to celebrate the relationships they had. As one of the characters says,

Isn't it amazing how important a person becomes when they die?

It's actually called 'sitting shiva', which means sitting for seven days. In the most orthodox households they will wear drab clothes and even cover the mirrors to exclude all concerns of vanity.

Such an event has rather fascinated me for some time and eventually I decided to write a play called *Sit and Shiver*. That's simply because as a child that's precisely how it sounded to me … *Sit and Shiver*. It seemed appropriate since it suggested to my young mind a group of people sitting in their grief and even shivering in their grief.

I turned to my own family for the characters, and I made the 'star' of the piece my Uncle Sam, my father's brother who had been blind for some years. Sam was a very wise old boy whose blindness hardly mattered a fig to him and who still did his daily perambulations round the East End. He was a delightful man, an ex-communist, vociferous reader in his sighted days and an early adventurer. Sam became fascinated by the history and legends of New York in the twenties and read the great American novels voraciously, such as Upton Sinclair's great epic *The Jungle*. Or the works of Herman Melville. He spoke of them with such passion, as if he were a character in them, which in a way he was.

He emigrated to New York as a young man and existed off the streets in casual work, labouring and of course tailoring. He was self-taught, an autodidact. He loved having a chat whenever I popped down to the East End for a visit and could quote Shakespeare by the ream. He was one of the driving forces behind the Jewish Defence when Mosley's fascists tried to march through the East End in 1936. My uncle Sam is honoured by being featured on the great mural *The Battle of Cable Street*, which still exists today on Cable Street itself.

Sam was a central character who seemed to pull everyone into their place when their petty obsessions and trouble had them veering off into negative waters.

I found an excellent Jewish cast headed by a part-time actor and fluent Yiddish speaker called Barry Davis. He was remarkable in that he played the entire role of Sam with his eyes closed and didn't miss a trick. Sue Kelvin played the daughter of the deceased and Linal Haft played her much nagged husband, a role which I then took over when Linal decided not to transfer with the play to the beautiful Hackney Empire. Leila Crerar played the gentile outsider who was engaged to the nephew, played by Russell Bentley. She was able to give a perfect outsider fascination to the event. The boisterous aunt was played by Bernice Stegers, the uncle by Frank Lazarus.

For the setting we had about seven boxes that were used as seats. To the left of the stage was a long table for the continuous feeding of the guests, with tea and cake which became very much part of the action of the play and was accompanied by the filling and refilling of cups, especially for my Uncle Sam, who, I remember, was seldom without a cup of tea in his hand.

Now, as the play opens and the guests arrive, there is much chatter about how wonderful the old man was and what a good and generous guy, but as the play continues there appear tiny cracks in the portrait, which of course widen, even though the faithful daughter (Sue Kelvin) passionately tried to seal them up as soon as they appear. I took the liberty of basing the dead man on my own father. I couldn't have had a better model to work from, even though at the same time I had a huge respect for his work ethic and intelligence. My dad was a rather strange dude. I remember him as a young child, picking me up by my armpits and I do believe, since I recall it so vividly, both the time and place, that it might have been the one and only time he did. As I grew older, I became aware of his absences from home and the neglect of my mother and watched the pain it caused her. I don't believe he could help himself, because in those days, unlike today, marriage and family was a lifelong commitment – it was not really for him. Every one of my ten uncles and aunts had lifelong partnerships, so the 'dead man' for whom we are all sitting 'shiva' was in many ways my dad.

The young man, the nephew, played so well by Russell Bently, is an actor who, to his shame, is not working and because of this feels less than whole as a person and even envies Uncle Sam, who is a trouser cutter! He confesses as much to Uncle Sam, who just won't accept such a contrast and boosts the young man's confidence by telling him that he, as an actor, is a messenger for the gods of languages.

Just before the first act is over, and after there has been much debate and conflict of opinions, especially when a rich friend comes in to pay respects (there is always a distant family member in every Jewish household who has made money), suddenly the front doorbell rings and in comes a strange woman, in her forties and still very attractive. She says she used to work for the deceased, called 'Al', in his small shop on Saturdays when she would help out, sew a button, do some alteration etc.

This new and rather becoming woman causes the slightest hint of alarm and suddenly, out of the blue, she confesses that she misses Al greatly, to which the daughter sagely replies 'We all miss him.' She then cannot stop the flow and, for the grieving mother, the earth opens wide to reveal a much larger corpse than the one that was recently buried. She is just revealing another skeleton in the closet. The visitor confesses tearfully that she in fact loved 'Al' and they had a child together! This rocks the whole family, except for Sam who still keeps them all from toppling over the abyss. The strange woman now leaves. The daughter is in utter shock and grief when Uncle Sam wisely says

> *Look, suppose one day your 'half-brother' would want to visit his lost family and he was a millionaire, you wouldn't kick him out would you? Or a great scientist, or a novelist …?*

The play winds down and ends up with Uncle Sam saying he used to study acting as a young amateur before he become a trouser cutter, and goes into the storm sequence of *King Lear* … in Yiddish.

I loved writing this play, and it was the first time I had ever put my own family into something I had written. It was such a rewarding experience as I had plunged into my own life and pulled out all those writhing skeletons and, at the same time, honoured them,

The play was very well received, and it looked good in the beautiful Hackney Empire. The reviews were positive and I played my modest part in it by playing the henpecked husband who in the end gets his own back in a roaring denunciation of his wife. It was a fantastic experience, and I had never before seen so many Jews in the audience. The bar at the back of the theatre was always kept open at the end of the show for your friends and guests, it was a very happy time. The Hackney Empire lost its fine administrator and the regime which followed refused to do 'drama'. No call for it, they said!!

32

RANDOM THOUGHT

Salome at The Gate Theatre, Dublin

To love a play usually means that it brings out the best in you when you bring it to the stage. You devote yourself to it as if nothing else on this earth could matter so much.

With Salome and its hyper-exotic language, I knew that I had to present the play almost as a ritual and very slowly so that not a single utterance was lost. Just as I had worked with actors using a metronome, in fact freezing the human frame, in Salome I chose to do the reverse. Slow motion intensified the actor's performance in quite a different way. Like any 'technique', it has to be done perfectly, and for the audience the effect was to captivate them and hold their attention. With the music played on a piano by Roger Doyle, the mood was set when the first two actors crossed the stage uttering the words 'How beautiful is the princess Salome tonight.' The audience seemed to be completely hypnotised. Furthermore, we did the entire play in slow motion. It toured the world. Was this biomechanics? I'm sure it comes pretty close.

33

ON THE WATERFRONT

Theatre Royal, Haymarket 2010

So this is how it happened. Many years ago I was sitting in Richard Eyre's office at the National Theatre, since all the rehearsal rooms were booked so I was put in the director's office.

I was casting the last few actors for my production of Kafka's *The Trial* due to open shortly at the National Theatre. There is a great view of the Thames downstream from the window, but what really caught my eye was a script sitting on top of his desk. It was a stage adaptation of the famous Budd Schulberg screenplay *On the Waterfront*. It was certainly a 'wow' moment, and I thought that it was simply an amazing idea to stage this classic movie. 'Oh clever Richard Eyre,' I thought, 'this has to be a winner.'

After my brief casting session I bumped into Mr Eyre in the corridor. 'Oh, Richard,' I said, 'I happened to see on your desk a stage version of *On the Waterfront*, what a brilliant idea, when do you plan to do it?' He replied that they weren't going to do it, that they didn't want to do another play taken from a film. 'Why don't you do it if you're interested?,' he replied.

I thought about it for some time. I read it and, whilst it contained the essence of the film, there were many flaws and clumsy interpolations, like the over-familiar 'narrator', but the script made a journey from Richard Eyre's desk to mine and sat there for a considerable time. One day, during a quiet period, I just decided to move the script from my desk to a rehearsal room. It was time to do a workshop on it. This has always been my mode of operation. So, my astute company manager Matt Cullum and I called up a few old regulars and began. Matt brought along some moody jazz music from the period and we began rehearsals.

Once you get into the rehearsal room, the once-dormant script starts to wriggle into life. The Beast awakens, it hears its name being called. I had a bunch of first-rate actors who were almost tailor-made for the roles. There were just a few of us there, maybe half a dozen, and we began. Now, we don't sit and jabber forever, since that's not our way. The more you jabber, the more you suck from everybody that special gem of spontaneity. One has to get up and get inside the script and let it take you where it will. Once the words are percolating inside the actors' mouths and bodies, it will tell you where to go. Sitting and talking certainly does not.

So, after a week of workshops, we all knew that we had found the 'key'; we knew it, and with the help of the Hackney Empire, who financed us to do a couple of nights' try-outs, we began. From the very first minute when the guys got on the floor and began, the script started to breathe, it came to life and I was so excited to see it.

On the Waterfront is a street play in that so many scenes are set on the street, which is of course the working-class territory. Matt hit the play button and the music flowed and the actors flowed with it.

We knew we had something really special, but it had to be cast really well and I was able to get some of the best. Simon Merrells, whom I had known for some time, played the Brando role, Vincenzo Nicoli played the Priest, with Johnny Friendly being played by John Forgeham and the rest of the actors coming into the other roles when needed. Slowly, we built up the company.

Alex Giannini, another Italian Englishman, played Friendly's evil sidekick Big Mac and was brilliant. He sewed all the separate pieces together and was a hell of a team player. I dedicate a few thoughts to him since he left us shockingly last year in his early fifties. I miss him like a brother.

After a few weeks, we were ready to go, but this time we had our live musician Mark Glentworth to whom I hardly had to say a word, he simply played as he felt the energy of the play touch him. And he was brilliant, able to find the exact tone for the scene.

As we progressed through this strange and atmospheric play, it grew in me so much that I felt that I was born to direct it. This was New York, Hoboken to be exact, and the sounds of actors' voices were expressive and dynamic. We felt alive to be doing it, perhaps more alive that we had ever been before.

We used an open stage, a few cane-backed old bar room chairs and that was ample for us. The streets, alleyways, docks were created by the movement and action of the actors and the sounds that emanated from the musician's fingers. Of course, the freedom of film allows the director to be totally realistic, and we had to see how we could replicate that on stage, and we would.

The first problem was the very opening when Terry Malloy was to coax the longshoreman Tommy out onto the roof, where the goons are already waiting for him, to put an end to the informer. Terry has one of Tommy's 'boids' (birds) and he releases it to Tommy, to distract him. Then the following event happens.

Johnny Friendly's goons are waiting for Tommy on the roof to throw him over. How we achieved that was, in fact, quite simple. A crack of a drum and the two goons are now with Tommy. They pull him back and then, in slow motion, thrust him forward. He appears to fall from a great height, also in slow motion. The drum cracks again as we hear him hit the deck. It was not necessary to see the actual act of crashing to the ground. It is always more effective to see the reaction.

The reaction was seen as a whole group rush to the body in total shock. Then they slowly part as their faces and bodies react in horror to what they have seen. It worked superbly and we didn't have to throw a stuffed facsimile of a body from the flies, the actor 'acted' out the fall.

One of the actors flies off to get a doctor and a priest, bodies whip round and up and down the stage, actors change roles and hats, and now we see the priest, striding on with Edie Doyle, sister of the mob's latest victim Tommy Doyle the longshoreman, who was brave enough to spill his guts to the law. They're appalled by this latest thuggery of the waterfront mob, and the priest, played powerfully by Enzo Nicoli, promises to do all he can, which is far from good enough for Edie Doyle.

Her dialogue is now bitter and searing as she accuses the priesthood of hiding in a church and evokes the spirit and acts of Jesus, who never took refuge in a church but came boldly out to face his oppressors.

Now, Friendly's cohort and slave master Big Mac, played as if born to the task by Alex Giannini, comes on and demands that the dock workers get to work. Our group, now with minor costume changes, are now warming themselves by one of those fires one always see in movies set in docks, usually an old oil drum. We mime all the actions of course, the hoisting of the sacks, the throwing them to others, changing positions, and they work like a perfectly trained team of workers to a drum beat.

Just now, Father Barry comes on with Edie, since she wanted to see what kind of life they are leading down there. Pop Doyle, her father, is absolutely gutted that his daughter is witness to the appalling conditions the dock workers have to suffer, and makes his feelings known. Our oldest actor, Sean Buckley, played Pop Doyle as if he were indeed Pop Doyle. Sean was the senior member of the group and had a wonderfully grizzled, worn look, as if he'd been through the mill. I was always so impressed by him, and I have to say that dear Sean has also left us recently and I will never forget him.

Now, Father Barry is outraged too by what he has seen and, once Big Mac is out of hearing, he suggests that the safest place for the men to meet and air their grievances is his church. They all agree to meet there.

Now, for Johnny Friendly's waterfront shack, where he sits with his goons, we simply used a bunch of chairs scattered in the centre with all the mob hanging out like a bunch of sleazy villains with Friendly in the centre. Terry Malloy lingers grumpily on the side lines, still bitter about being set up for the hit on Tommy. The goons wear trilbies and look mean, although these are the very same actors who are playing the dock workers! Yet you would hardly know, so swift was the transformation.

Here, we get introduced to the bad guys led by Johnny Friendly. The 'Accountant' reading out the figures, Charlie the Gent sat comfortably in his smart camel-hair coat. Friendly is a killer with no conscience, but he still has a weird sense of humour. He's a bit miffed that Terry is so off colour. Charlie, who is actually Terry's smart brother, attempts to mollify him. It's business as usual since they got rid of the

'dodgy' character Tommy, who was going to break the secret code of D and D –
deaf and dumb.

No sooner have they left than they are changed into dock workers; the chairs
are now placed in two rows to represent the interior of a small church. Enzo Nicoli
now enters as Father Barry. He removes his dock worker's jacket and scarf and in
seconds he is the ruddy-faced, pure, Father Barry and looks it to a 'T'. Father Barry
questions the men, begs them to confess their sins of the corrupt union, but they
are reluctant to break the code of Omertà, or 'D and D'.

Now, we have to show the union's mob getting ready to attack them with baseball bats, but the only spare bodies upstage are Johnny Friendly and Big Mac. So
they enter from the wings and bang their bats, which, accompanied by the whack
of the drums, is deafening. The dockers all run in fear but, not knowing which way
to go, they fly in all directions. Now the audience can't tell who are the thugs and
who are the workers in the melee. We suddenly freeze the action upstage and go
into slow motion. As each worker approaches he gets whacked. All the workers
are trapped between me giving my best, meanest Johnny Friendly, leader of the
crooked union, and Big Mac. They were whacked backwards and forwards. It's a
highly dramatic moment. Terry Malloy escapes with Edie.

This is also accompanied by some eerie music to match the rhythm of the
beating of the men, but curiously this is oddly beautiful, as the men seeking escape
go from left to right but also in slow motion, revealing clearly their agony and

FIGURE 33.1 *On the Waterfront.*

confusion. The scene dissolves leaving Terry Malloy growing closer to the beautiful young woman Edie Doyle.

A scene which might have caused us problems was the one when Edie Doyle visits Terry on his waterfront roof where he keeps his pigeons. This is a pivotal part of the film and cannot be omitted just because the stage can't handle such scenes, and we were determined to lose absolutely nothing of the film.

I knew that there was only one way of doing this scene, and that was to 'act' out the birds. Of course, this would come to me naturally, having been steeped in mime, but this doesn't automatically mean that it could work for every problem moment when transposing a vital element from film to stage. But, believe me, it works for more cases than not.

That's the beauty of 'mime' and its magical element to solve, in the simplest way possible, intransigent problems.

So, when we came to the scene I knew in my heart that it would work and so I had no difficulty suggesting to my group of male actors that they impersonate pigeons. I set the chairs in two rows and we put the front row sitting on the chairs and the row behind sitting higher on the back of the chairs, so they appeared as if on a higher ledge.

They then impersonated the soft whirring sounds of pigeons, accompanied by the movement of their heads and arms. It was quite stunning and worked beyond our expectations. It showed how theatre can entertain by transformation, by acting out what would seem to be impossible. Then, when Terry comes on and shows Edie his 'boids', the effect was stunning. For this was sheer theatre, when you challenge what theatre can do, the further you escape from the simple world of naturalism.

The next 'problem' to be solved was the menacing car drive when Charlie the Gent, the brother of Terry, tries to persuade Terry to keep D and D for a considerable reward. It was such a powerful and deeply moving scene that we had to do it as they did in the movie. They're in a car, so again we use our wonderful protean chairs. The driver, played with perfect menace by Dominic Grant, is sitting in the front and the brother gets in the back. Runty Nolan mimes the driving wheel while the two men do their scene. The light pin points the scene. Now, what makes it work for me was less the simple mime of the chairs pretending to be the car. It was the sound made by the cast offstage, a slow but steady growling, steadily rising. Very steadily the car's growl becomes even more emphatic until it becomes animalistic. The growl of the engine becomes the low and savage growl of predatory beasts in the jungle. The roaring now becomes a howling as the 'beasts' draw near their prey.

Then comes the shocking and brutal murder of Charlie the Gent, because sadly or unfortunately Charlie couldn't keep his brother Terry in order. The mob had gone too far with their killings and Charlie was no longer relevant. He had to be got rid of. The mob thinking that such a shocking act of violence would put a break on Terry's big mouth. Of course, it had the opposite effect.

Terry decides to take revenge and recklessly comes alone to Johnny Friendly's bar. After a brief spat, they engage. Friendly takes a dock worker's vicious-looking hook. Terry is able to dodge the nasty sweeps of the hook but then the others step in to collectively beat the hell out of him. They all surround him and what makes it one of the most hideous beatings I have seen on the stage is the pounding of the drum for twenty seconds. At least eight men are pounding the life out of him until he is a broken wreck of a man.

Now, I planned something rather strange and I don't really know why I did it. It's the play's end, except for a brief scene with Edie and the priest, and I ask Terry Malloy, Simon Merrells, to very slowly raise himself and get into the line-up for the curtain call. He agonisingly staggers to the back where the other actors are already standing, and they are softly egging him on. The curtain call has been made to be part of the play! The audience at first are perplexed, but on the second bow they burst into applause.

I love this play. I think it's time to do it again.

34

OEDIPUS

Edinburgh Festival 2013

I wrote my adaptation of *Oedipus* sitting in a trailer while endlessly waiting to fulfil my role in a movie called *Revolution*, directed by Hugh Hudson. While grateful for the work, I felt little for my slender role in the film, which, however, was beautifully shot. So I began my usual scrawl. I have been fascinated by the Oedipus story for many years and had written my modern version called *Greek*, which continues to be played around the world. Now I was going to write my classic version. I consulted two or three versions and then shaped it to my taste both in writing and in directing. I felt that I still had not told the full and original story, so now was an opportunity. I was sitting in a movie 'trailer', which is a place of no distractions, no commitment, no responsibility, except to shoot your brief scene which then takes forever, so you are at peace. A perfect sanctuary to write in.

I finished the play and then waited for it to marinate in my brain before beginning the terrifying task of committing it to the stage. It felt good, and I rustled up my usual subjects to act in it. Simon Merrells, with whom I had done *Waterfront*, was Oedipus. Enzo Nicoli was the scheming brother-in-law to Oedipus and Louise Jameson was Jocasta. Before we were all cast I worked with a few actors who were available, since it was a workshop, and actors came and went for the first weeks.

Actors who see, even intuitively, the value of the work, will stay … Others who have never done this kind of work before will be tempted to try it out, taste a morsel and then, feeling it too unfamiliar, will flee. Eventually, you will have your core – a little like the seven samurai, who were chosen after the less committed were tossed out.

For me the main motive for delving once more into the Oedipus legend had to be a strong sense of identification with the main character. A man somehow destined to be thwarted at every juncture. Blazing in his youth with a passion and violent temper, and yet bold and fearless in taking on and defeating dangerous adversaries. A darling of the state for defeating the loathsome Sphinx, risking his life and eventually wedding the glorious Queen Jocasta as his reward, and siring two beautiful daughters. But then some early crime comes back to haunt him even though basically in a court of law he would have been found innocent, since the killing that he was accused of was motivated in self-defence. Nevertheless, the lesson is that you cannot defeat the gods, or Fate. It has a horrible twist to it. Then the cats leap out of the bag at every juncture.

We began our workshop in a studio in Hoxton. Such times are the most exciting for me, since without a theatre to show it, without a commission, without a producer, I just went ahead and hoped for the best since there is nothing worse than waiting for the dummkopfs of our industry to smile down benevolently. I had no idea for the shape of the play but I knew that, once I started, those microscopic germs of inspiration would rise to the surface once they were called. They will not come if you just sit and brood about it.

I had as yet not found my Jocasta, so in the meantime I asked one of the group, a young, elegant and good-looking man called Chris Hogben, to read it for me. When he started reading Jocasta's lines I was simply enchanted by him. His delivery was perfect, delicate, concerned and he moved simply and beautifully without over-feminising. However, I decided to go the conventional way and found an actress. Louise did her very best and was really an ideal Jocasta, but my mind kept going back to Chris and so I made life a little difficult for her, but she eventually came through well.

Actually, my mind did keep returning to Chris Hogben, and this may have muddied the water when directing the present Jocasta. However, when I did the show for the Edinburgh Festival after Nottingham, several actors were not available and I recast Jocasta with Anita Dobson, who was equally good as Louise.

One day, when I thought that we had a goodish first act, I did invite a couple of producers in, who so very kindly offered to put an encouraging trickle of money in, but that was all. Still we forged on. I saw it in typically ensemble terms of a moving swirling chorus, and it was working, just about. However, we had discovered a genius musician in John Chambers, who created the most extraordinary soundscape which lifted the play to quite another level. He just sat with us and played as he saw fit or felt inspired … We then broke rehearsals as I had some bread and butter TV job and took off for a few weeks. But as I was away and thinking about the show I had a eureka moment.

I saw in a newspaper that was covering the Greek economic problems an image that seemed perfect. Here was a striking photo in the paper of a group of Greek men sitting at a long table, each had a typically flat working man's cap on, grizzly unshaven chins, and then I knew that I had the form, style and shape of the play. Whilst away I was so excited that I asked Matthew Cullum, who was my assistant director and company manager, to call the actors in and just start with the entire cast sitting at the table. It was perfect; they didn't just sit but draped themselves, and it was of course the perfect image of *The Last Supper* by da Vinci, which I had used for another table tableau in my production of *Messiah*. Oedipus begins the play by questioning his devoted disciples about their woe, which allows the audience to become familiar with the plot. The cast squirm, leap, beg, howl as they relate to Oedipus the horrors of the plague they are going through. Oedipus reassures them that his brother-in-law Creon is on his way from Thebes, where he has been consulting the Oracle. Creon soon arrives with his news, which at first is so good that it inspired the cast to rise from their chairs and perform a typical Greek dance. Then he joins the table and relates the story he heard from the Oracle about a murderer who slew the King and who is still at large in the Kingdom. Creon then relates the story of the meeting at the crossroads.

> *Daylight, cut down, robbers' pounding clubs*
> *It's hot, sun's blinding my eyes, the dust is rising,*
> *The horses shriek to a halt, rear, we jolt forward,*
> *Horses paw the ground, champing at the bit.*
> *Through the haze, a man, or men standing*
> *Grinning, outlined shadows, the light smacks your eyes.*
> *Breathing horses, otherwise deadly quiet,*
> *A shout, the echoes bounces off the hills,*
> *'Get back, get back or else you'll feel my wrath!'*
> *A naked blade is drawn, bright dazzling, the King's.*
> *The robbers, bandits grin, spittle shines their lips.*
> *A crow wheels in the sky, the suns behind them,*
> *Outnumbered, the clubs rise and fall, rise and fall*
> *Just like they were crackling walnuts …*
> *I turned and fled and didn't turn back to look.*

So Creon relates the story, apparently by a witness, one of the King's guards who escaped … obviously the guard is lying since King Laius was killed by only one man, and would be furious that they could not protect the King from one solitary man.

The story is so utterly descriptive that I felt it should be acted out and not just told, and so we experimented with a few ideas, even to the cast creating with their bodies horses and chariots … eventually I recalled Jean-Louis Barrault in that great 1940s film *Les Enfants du Paradis* creating a scene using just his body, and it was quite wonderful and most theatrical. So I got up and tried as best I could to demonstrate how a single man can relate an event using only his body. So my brave cast got up and tried. Eventually Anthony Barclay seemed to capture the trick of expressing the text physically while Creon speaks the words.

Naturally Anthony performs it on the table as if in a Greek taverna. It was a superb piece of storytelling!

As the dead story unravels, the Shepherd who found Oedipus as a baby put out to perish is recalled to tell his tale and all the links fall into place. Oedipus sinks further and further into the terrible web that he himself has woven. When on a second outing we had Anita Dobson play Jocasta, her wrought passion further tightened the screws. She decides to commit suicide by hanging herself. This is usually done 'offstage', or as the Greeks would say 'obscene', from whence we get that word, something that is not and never meant to be public. Of course we must do it *on* stage. This must be seen as it would in a film.

We can if we wish show the distressing scenes, which usually occur offstage, while being described very elegantly on stage. But here we combined both approaches, seeing Jocasta hanging, while her plight was beautifully described by Chris Hogben on stage.

We had Anita take a long silk scarf and wrap it slowly round her throat. She then stretches out the arm holding the scarf, and then gently sways using the ball of one foot. While doing this, a chorus member describes it in vivid detail. The image of her dying combined with Chris Hogben's text was quite electrifying, and Anita's sublime movement rendered this unforgettable. She has hung herself and the image was as perfect as it could be.

Oedipus now enters and the chorus continues to relate the dreadful story. Simon Merrells as Oedipus now enters, sees his wife, very gently unravels the scarf and sets her down. Then, having taken the pin from her scarf, stabs his eyes and falls blind onto the table, whence he retrieves a simple white mask with blacked-out eyes. He then goes into a rather overlong harangue about his guilt, his sins, his terrible pride which called for his downfall. Creon has had enough and eventually orders him out of the palace. This is done most unceremoniously by the chorus, who seize Oedipus, step back to give more thrust and almost hurl him out the door.

CREON: *'Now we have cleansed our house!'*

This demands a celebration and so, with the atmospheric music from our drummer beating out a powerful rhythm, the cast celebrate in percussive gestures, reaching an almighty climax as the scene freezes. The mighty Creon, arms outstretched and baring his great white teeth, is smiling like a smug tyrant.

Slow fade.

We played most successfully in Nottingham and then in Liverpool. Vincenzo Nicoli played Creon in both places, but when I booked the Edinburgh Festival he had another job and stepped out, so I stepped in. Quite a task to follow our wonderful Enzo. It was an enjoyable role and I quite liked it, though I wasn't in love with it. After the first week I suffered a painful back affliction and had to be operated on as soon as possible. My very capable and devoted assistant Matt Cullum, once a superb actor and now my production manager and assistant director, was able to memorise the lines swiftly and took over, apparently most successfully. He learnt the entire part in two days and went on without the book. I'll call him 'Braveheart'.

We were unable to get anywhere to have us in London, regrettably, and so the play was put to sleep until the following year when we were invited to North Carolina to a charming place called Charleston, where of course President Lincoln was assassinated.

Sadly, very, very sadly, we have never had the opportunity to show this play in London, which is a great pity, for I do believe that it was one of our most inventive and well-acted productions. Still, there is time …

35

THE HAIRY APE

The Odyssey Theatre, Los Angeles 2015

This is a play I have been wanting to do my whole life. It is Eugene O'Neill's howl of passion from the very depths of his soul … Maybe his paean to the gods. It is a shipboard romance like no other. I have never read anything like it before or since, and no playwright can possibly compete with this most astonishing work. It is inspiring. It touched me deeply, since I could see myself writ large. A *cri de cœur* for the common man. And of course in our feeble, middle-class, middle-of-the-road theatre, it is seldom if ever done.

It seemed to cling to me over the years, and then over the decades it remained in the chambers of memory, like a ghost just waiting to be summoned up and impatient with me for not heeding it. But at last, I did, I had to, I could no longer wait. Yank, the protagonist in *The Hairy Ape*, was written as if brimstone were burning in the soul of O'Neill, and it spoke to me over and over again. I just had to let it out and allow it to burn up on stage. As usual, our feeble caretakers of theatre had little time for this masterpiece and so rejected it. Once again I had to do it myself. Fortunately I had an ally in Los Angeles, the Odyssey Theatre, who wanted my work and were always enthusiastic to embrace me.

During an early fallow period, myself and a few actors decided to hold workshops each weekend above a pub called The Camden Head in Camden Passage, Islington. Bruce Miles, an actor I had worked with at the Citizens Theatre, Glasgow, and an Aussie export, had encouraged it. I recall the very first day of the workshop – as I walked up the stairs to the first-floor studio, I said to Bruce, who was just in front of me, 'My heart is trembling with excitement!' We all decided to perform pieces from our favourite plays. Having just read *The Hairy Ape*, I chose to do a piece from the explosive character nicknamed 'Yank'. The language was awe-inspiring, I felt no British writer could ever begin to rival this. I thought that one day I would attempt to do this masterpiece. Although I tried to interest producers, it was made more difficult by the fact that there had been a production in London a few years earlier!

The time had come, and I once more flew to Los Angeles to begin work. Many weeks were spent trying to cast the damn thing, but most of the actors were just not up to it, and betrayed their ineptitude all too easily when trying to tackle the great sinewy language.

Initially one has a limited choice of actors who are willing to do what in LA is called a 'showcase'. So, after going through the grind and filtering out the dross, you eventually find your group.

Eventually, after a month of auditions, I found a willing and able group of rough and keen actors headed by Yank, who I decided should be played by a black actor.

He just seemed to fit. As a black actor representing the struggle of black people in the 1920s, Haïlé D'Alan identified with the outsider status of Yank. Yank is a simple man with extraordinary aspirations, and with his undiluted power leads the group by example. 'Soul' is what reeks out of Yank. When it was done decades ago in America, the legendary black singer Paul Robeson played Yank. This young man Haïlé D'Alan gave one of the most exciting auditions I had heard, and I knew from his first reading that this man was born to play the role. He was powerfully built, with a dynamic presence, and I knew that, with him, we were certainly on our way. During the early workshop process, we were still weeding out those whose lack of commitment was revealed after two or three sessions. Now that we had found our cast, I told them what I felt about the play and they all concurred. I made the point, albeit with humour, that they should approach this project as if their lives depended on it, as if this were the last thing they would ever do on stage. They all responded with great glee to the challenge. After all, this was no ordinary play. For me, I did feel that my life depended on it, so I would not even begin to do it unless I was sure of my band of soldiers. Haïlé D'Alan made a small speech to me that certainly carried his conviction in the project. He said he would certainly give everything he had in the service of Eugene O'Neill and to me. I was much touched by his confession.

I decided the stage would be open and bare, slightly raked, with a ramp on one side, which would come into use for the scene in the zoo when Yank meets his tragic end in the arms of a huge gorilla.

Scene One: We are introduced to the stokers in their living domain, the bowels of a great ship. They are released from the engine room, where they spend their hours piling coal into the giant ovens. Now they are free, an abandoned, drinking, shouting, jostling, mock-fighting mob, all in a frenzy. The human beast at play. Their voices are quick, percussive roars. I knew that this scene must hook the audience from the beginning, and beginnings of plays are terribly important, but they must be able to understand the broken text.

We worked many hours on this opening, until they became a highly fluid mob, throwing and catching beer bottles, spinning, dancing, jumping, crawling into each other's arms until Yank comes in and, like a great alpha male, dominates the scene. He is a force to be reckoned with, and all of them must adjust their moves to his presence. When he moves, he eats up the stage. When he's excited and begins one of the great arias of the play, he is magnetic. When he rebukes one of the old-time workers, who complains about the heat and the dirt, and the stench of the coal room, he declares that he is a piece of the ship, he is the coal, he is the steel plate, the steam, the pumping engines and is proud to be so. He is exalted by his position, as one who keeps 'this old tub alive'. It is one of the great speeches in all modern drama, but perhaps means a lot more if you've been a worker, a common labourer, when you can really identify with him.

> *Say, listen to me – wait a moment – I gotter talk, see. I belong and he don't. He's dead but I'm livin'. Listen to me! Sure I'm part of de engines! Why de hell not! Dey move, don't dey? Dey're speed, ain't dey? Dey smash trou, don't dey? Twenty-five knots a hour! Dat's goin' some! Dat's new stuff! Dat belongs! But him, he's too old. He gets dizzy. Say, listen. All dat crazy tripe about nights and days; all dat crazy tripe about stars and moons; all dat crazy tripe about suns and winds, fresh air and de rest of it – Aw hell, dat's all a dope dream! Hittin' de pipe of de past, dat's what he's doin'. He's old and don't belong no more. But me, I'm young! I'm in de pink! I move wit it! It, get me! I mean de ting dat's de guts of all dis. It ploughs trou all de tripe he's been sayin'. It blows dat up! It knocks dat dead! It slams dat off en de face of de oith! It, get me! De engines and de coal and de smoke and all de rest of it! He can't breathe and swallow coal dust, but I kin, see? Dat's fresh air for me! Dat's food for me! I'm new, get me? Hell in de stokehole? Sure! It takes a man to work in hell. Hell, sure, dat's my fav'rite climate. I eat it up! I git fat on it! It's me makes it hot! It's me makes it roar! It's me makes it move! Sure, on'y for me everyting stops. It all goes dead, get me? De noise and smoke and all de engines movin' de woild, dey stop. Dere ain't nothin' no more! Dat's what I'm sayin'. Everyting else dat makes de woild move, somep'n makes it move. It can't move witout somep'n else, see? Den yuh get down to me. I'm at de bottom, get me! Dere ain't nothin' foither. I'm de end! I'm de start! I start somep'n and de woild moves! It – dat's me! – de new dat's moiderin' de old! I'm de ting in coal dat makes it boin; I'm steam and oil for de engines; I'm de ting in noise dat makes yuh hear it; I'm smoke and express trains and steamers and factory whistles; I'm de ting in gold dat makes it money! And I'm what makes iron into steel! Steel, dat stands for de whole ting! And I'm steel – steel – steel! I'm de muscles in steel, de punch behind it!*

This is male force in all its magnificent glory and he revels in it. He is so proud of his physical power, as if it were God-given. As Haïlé performs his speech, he uses the stage so freely. The group follow him almost like a flock of birds, crouch by him, in all positions of support, all ready to support his needs, to be his very willing disciples.

Now we accompany all of this with a well-paced drum that follows and amplifies the strength and character of the group, the combustion of their moves ... The more we rehearse, the greater the cohesion of the company, they are turning onto a magnificent ensemble! For the beginning of the piece, I had all the actors exploding onto the stage, but then I decided that it was maybe just a little too contrived, too noisy for its own sake, and decided to change it. We dragged two, long, low benches on stage. I suddenly felt that we should start slowly and quietly and then erupt. So

I asked them just to walk on quietly, in the attitude of their character, and slowly sit on their benches. Let the audience see what you are like. Let them see how awesome you look, grubby, tattooed and simply menacing. It was perfect.

So, for the first moment, they just sat there to be examined, scrutinised, both admired and slightly feared. The drum let out an almighty thwack and they were off. Now there is a meeting of two worlds as the old sailor, the last of the coal stokers, in a very moving speech, remembers the great old days of sailing ships, steering by the stars with the wind in your face and the pungent, sweet smell of the sea in your nostrils. This holds their attention for a while as the group sway to the nostalgic memories of the past. Then the new, brutal world of Yank rips into his elegy, with all the passion of the new industrial world of smoke and engines and coal. The old world and the new. After Yank's brilliant castigation they all move off the stage like stooped, muscle-bound men; they resemble apes.

Now we see two most elegant ladies, occupying the stage, sitting comfortable on the deck taking in the sea breeze, the sparkling spray and the fresh air. The younger woman is with her guardian, her aunt, they are on a sightseeing trip to Europe, where the young woman plans to introduce herself by some self-consciously virtuous actions, by going down to the East End's Whitechapel and seeing what she can do to aid the poor and depressed homeless and unemployed while dressed in the most expensive silks. She warbles on about how she wants to do some good in the world. Her aunt of course mocks her self-conscious virtue signalling. For a start, the niece wishes to see the ship's vast engine room, where the workers pile coal into the roaring ovens. A young, well-attired officer offers to escort her down.

Now we enter the bowels of the ship. I eschewed the idea of building giant ovens and merely rigged a barrage of powerful red lights illuminating the stokers as they pile the coal in. They are stripped, muscled and gleaming like marble sculptures, and in unison taking their shovels and pouring the coal in. I even decided to do it without the shovels, I just wanted the men to mime the whole process from stooping, thrusting their arms down into the coal, slowly lifting the heavy coal onto their shovels and then hurling it into the open mouths of the oven and all in semi-unison like a huge multi-limbed beast.

They begin, at first one at a time, until they are all heaving, thrusting, bending, howling, groaning and shouting. Whilst they are doing this, Yank suddenly becomes aware that the stokers around him are gradually ceasing their work. The naval officer escorts his young passenger into the ship's bowels for a glimpse of the lower orders … Yank goes into one of his animalistic rages, which is awesome to behold. Unbeknown to him the niece, sheltered behind the officer, is watching all this with a mixture of fascination and sheer horror. Yank now turns and sees her … They stare at each other for a few seconds, while she, frozen now in fear, can do nothing except give vent to the monstrous thing she has just seen by shouting 'Oh! The filthy beast!'

The poor woman then passes out, having never witnessed anything like this before in her precious, protected life. Yank cannot help but brood on the insult the young lady has given him and feels as if she has passed some stain to him, some insult that cannot be washed away.

Now in the next act he has been discharged and is idly wandering around New York City, astounded by the sights, the people and the stores with all their useless and expensive baubles. He is out of his natural environment, which is the ship and his co-workers. On Fifth Avenue people avoid him as if he is not there, and don't even acknowledge that he exists, but are aware enough of him to call the police, who swiftly come dressed in their blue bobby hats and armed with billy clubs and beat him to the ground.

Where can he go? He is 'Yank', a confused, simple-minded beast with no home and no human contact. Even the Worker's Union, into whose office he stumbles seeking a connection, throws him out, since they feel that he is far too violent and might harm their cause. Yank then makes a heart-rending plea to the moon, expressing his suffering and most of all his confusion as to why he is never accepted. Eventually he wanders over to Central Park, where he suddenly hears the roaring of lions and, investigating further, finds the zoo. He wanders idly in. Now this is the climax of the piece as only O'Neill could do it.

He is drawn to the chattering of the monkey house. Now our group of actors are absolutely ready for anything. The projection on a large screen at the back of the theatre is of course of Rousseau's painting of the jungle. The chattering gets louder and on the ramp are assembled all the actors bar one, as wild chattering monkeys, shrieking, jumping up and down with excitement, beating their chests as they see this human monster before them. They almost appear to laugh at him.

The scene is all the more remarkable for the fact that our brilliant ensemble created it in seconds. I merely said that we need you now to be monkeys on the ramp, reacting to the presence of Yank. They immediately leapt onto the ramp without a moment's hesitation and before my very eyes became a family of wild, chattering simians. I laughed at their audacity, their keenness, their abundant enthusiasm. In fact I almost wanted to cry … Now the monkeys flee since coming up just behind them is a mighty ape.

I thought long and hard about this and decided that it had to be played by one of our team, and fortunately we did have a mighty large member of our group who could do it and do it well. His name was Jeremiah O'Brien, and he really needed no animal head or feet, although we did briefly try them. He came on just in a pair of black briefs and nothing else except for a pair of black leather gloves which seemed appropriate. The ape was him. He had studied via video ape-like moves and was as perfect as he could be. Yank sees this great creature behind its bars, staring at him. And then, suddenly, Yank feels a strange bond between them. There is a spark of connection. Yank feels he has found a fellow compatriot, a like-minded soul locked up, imprisoned in a way like Yank is. Imprisoned by society, unable to escape. Yank slowly unlocks the cage and lets the great beast out!

The ape leaps down from his cage and just stares at Yank in puzzlement. Yank greets him like some long-lost cousin. He speaks to the ape, who just stares back dumbly. Eventually, Yank extends his hand in a way of greeting his new friend. The ape just stares at it, but then slowly takes the extended arm. He draws Yank to him and almost lifts him off his feet and crushes him. As his ribs are cracking, Yank still has the same old insane spirit to whisper with his dying breath 'Hey, I didn't ask you to kiss me!' Yank's last words sadly confirm that he is still alone, even the gorilla didn't accept him. He dies.

The play opened to the best reviews one could hope for. Many of them were eulogies. I could not have been more proud of this group of actors who gave so much of their lives to it and with such energy. For this rehearsal period, they had worked for absolutely nothing!! I felt that all of these guys were now my friends, like Yank, I had bonded with my brothers and sisters. Maybe there is a bit, or more than a bit, of Yank in me, yet I also think there could be a bit of Yank in all of us. Probably that's why I had such a strong connection with O'Neill's masterpiece.

One day I hope to do this play in the UK. Rather sadly, this is a seldom-performed play since most producers and actors connect more to the ever-whining humans and their griefs in *Long Day's Journey into Night*. They are not so turned on by plays about 'apes', even human ones.

So, my thanks to
Haïlé D'Alan
Paul Stanko
Joseph Gilbert
Jeremiah O'Brien
Andres Paul Ramacho
Anthony Rutowicz
Benjamin Davies
Katy Davis
Jennifer Taub
Dennis Gersten
Christopher Scott Murillo – Scenic Designer
Christopher Moscatiello – Sound Designer
Will Mahood – Percussionist
Savannah Harrow – Stage Manager, Associate Producer
Katelan Braymer – Lighting
Beth Hogan – Producer

36

ACTORS I HAVE ADMIRED, LOVED AND EVEN CRIED OVER

Patricia Neal

I was just in my early twenties when a playwright called Ian Dallas took me in hand to awake my consciousness for theatre. I am so grateful to him. He took me to see *Suddenly Last Summer* at the small Arts Theatre in the West End with Patricia Neal in the starring role of this most shocking and terrifying of Tennessee Williams' plays. Patricia Neal played a woman who had witnessed the brutal murder of her poet husband. He was massacred by a group of starving street children, who then went on to cannibalise him! The poet's over-adoring mother has her committed, since she cannot believe the story she has told and is considering having her lobotomised.

During the play, Patricia Neal is obliged to recount the story to the examining psychiatrist. She does this, and I confess this was one of the most harrowing performances I had ever seen. Under just one bare lightbulb she goes through the gruesome details in this most extraordinary of plays. I have never forgotten that impressive performance. When the film came out, with Elizabeth Taylor taking over her role, I was more than sorry that the film company could not use Patricia Neal. Poor Miss Taylor was only just adequate.

I have always loved this remarkable actress, having hitherto seen her only in films, but even just on screen she was outstanding, especially in the film *The Fountainhead*, based on Ayn Rand's remarkable book. In the book, the architect played immensely well in the film by Garry Cooper is a man who cannot and will not compromise. His personal aesthetic is to create unique buildings according to his own principles and not be curtailed by popular taste. His structures are wild, ambitious and totally daring. Hence his work is seldom demanded by the purveyors of mass taste – sounds familiar?

One day, as he was observing work on a building site, he comes across one of his chief critics, an overbearing man of low abilities, who had helped destroy the architect's career. They meet and the critic tries at least to establish a modus vivendi. The critic says, in a rather jovial manner, 'I don't suppose you care for me much, do you Mr Roarke?' To which the architect replies 'Not at all, I have never read you.'

A perfect answer. When I first saw this film in my teens I was strongly influenced by it, and I tried to make the architect's credo my own.

Zero Mostel

Now, by coincidence, at the same theatre a short while later I was taken to see *Ulysses in Nighttown*, based on James Joyce's *Ulysses* and adapted and directed by Burgess Meredith ... What an explosion of a production, and light years from anything else available to be seen in London. What made it such an astounding experience, apart from the staging, was the great titan of American theatre, Zero Mostel. He was such a great monster of a man, whose sweating face and huge head was covered by a comb-over. Those few black hairs perfectly suited the character, and he acted with an aplomb and energy which were inspiring.

I don't think London had seen anything like him, and I admired him greatly, for, fat as he was, he moved with the delicacy of a ballet dancer. He shone in whatever film he was in, and I was most impressed by the roles he chose. He always played the wretched outsider as in a Woody Allen film, where he was a stand-up comic who was seldom employed since he had been exposed as a communist. No matter how great his talent, he was condemned to perform in out-of-the-way dumps in the Catskills, loathsome summer resorts. Woody Allen plays the 'front' and uses his own name as a cover for those black-listed by the right-wing commie-bashers. Zero's death at the end of the film is terribly moving, and only an actor of his depth could do it. Before he commits suicide, he gives the waiter who has brought up his final drink a large tip. At the end we just see the open window with curtains gently fluttering in the wind. Oh my god, did I identify with him!

Laurence Olivier

Olivier seemed to affect me as a neophyte actor almost more than any other player on stage. I had been watching him closely for years, mainly in films, where his captivating voice rang in my young ears as the finest music and his rising crescendos in *Henry the Fifth* thrilled me as no other actor has ever done. Who can hear his great and rousing exaltation to inspire his troops whilst on a horse and crying out 'God for Harry, England and St George ... Geooooooorge!' without being stirred? One would go through fire for him. I first saw the great man live at The Royal Court Theatre in Ionesco's *Rhinoceros*, which Orson Welles directed. As Bérenger he was superb at playing the underdog, which he did with such care and skill as if to show that he can still soar in the opposite direction to his superheroes. I still recall Orson Welles standing just behind me in the dress circle cueing the lights, since he had not yet completed them before the first night.

But it was on seeing Olivier as Othello that I was totally struck dumb. He had played in this role at The Old Vic for a short season and now was opening at the Chichester Festival Theatre. The entire run was of course sold out. Every paper had saluted his performance as one of the theatrical wonders of the twentieth century. It just so happened that I was playing in a TV production of *Crime and Punishment* and was working with one of Olivier's close acting allies, Esmond Knight.

Esmond was one of the old-school English actors. He was badly wounded during the war, which left him half blind, but he continued his acting career. I mentioned how much I admired Olivier, who was about to open in a season at Chichester.

To my astonishment he offered to get me tickets! 'Just say you're going with me.' This I swiftly did, and since I was free the next day I was able to see his perform-ance. With my girlfriend at the time, Anne, I boarded the train for Chichester at Victoria station. All this was accompanied by a tremendous sense of expectation. When arriving at the box office and requesting my tickets I had to lie and say unfor-tunately Esmond Knight was unable to come tonight as he was still in rehearsal for the TV play we were both doing. A sour-faced manager eyed me most suspiciously, but there was nothing he could do and we were guided to our most congenial seats not too far from the front of the stage, which was, as I remember, a thrust. We then heard through the speakers 'Ladies and gentlemen, would you please take your seats, as the curtain will rise in three minutes' time.' That was a voice like no other. Of course, it was Olivier's. He had recorded his voice for the warnings to the theatre-goers. We sat and waited. There was such an air of high excitement that was palpably felt by the entire audience. I saw the critic Bernard Levin sitting a couple of rows down, as this was Olivier's first night in Chichester. Once again, Olivier's dulcet tones rang out, warning patrons that the curtain would rise in one minute's time.

I was even nervous for him since I felt such a bond with the great man. Such enormous anticipation from the world out there for everything he did. The lights were lowered and the house was hushed. The silence was so great that you might have been forgiven for thinking that the house was empty. After the initial scene with Iago and his foolish opportunist Roderigo, when he provokes Brabantio with sordid tales about his daughter Desdemona, we come to Othello's entrance. From out of the darkened stage at the back of the theatre and slowly coming into the light strode Olivier.

The house was even beyond silent now, for now they were witnessing one of the great acting masters of the western world. He sloped in, walking very casually with a slight what you might call African walk from the hips. He was beautiful in his brilliant white costume, which contrasted so greatly with his brown painted limbs and face. We were hushed, and then he spoke the first lines to Iago ''Tis better as it is,' and his voice had been lowered at least by a whole octave. It was deep without any strain, and while he spoke he so very gently he waved a long red rose that he had entered with, occasionally raising it to his nose for a casual sweet inhalation. Breathtaking.

A scene later he is making his justification to his interrogator. Relating how his wooing won her, 'Her father loved me, oft invited me, still questioned me the story of my life,' a very long monologue which he performed effortlessly and which included some sly humour. By now we were all totally enchanted, but of course it is when the play progresses and Iago sows those little poisonous seeds of doubt that the play begins to cause pain.

It is when Iago begins so cunningly to drip his poison into Othello's ears that we see moment by moment the insidious effect that Iago's vile concoction has on Othello. Slowly, oh so slowly, we watch with chilling fascination Othello's face gradually change until he can bear it no more and, like a provoked bull, Olivier erupts. He erupts like no man has ever seen or is likely to see again. Frightening, pathetic and terrifying all at once. And as he begins his tormented dirge …

> *Farewell the tranquil mind, farewell content!*
> *Farewell the plumed troop and the big wars*
> *That make ambition virtue! Oh farewell!*
> *Farewell the neighing steed and the shrill trump,*
> *The spirit stirring drum, the ear piercing fife.*

Olivier doesn't merely announce his bitterness that his life from this point on is slipping away from him, he chooses to enact it, as if sadistically thrilling himself with the thought of his glorious demise. His vocal chords are stretched to the limit, making sounds unheard of in our modern age of restraint, but here we hear the sound of the fife as he raises his voice to enact it whilst his body twists and turns, totally uninhibited, not only releasing his fury, but indulging it. We watch silently, stunned, hardly breathing, as if watching a living sacrifice, and then when the great master reaches those incredible words Olivier feasts on them like a raging beast.

> *Like to the pontic sea,*
> *Whose icy current and compulsive course*
> *Nere feels retiring ebb but keeps due on*
> *To the Propontic and the Hellespont*
> *Even do my bloody thoughts, with violent pace*
> *Shall nere look back, nere ebb to humble love*
> *Till that a capable and wide revenge*
> *Swallow them up …*

Olivier has this rare ability to ignite fires within his soul that we can scarcely imagine and yet still he keeps up this energetic response to the drug that Iago has delivered and doesn't let up, he has become narcoticised and now cannot step back to reflect a moment. It would seem that, in some ways, Othello's vanity and pride are far too receptive to noxious thoughts and he cannot step back and yet, what Olivier does so profoundly when he reflects of Desdemona … 'So delicate with her needle! An admirable musician' … for just a few seconds the great beast crumbles, his voice adopts a soft, pleading tone almost on the verge of tears until Iago, seeing that he might lose his impetus rushes in to say 'She is the worse for all this …'

We see this poor man just perched on the edge of a chasm, almost wanting to be toppled back into the familiar warmth and comfort of his former life. But with each yearning to be relieved of this monster in his head Iago sticks him with barbs until the great bull collapses. I recall that night so well, and as the light dimmed on the first act the entire audience was in a state of shock. Nobody clapped, not a soul could even speak. After what we had just witnessed it felt that speech was empty. What could we say after that, that didn't sound small and puny. 'Shall we go for a drink?' After a couple of moments the audience slowly shuffled to their feet and discovered a sense of who they were.

By the end of the play we, the audience, are both traumatised by what we see an actor is capable of and at the same time thrilled to have witnessed this sacrifice, for that is what great theatre is in some way … A sacrifice. We travelled back on the train to Victoria, our minds so full of what we had seen. We had changed, we had been enlivened. It is rumoured that in the gentle green swathes of Chichester, ageing spectators who had lived their later years in peaceful celibate calm had that night felt some strange and mysterious fire ignite their loins. I even felt it myself.

Alec McCowen

I saw him play Mercutio in Zeffirelli's stunning Italianate *Romeo and Juliet* at The Old Vic. In fact, his performance was so daring, so alert that it had the effect of making Romeo look rather awkward and underwhelming. How hard for a Romeo to be playing on the same stage as McCowen! McCowen had trained his voice until it had achieved a piercing brilliance so that when he spoke he actually gave you even more than the lines themselves.

I had not long left drama school when I had to see Zeffierelli's production of *Romeo and Juliet* at The Old Vic Theatre. The production was very atmospheric, the curtain opening onto an amber-lit, dusty market street in Verona, with carts laden with fruit being pulled or pushed, crowds jostling each other and noisy street performers, pure commedia dell'arte. Quite wonderful.

However, in spite of the star-crossed lovers being quite adequately played by John Stride and a young early Judi Dench, it was when I heard the startling, ringing tones of Alec McCowen that I knew I was in the presence of an actor of immense talent. His voice had that piercing English tone which had just a touch of Tunbridge Wells about it, brilliantly articulated and so intense that lines just leapt into your ear like darts. He became the lines and marshalled his voice to serve Shakespeare in a way that very few actors could.

He was also compelling to watch; in fact, not only you could you not take your eyes off this small, lithe figure, but he seemed unfortunately to obliterate any actors who came within his sphere. So Romeo and Juliet seemed to fade before your eyes and their emotional blathering carried no real importance, since when McCowen was on stage he just amplified the play. I started actually to feel for the other actors.

McCowen had such a delivery it felt like he was preaching to you from a pulpit. He actually went on to learn the gospel according to Saint Mark and performed it as if he were a spectator at the time, relating the event with tremendous enthusiasm.

Many years later he actually came to my own one-man show that I did at the Garrick Theatre. He wrote to me expressing his pleasure with my show, and we became friends, if only as far as witnessing each other's shows and exchanging many letters. He seemed to be forever young, although he died a short time ago. He is much missed.

Robert Hirsch

I first came across the great French actor Robert Hirsch of the Comédie Française in my last year of drama school. The Comédie Française was appearing in London as part of the celebrated world theatre season that was then a yearly occurrence. It was masterminded by the great impresario Donald Albery, and it was the season of the most celebrated companies in the world that fired my excitement for theatre above all else. For here you could see some great companies who were to perform for at least a week at the Aldwych Theatre in the West End. The Comédie needed extras for one of their productions for the crowd scene in the Feydeau farce *Un fil à la patte*, or *Cat among the Pigeons*. A tremendous opportunity for me to actually see the Comédie Française close up. About a dozen or so students turned up, and the director Jacques Charon put us through our paces and instructed us how we had to burst into the living room, where I believe a wedding was being celebrated. It was beyond thrilling to be this close to this legendary company. They all looked so elegant, and the women were so beautiful, that it made me feel we Brits were just like country bumpkins.

For the afternoon dress rehearsal I sat in the stalls, since our crowd scene came much later in the play. Suddenly I saw this extraordinary apparition make his entrance. He was just descending the stairs and I can swear that I had never seen anything like it in my entire life. Robert Hirsch had a physical flexibility that was awesome to behold. With a ridiculous makeup of a simple doddering man he made an entrance that was so absurd, so ridiculous that by the time the actor had descended the stairs, the audience gave him a huge ovation before he had even begun to speak. I was also astounded by his delivery. He played the role of Bouzin in one of Feydeau's most famous comedies.

After I had played, or rather appeared, with the company for the run, I did manage to briefly speak to Robert Hirsch on the last night as he was ascending the stairs after the curtain call. I told him that I was amazed by his skill and bravura performance and that it had inspired me as a young actor to be as brave as he was. 'Oh, thank you,' he answered, 'so very kind of you,' in of course perfect English, and Alain Feydeau, who was the grandson of the playwright George Feydeau and was standing nearby, immediately asked me to join them at the famous Rules restaurant which was just around the corner in Covent Garden. I did so, and thence began my friendship with the Comédie Française.

Some years later Alain Feydeau was visiting London and I took him to his grandfather's play, which was now being performed in English at The Old Vic. Albert Finney was playing the role of Bouzin that Robert Hirsch played in the original production. And it felt like I was seeing a completely different work. While Finney was an excellent actor, he was not a farceur.

Robert Hirsch died just two years ago. I felt privileged to have seen this quite amazing man.

Marcel Marceau

I first saw this magician of movement in London at the Palace Theatre when I was about twenty and I was, like most people, enchanted by this astonishing manipulator of gravity, for indeed he did seem to float before your eyes. His face was painted like a doll, and atop his head was a barbarous bundle of hair. This was art, this was theatre, this was drama at the very highest level, and nobody could even begin to rival him. This was art, and in his dazzling white pantomime costume he was as perfect a human figure as I had ever seen.

But from where did this originate? And what had Marceau seen that had sowed the seeds of desire to turn himself into a moving artwork? I know that he trained with Charles Dullin and Étienne Decroux early in his career, before eventually devising his own one-man show. Decroux was still alive and teaching at his private studio on the outskirts of Paris in 1965, since I attended one of his classes and I have never forgotten it. A group of young students sat at one side of the room as the audience. He then simply gave a one-word title to what you are then asked to perform, i.e. preparation, hunger, desire, fear, boredom. He then asked for a volunteer to come and perform. Within a few seconds, two young students leapt onto the stage. Of course they were already highly trained by the master. They begin. It was stunning and the whole room was deathly silent. The students moved without effort, but with immense concentration as they read each other's gestures and each find the apposite response. I watched spellbound. It was unlike anything I had ever seen. But in spite of this, I then volunteered. I performed 'preparation'. I moved painfully slowly and froze until a movement came out of me and then froze again as if uncertain whether that was the right way. To my astonishment he then praised me and held me up for special attention, commenting on how the changes of mind and uncertainty were clearly expressed in the movement.

When I saw Marceau, his *The Cage* performance was an extension to what he might have learned with Decroux. A man is walking (*marche sur place*). He comes to a barrier and can move no further. But then he discovers a door. Much relieved, he opens the door, but then finds himself in another room, a smaller room, and he continues his journey, but soon enough he finds another door. Again he manages to open that door, the next room is considerably smaller than the last. Now he is crouched and he attempts once more to find the opening. He does, but the last room is smaller still and he can no longer move but still manages to open the smaller door, albeit with great effort. He does this, and can only just arduously thrust his arm out, then he expires. These works are unique and highly symbolic of the condition of the human race, which continually attempts to escape from one situation only to trap themselves into something much worse. We can't escape.

The mask maker. A man is making masks and, as he nimbly finishes one, he thrusts it onto his face, which immediately freezes into the position, and then just as swiftly takes it off and returns to his own flexible human face/expressive face. He then takes another mask, and with a swift movement of his hand slaps it on his face once more. A completely different face now appears, perhaps comic. He struts around with this new expression firmly in place and then once more, using both hands, peels it off. He is enjoying his work. In fact he seems to relish it to the extent that he now plays with the differing masks, throwing each one on for a few seconds and then changing them. So Marcel's amazing, pliable face is doing all of the work. Now he comes back to the comic mask once more, but this time as he attempts to pluck it off his face, he can't. It has become stuck! He attempts vainly to peel it off, and with great effort puffs and pants, twisting his body this way and that, but the comic mask remains ... He twists again, crashes to his knees, does everything to remove the mask, but he can't. A tragedy is unfolding before us as he grins maniacally as the comic mask which now won't leave him. The horror that it may never leave him is now almost a certainty, is he dying, trapped by that monstrous mask that he has created? Then, just as we are giving up all hope, he peels it off. The relief in Marceau's beautiful face is immense. He looks at the masks, but will not play with them again. I had never seen anything quite as astounding in my life, and of course this made me all the more determined to attempt to learn the great magician's tricks.

37

FINAL CHAPTER

It was 1947 and the Second World War was well and truly over. We had been evacuated to Luton to avoid the bombs, since we were living in the East End of London. Most of Ma's relations, including her brother and sister, had emigrated to New York in the twenties, as did she. But Pa got lonely for his family, as they were all still in the East End, so she obligingly returned, back to London, but she missed New York badly. I had not yet been born. I came to life in Luton more or less, although I do remember the bombs being dropped. The horrific wail of the sirens, like a huge wounded dinosaur, and going to shelters in Whitechapel Underground station. That's when we were evacuated to Luton. When the war was over, all I heard from Ma was 'We're going to America.' America, America was all I heard. I certainly had a taste for it, since Ma's relations were always sending big food parcels over with half a dozen comics especially for me. I loved those comics. Loved the stories, the colours and especially the smell. That smelled of America for me.

Well, one day, the big moment had arrived and we were destined to go and we went, without Dad of course. He had things to do, deals or whatever to wind up, and when he had done all those mysterious things he would jump on the Queen Elizabeth and join us. Promise. Yes, we had, my sister included, all sailed on the Queen Elizabeth, the very first one of the Queens. It was an adventure above and beyond anything I had ever experienced. When we were driven to the docks at Southampton, I saw this huge wall in front of me, which I took to be some giant warehouse until I learned that it was the side of the ship.

Once on, Ma and I shared a two-tiered cabin and Beryl, my sister, had to share with someone else, since of course we were in tourist class. So the ship was one colossal adventure of my life and I explored the labyrinthine bowels of this magnificent ship from morning till night. Eventually we arrived and mum's family were waiting for us. We had arrived at dawn and the morning was just beginning to lighten up and I saw the huge scrapers of New York's Manhattan in front of me! It was a dream, it was a miracle, it was a fantasy. In fact I thought I was in a movie and half expected Captain Marvel to fly over the city to welcome us.

It took some hours to disembark. We had one great trunk and bits and bobs. And we didn't require it during the voyage. Eventually we trod down the gangplank into the waiting arms and weeping eyes of my aunties as they hugged mum and met me for the first time in their lives. I slid into the back seat to where my aunty Doris was seated, and she took from her bag a Hershey bar. This was the first time I ever tasted that almondy crunch. I was happy, oh so happy. I was in heaven. I was in America.

We were driven to the Bronx, a gutsy racial mishmash of a borough, and as we got out of the car to enter my aunt's apartment I saw coming excitedly towards us Pearl, her daughter. She was carrying some groceries for our evening welcome, in one of those large brown paper bags I had seen so often in the American movies that we virtually lived on in Luton. The food and chatter that evening were both unforgettable. It was inevitable that after devouring strawberry ice cream for the first time I should return it all to the toilet bowl.

Next day my dear cousin Morris, the daughter of mum's sister, my aunt Ray, drove us to their lovely but modest middle-class home in upper New York called Nyack. Nyack is full of those charming washboard houses and white picket fences and sleeps contentedly by the giant Hudson River. Aunt Ray poured me a cold glass of milk as soon as we arrived. Wow. It really was icy cold and the very first time I had experienced anything from a fridge; in Luton we were unfamiliar with such luxuries.

Cousin Morris had what was commonly known then as a drug store, which was a mixture of dry goods, medicines and useful bric-a-brac for the house. But at one end of the shop was a very appealing snack bar. A shortish bar on the left side as you entered, with half a dozen tall stools, a counter and two "coloured" girls ready to wait on you. It was charming beyond belief. I was allowed to use it just once during the day and order whatever I wanted. I was certainly in paradise.

But what cousin Morris did next was entirely beyond any dreams I had. He took me to the men's clothing store opposite the drug store and had me fitted out, with not just one but two glorious suits! And to top it all, the suits were accompanied by long trousers! I was utterly beside myself. Each morning as I got up with Morris to accompany him to work, I slipped into my long pants and felt like a young man. I had left childhood behind. That was an old, dull period sleeping quietly in Luton.

Next I heard, for the first time, a name that I would hear again and again. When we got home that evening aunty Ray had complained that one of Helen Hayes' dogs had barked furiously at her as she walked into town. Helen Hayes herself had rushed out of the house and apologised to her. It seemed quite important to her that it was one of Helen Hayes' dogs that was responsible. I later learned that Helen Hayes was a famous Broadway star. In fact Miss Hayes was known as 'the First Lady of the American Theatre', born in October 1900 and dying in Nyack on the 17 March 1993. So the grand old lady spent over half a century in Nyack, New York.

So, it being 1947 when her dog barked at aunt Ray, Miss Helen Hayes would have been forty-seven. Soon enough this brief idyll was over and we were driven back to the Bronx to an address I would never ever forget, simply because America was to be torn away from me too shockingly soon. However, for now we were ensconced in my uncle Joe Hyman's old-fashioned Victorian house, on 308 East, 173rd Street. Joe let rooms to a regular bunch of working-class lodgers, for whom the house was not just a sanctuary but a cosy community. That afternoon after we arrived, Joe showed us our lodging on the very top floor, the attic, in fact, where we shared the space with a hospital janitor called Chris. His room was on the back side of the building while ours was on the front facing the street. We shared a tiny kitchen and one toilet. For baths we would go downstairs and use uncle Joe's. Joe mostly hung out in the large living room on the ground floor. He had a record player, which I found simply fascinating, and I played over and over again 'Peg o' My Heart', I seemed to be very attracted to that. Joe was a great grizzly old sport, who had once emigrated to New Zealand and served in the Armed Forces. Then he worked on the New York waterfront as a docker, but now he seemed to be in retirement. His wife, my aunt Alice, wore her hair piled high in what might be called 'Lynch' mode after the director's famous first film *Eraserhead*, where the hero has his hair piled high and flat-topped. Eerie.

Now at that particular time I was taken to the local school, P.S. 70, which was just a block up the road, I was speedily becoming an American citizen. My teacher was a very kindly and civil man called Mr Rich, and I really liked the classes, since they seemed to be a term or two behind England, which gave me the opportunity to catch up on my maths, which was awful in Luton. Once at school, first thing in the morning we would all assemble in the gym and do the rounds of the gym floor, doing exercises such as pull-ups, as many as we could, no fewer than four, but six preferable, and then we would practise passing the football American style. Then we would assemble in the hall and pledge our allegiance to America. I enjoyed that. Finally, we were asked to sing a hymn-like song written by a Japanese refugee who found sanctuary in America and wrote a song of gratitude. It went 'I love life, I want to live ... etc. etc.' I have never forgotten the music to that song since we sang it every morning. We never had any of these rituals in Luton, just dreary morning prayers. Here I felt I was part of America, I was encouraged to be proud of my new nation and nobody was ever physically punished. Hoorah!

The days were full and I made friends easily, since young American kids were so easy to make friends with. The nights were drawing in and it was getting cold, and sometimes mum and I, accompanied by the lodger Chris, went to the movies since Ma was bitterly lonely and was just happy to get out of the attic. I remember seeing a wonderful creepy film called *The Invisible Man*. Before the film started they even had a live show of some acrobats. I do believe that was the custom in those days at these suburban movie houses.

For a weekly treat, cousin Morris would drive with his mother and pick us up in the Bronx and take Ma and I out to lunch. We had to have a drive about first and be taken on a tour of the Bowery and see what seemed like scores of men just lying flat in the street, dead drunk. It was a shocking sight that they just took for granted. Then we drove through the financial district and he showed us how it was totally deserted on the weekends. Then we drove around Central Park, and then it was lunch, which was always a Chinese and which we all enjoyed. After that he took us back to the Bronx, and dumped us quite happily since aunt Ray had a favourite TV programme that she couldn't bear to miss.

Now Ma was bitterly lonely as Dad did come out, but only for a couple of weeks, since he was outraged that Ma's family had not been more helpful. But I thought that they did what they could, which was to find a place to rest our heads and for free until the man of the house came and found a job! So he left us high and dry, and one day I came home from school and he was no longer there.

Mum had by this time had enough, since she had no man and no home to care for and was just wasting away. There was a young woman called Paula Mansfield, who was the daughter of mum's other brother, Alf, who was once a famous boxer as a flyweight, but sadly lost his sight over the punishing schedule he gave himself in the ring. Mind you, he did fight the great Welsh champion Jimmy Wilde, who became a legend. He had at least three fierce matches with him but was defeated each time. Paula wanted to be in show business and was always doing her calisthenics in Joe's living room. She was a friendly, funny girl and, having been born in Manchester, never lost her Northern accent.

Mum couldn't wait to go home to what she had known and was familiar with, and tickets were bought. My sister had no intention of crawling back to that bombed-out shit hole which used to be the East End and, having got a good, well-paid job in a deli where she was simply adored, she decided to stay for another year!

To make the most of our last few days, Ma and I would go out, take the bus to Broadway and see movies. There was a movie running on Broadway called *The Gangster*, starring a beautiful skating star called 'Belita'.

Now coincidence of coincidences. Whilst on the boat The Queen Mary, as a special treat, we in tourist class were entertained after supper by playing bingo, or, as it was sometimes called, 'housy housy'. Well, this time I actually won. As I stepped up to receive the winnings, the compère made an announcement that the movie star 'Belita' would be the person giving it! I was beyond astounded and delightedly told her that I had seen her starring in the film *The Gangster*. I think she was quite taken by this, and we chattered happily for a few minutes. I even asked for her address in Hollywood. She said she lived in Beverly Hills. That was the first time I had heard of it. She wrote down her address, and I promised to write. But by then I think she had had enough, and she said she had to go back to her cabin. I walked her to the door, but not before saying 'You don't get many movie stars travelling tourist class.' Suddenly she stopped for a brief moment, turned to me and said 'We're just slumming!'

I should also mention that, during our time in the top attic floor in the Bronx, the actor Marlon Brando was playing on Broadway in *A Streetcar Named Desire* by Tennessee Williams. So each night, while poor mum and I and sister Beryl were gloomily tucked up in bed in our dreary attic, Marlon was stunning the world at the Barrymore Theatre on West 47th Street!

Almost exactly forty years later I would be directing my production of Kafka's *Metamorphosis* at the same Barrymore Theatre with Mischa Baryshnikov.

On the first night, I watched from the deli across the road with its window opening out onto the street as the shining limos drew up and deposited their elite human cargo onto the pavement outside the theatre. Sir Isaac Stern, Martha Graham, David Bowie, Joe Papp, Nancy Reagan, so many others. After a few minutes I decided to slip in unnoticed and watch the press night. It went well. As well as I could have expected, and the cast were confident and sure of the lines.

After the show our producer Lars Shmidt had us 'creatives' to dinner at a private room at the Carlisle Hotel, one of New York's finest establishments. We chattered merrily over supper while I knew Lars Schmidt and his co-producer, the doyen of American producers, Roger Smith, were anxious about the reviews. They had every right to be. At about midnight Lars excused himself to go out and buy *The New York Times*, since its review makes or breaks any Broadway show. It's almost pathetic that a group of grown experienced men should be so beholden to the idiot who was writing for *The New York Times'* theatre section. His name was Frank Rich. Now, as it so happens, I had another show running in New York at the same time, namely *Coriolanus* with Christopher Walken and Irene Worth at The Public Theater on Lafayette. Frank Rich had given this show the highest accolades of the Shakespeare marathon season that the theatre was mounting.

He simply raved about it, declaring it to be the best of the bunch so far, and so we did have high hopes that I was already in Frank Rich's good books.

After a short while Lars entered the room with the longest face I had ever seen on him. Frank Rich had not only reviewed it but damned it to death in the stupidest comments I have had the misfortune to read. It was totally unbelievable. My partner Clara and I almost had to laugh at the reaction to one critic's silly review, and I was so proud that coming from a civilised city like London with half a dozen daily papers we would never be in such a position as these pathetic New Yorkers with their one review. However, the play continued to run with its million dollar advance until Baryshnikov decided to pull the plug on it after just six weeks. The show also had some rave reviews from smaller journals and on radio, but these did not count for enough to outweigh *The Times*. Such a shame. That night the audience were overwhelmed and gave it a standing ovation.

Couldn't wait to get back to London to stage *Salome* at the National Theatre.

The sixties

So it was in the sixties that there suddenly came from the USA an explosion of talent the like of which we had never seen before. Most, if not all, came from disenfranchised youth, the hippy movement, rock music, anti-war demonstrations, partly drug culture and the revolutionary youth movement. So theatre groups were formed, dedicated to creating dynamic performances based on themes that shaped history or mythology. While the Broadway theatres still belched out the same old formulas, those cosy, wholesome plays like Neil Simon's *Brighton Beach Memoirs*, to cosy audiences which loved seeing their own lives rolled out by charming middle-aged actors who were then obliged to endure slave labour in year-long runs of eight shows per week, the alternative theatre was changing and bringing drama to life with groups like The Living Theatre, formed in the late forties by Julian Beck and Judith Malina, and La MaMa, formed by Ellen Stewart in 1961. Joe Chaikin was a member of The Living Theatre before founding his own theatre company, The Open Theatre, in 1963. What distinguished most of these adventurous groups was the collaborative nature of their work, where ideas fermented in unison, through pooling of ideas and intensive improvisation. I was fortunate enough to see Chaikin's master work *America Hurrah!* at The Royal Court, and could not have been more impressed by the ease with which the actors worked together, how they bonded, which was the result of breaking down those old barriers in the legit or straight theatre. This method worked, and still does, against the dictatorship of the director, the autocracy of the playwright and the pliant subjugation of the actor, who has little to say but to learn their bloody lines.

The actor must learn to suppress their own feelings, ideas or flashes of inspiration lest the director feels sidelined, God forbid that you as an actor should make a comment to another actor as I did in a revival of *The Birthday Party* that was to be staged in LA directed by William Friedkin, forgetting for a brief moment that I was in the straight theatre. The director began screaming at me, 'Don't you dare give another actor directions!!!' I was for a moment totally shocked, not believing that anyone could be so dictatorially possessive that he could behave like a raving lunatic. But, when I recovered, I simply walked out. The fresh air felt good. In the end it turned out that the director couldn't replace me, so the show was cancelled.

That was the last time I worked for anyone else, except for a brief, or not quite so brief, ten-week run in London where I played Saddam Hussein in a brilliant play by Anthony Horowitz called *Dinner with Saddam*, which was calmly directed by a civilised Lindsay Posner. But still the stale odour of straight theatre lingered over it when the stage manager used to call me to give me the director's notes whenever I might just stray a tad.

So watching these adventurous and boldly inventive companies did somewhat steer me into the way I would wish to go. When The Living Theatre staged *The Brig*, which was about life in a naval prison, I thought that no theatre could ever be better. It stunned, shocked, amazed, delighted and moved me. These guys (the actors) were just beyond acting, beyond anything I had ever seen or was likely to see here.

I saw La MaMa for the first time at the little Mercury Theatre in Notting Hill, performing a remarkable play called *Futz* by Rochelle Owens. The writing and the staging came brilliantly together, as it was staged by theatre genius Tom O'Horgan. The movement was unlike anything I had ever seen before, and of course I have never forgotten it. Then he directed *Hair*, which was an anti-war musical with the most lyrical music I have ever heard in a musical. This was staged in Joe Papp's theatre in Lafayette, New York.

When I worked for Joe in New York directing *Coriolanus*, Joe used to tell me how the show originated. Apparently Joe Papp used to teach at a university just an hour from New York and one day he shared a carriage with the composer Galt MacDermot. During one of their journeys, since Galt was also teaching, the composer suggested that Joe might like to hear his new work entitled *Hair*. Joe was used to being hustled, since it was now that he was about to start his season at The Public Theater, but to appease the young man he suggested that he stop by the theatre one afternoon and play a couple of his songs.

The composer duly turned up, and Joe called some of his office staff just to give the composer a semblance of an audience. The composer sat at the upright piano in the rehearsal room, and Joe and a few of his staff sat down and patiently prepared to listen for a few minutes. Apparently he began with 'This Is the Dawning of the Age of Aquarius' and the whole staff and Joe were quite taken with the lyricism and brio of the piece and now paid him a little more attention. MacDermot then went on to go through the entire score, and by this time Joe was convinced that he had stumbled across an amazing talent. His staff were awestruck, moved and highly responsive. Joe had planned to open his inaugural season with a good, rather stolid piece of British drama called *Armstrong's Last Goodnight*, but now he simply changed his mind. *Hair* opened, quickly became the biggest hit in New York and soon was to play in every major city in the world.

Something was happening in world theatre which was changing the predictable style of drama and this feverous germ was infecting the theatre everywhere. The Polish director Tadeusz Kantor stunned cities worldwide, including London, with his *Dead Class*. The entire production was played behind several desks, and the movement was percussive and dynamic and thrilling to watch. Articles were being written by 'prominent' avant-gardists complaining that London too had its Becketts and Ionescos, but they were being ignored in favour of the tried and tested and umpteen revivals of *The Cherry Orchard*. When the large institutions did take a mild risk, they congratulated themselves forever and a day. But people, that is, mainly young actors, directors and writers, were picking up the vibes, and London was awash with new, adventurous theatre groups and most significantly the Arts Council of Great Britain was subsidising them.

I had already produced and directed three major works before I dared to write to the Arts Council to see whether I could avail myself of the funding that other groups seemed so easily to get hold of. To my astonishment I had an early response requesting that I enclose a budget of my needs for a year. Naturally, in my modesty I made a small request, but then I doubled it and it was still quite modest and they granted it! Eureka. I was now in some ways respectable. Experimental work was now being recognised, even if emphatically not by the straight predictable theatre, but by the Arts Council of Great Britain, and I was indebted to them.

However, now I had to have a schedule of works, a budget itemising all my costs and also projected losses. I needed an accountant. Badly. I eventually found an administrator, which was the first step to establishing a bona fide company, and then a touring manager, which was easier said than done. Eventually we managed to find dates, and often the Arts Council would help us by booking tours for us, which we would always be glad to accept.

I was beginning to find my way. No longer would I be obliged to hustle my agent for mindless TV work, although I still did take on commercial work from time to time since I needed to earn money between the gigs that we did. Now I was not afraid to take risks and lose money, since it was the state's money, and I was encouraged to keep searching and experimenting. The Arts Council recognised this and seemed to recognise me. With Arts Council money I could then put together my version of Kafka's *The Trial*, show it at The Roundhouse and then tour it through Europe.

Now that I had the Arts Council as a financial supporter I had the freedom to continue exploring my theatrical ambitions. The amount received each year was a powerful spur to me. However, I was appalled to notice in trade magazines like *The Stage* etc. other theatre groups bitterly complaining that their grants didn't fulfil their ever growing need or did not keep up with inflation. I was somewhat taken aback by their whining, but of course then I realised that many of these groups or their artistic directors were smart 'uni' people who had happily lived off the state all their lives. They had spent three years at uni living off the generosity of the welfare state, or their parents, and then continued to live off grants at drama school. However, I was deeply grateful to the Arts Council of Great Britain for being behind me and, despite no longer claiming any grants, I am still everlastingly grateful to them.

I continued touring and rehearsing plays with funding for at least ten years and then I went on my own. The last time I applied for a grant was in 1980 when I directed and played *Hamlet* at the Edinburgh Festival. This exposure made it possible to tour our production all over Europe. It was seen by the great Belgian impresario Jan de Blik. In London the reviews for the show were beyond nasty, ignorant, pathetic, stupid, crass, banal etc., but this in no way affected de Blik, who put us on a tour to all the great theatres of Germany, ending up in Paris where, as I have already mentioned, we were the guests of the great French maestro Jean-Louis Barrault. On the last night of our three-week booking we were honoured by the elite of French theatre coming to see us. And when Andrzej Wajda, Poland's greatest film director, came backstage with his two little children and said this was the best *Hamlet* production he had ever seen we were so honoured, so fulfilled that it completely took away any bad taste left by the barbarians in London.

However, since *Hamlet* did lose a great deal of money, both from the Arts Council and mine, I was determined to stick with a two-hander and wrote *Decadence*. It was the distillation of the mores of the class wars in England, and I was still not content to write or perform anything that was not compelling. We played it in Edinburgh, then Los Angeles, and then ended up in the West End at Wyndham's Theatre. I was most relieved and this time even changed my attitude to the critics, since this time they praised the show to the skies.

I was now quite comfortably forging a reputation as a kind of minor avant-garde figure who occasionally titivated the masses.

Well, about this time Peter Hall was about to take over the National Theatre and was keenly looking for plays that could occupy the Cottesloe Theatre, since the early mandate for that rather beautiful smaller theatre was to be 'the nation's theatre for Great Britain', and it would host guest productions of new and innovative works that ought to be seen outside the provinces. I received a call that he would be interested in meeting me. Oh my God, I was fraternising with the establishment. I met him for lunch, which we took in his office, and I shall never forget that event till the end of my days.

I had in fact auditioned for him when he was running Stratford, though of course he wouldn't remember that, but now I was a director myself as well as an actor and had my own company, so he paid a little more attention to me. After our lunch of roast beef and salad he was kind enough to give me a tour of the Cottesloe that was in the final stage of being built. I must say I very much liked the crisp functionalism of the building. Soon he invited me to bring my work there and suggested that we started with *East*.

This we did, to great effect and packed audiences, and it was the National's company manager Michael Halifax who approached me with his large diary in hand and asked me to do another show the following week but just for a few performances to fill a gap. Fortunately we were still doing the odd tour of *Metamorphosis* with Terry McGinity and Maggie Jordan, a remarkable Scots actress. That was also sold out in advance, and I was beginning to feel that I had won a place in the heart of the National as a distant relative brought in from the cold. That I would be continually asked to help fill the Cottesloe. Sure enough, on the last night of *Metamorphosis* he approached yet again with diary in hand and asked for yet another show just for two nights the following week. I cannot tell you how thrilled I was to be asked and how proud I was, even if I noticed that Peter Hall didn't seem to make it to any of my performances. Yes, I said, I could without doubt.

We were again sold out well in advance and were beginning to gain some sort of reputation, so much so that Sheridan Morley did a profile on me for *The Sunday Times*. A whole page, no less. The following weeks the National Theatre went rather quiet and I had no more calls from Michael Halifax. In fact, that was that, I was not to hear from Peter Hall again. What a shame.

Never mind, I knew that it was my destiny to find success only when I did it myself and not have to put myself in the position of having to beg for an opportunity to show my work. On the other hand, once I had begun, by writing, directing or acting, most often with a group of willing and idealistic actors, an opportunity might then come up with a company that needed to fill a space. Paradoxically it was the commercial theatre that always came to my aid, since they had no swords to cross with me and just wanted to put bums on seats. All you needed was the money!! For me it would never be a problem, since the most important element of the theatre was the product. Once I had that, I would never turn down an opportunity that had been offered, even if I had to beg, borrow or steal.

But I would never fail to remember that it was the Arts Council that gave me a kick-start. Whoever it was that put their hand up when my application was mentioned, I thank you from the bottom of my heart.

Such was my naivety in regard to the shabby ways of the directors of theatre that I thought that by writing to them every year or so, after their having seen my latest work, or even read about it, they might be inclined to open their doors a wee bit and let me in.

But I did not have the imagination to realise that they would never permit that in a thousand years. But they might if there were an emergency, like there had been at the National, when Richard Eyre invited me in to direct and perform in *Salome*. This fortuitous and sad event occurred when Olivier passed away and there was a great yawning gap which had to be filled. I did so happily. Thank you Larry.

On 24 March 1874, in Budapest, a child was born who was to captivate the world. His name was Ehrich Weiss, but he was later to be known as 'The Great Houdini'. Of course, like all young kids, I was fascinated by this man who was born in Budapest. Also I felt a strong connection to him since my grandparents were born in Bucharest and, like Houdini's family, felt the need to escape to the cleaner, freer air of America.

There was something about Houdini, this Hungarian Jew, that was especially unique. For the Jews of Eastern Europe could not easily enter the theatre since they were far too 'foreign' and had these ghastly accents. They were not part of the host society and not familiar with their mores. Their women were far too dark and saturnine and lacked the rosy pink porcelain features of English ladies. It would be rather an impossible leap to be accepted after the first generation but a little easier for the next generation.

However, the early immigrants still had a love for the theatre and many had been actors in their old countries, so what did they do? Open their own theatre in the East End of London, called The Grand Palais, where they performed in Yiddish!

The Grand Palais was very popular and packed most nights, although I had no interest in it at the time and neither did my family. What they really had an interest in was The London Palladium and seeing all those famous and beautiful American stars who came over here to thrill us all.

Houdini was a first-generation American, was a splendid athlete at school and soon became known as a brilliant illusionist and escape artist. He opened his first show, a dynamic act with his wife, which he called *Metamorphosis*, and never looked back.

INDEX

Note: page numbers in *italic* denote photographs.